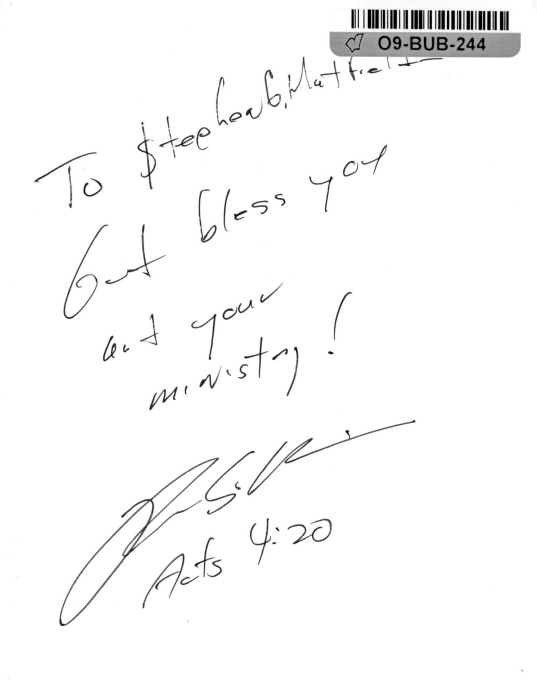

To Stephen B, Mattfield

God bless you

and your

ministry!

J. S.

Acts 4:20

BREAKOUT
CHURCHES

OTHER BOOKS BY THOM S. RAINER

The Unchurched Next Door
Surprising Insights from the Unchurched
Eating the Elephant (Revised edition) (coauthor)
High Expectations
The Everychurch Guide to Growth (coauthor)
The Bridger Generation
Effective Evangelistic Churches
The Church Growth Encyclopedia (coeditor)
Experiencing Personal Revival (coauthor)
Giant Awakenings
Biblical Standards for Evangelists (coauthor)
The Book of Church Growth
Evangelism in the Twenty-first Century (editor)

discover how
to make the leap

BREAK(O)UT
CHURCHES

thom s. rainer

ZONDERVAN™

GRAND RAPIDS, MICHIGAN 49530 USA

ZONDERVAN™

Breakout Churches
Copyright © 2005 by Thom S. Rainer

Requests for information should be addressed to:
Zondervan, *Grand Rapids, Michigan 49530*

Library of Congress Cataloging-in-Publication Data

Rainer, Thom S.
    Breakout churches : discover how to make the leap / Thom S. Rainer.
      p. cm.
    Includes bibliographical references and index.
    ISBN 0-310-25745-X (hardcover)
    1. Church growth. 2. Christian leadership. I. Title.
  BV652.25.R365   2004
  253—dc22   2004008376

Illustrations copyright © 2005 by Jess W. Rainer

Interior design by Tracey Walker

Printed in the United States of America

05 06 07 08 09 10 11 / ❖ DCI / 10 9 8 7 6 5 4 3 2 1

*This book about the greatest
is dedicated to the greatest family
The greatest sons
Sam Rainer
Art Rainer
Jess Rainer
The greatest wife
Nellie Jo Rainer
always with love*

CONTENTS

ACKNOWLEDGMENTS

I am a man most blessed.

Many years ago, a high school football coach named Joe Hendrickson introduced me to the Savior, about whose church I write in this book. For more than thirty years I have known the love, hope, presence, and power of Jesus Christ. I could have no greater blessing.

I grew up in a home where I knew the love of my mother, father, and brother. Though just my brother, Sam, and I are still alive, I remember regularly the incredible joy of being raised in a loving home. The blessing is incalculable.

I wake up each morning passionate about the vocation to which God has called me. Whether I am teaching, writing, administering, speaking, preaching, or consulting, I get to do what I love most. I love Christ's church. I love communicating the work of the church, the hopes of the church, and the struggles of the church. I am blessed to be able to do that which is my passion.

My primary vocational title is dean. The team of people with whom I work at the Southern Baptist Theological Seminary is incredible. The leaders of the executive cabinet are second to none. And the school I had the humbling honor to found over ten years ago is the best place on earth to work. I cannot express sufficiently the love I have for the faculty, administrators, and secretaries of the Billy Graham School of Missions, Evangelism and Church Growth. The blessing given to me by these men and women is an undeserved gift for which I thank God regularly.

How does one express adequately the emotions that come with the research and writing of a book that in many ways fulfills a life's dream? I must begin by first thanking the Zondervan team for their leadership on my third book with them. My specific gratitude goes to Paul Engle, Jim Ruark, Alicia Mey, and Mike Cook for their direct input and editorial work on this book. But the Zondervan team is so much more than these four people. I wish I could take the space to name every person involved in this project. It is a blessing to serve alongside this Christian publisher.

I am grateful to Jim Collins for his tremendous work in *Good to Great*, which inspired this study and this book. I am also very appreciative of his willingness to grant an interview at the onset of this project. The work in this book, however, is entirely mine. Neither Mr. Collins nor his organization endorsed or even saw the research at any stage.

This book is not my book alone. The research team pictured on the next page did the work. They labored on what we would soon find was the most difficult and arduous project we have ever done. But they persevered. They did their work with excellence. They are a blessing.

This book is about thirteen breakout churches. You will hear their stories many times. My deepest gratitude goes to all of those in these churches who made the research and this book a reality. It has been a blessing to see God's work in your churches.

On the dedicatory page, you see the names of my family: Nellie Jo, Sam, Art, and Jess. For you who have read any of my previous books, you know how much my family means to me. But what you cannot know fully is how much they contribute to my ministry. I discuss almost every aspect of my work with them. They give me feedback, encouragement, and constant love. I could not write books if I did not have the unconditional support of my family.

Sam: Thank you for your passion and zeal for this work and for life in general. Art: Thank you for the incredible leader you have become and for the tenacity and determination with which you approach life. Jess: Thank you for your deep compassion and creative mind and for the illustrations you created for this book. Nellie Jo: Words are not enough. I could not imagine a love any deeper than my love for you. This is your book, doll. You deserve every credit and accolade that has come my way. God knows how much I love my family. What an immeasurable blessing!

I am a man most blessed.

May the blessings I have received be used to bring glory to God, the only one who is worthy of the glory. And may you, the reader, be blessed as you take the pilgrimage of which I write, the journey on which good is never enough.

THE RESEARCH TEAM

First row (left to right): Doug Whitaker, Joong Shik Kim, Michael McDaniel, David Bell, Laura Cruse. *Second row (left to right):* Stuart Swicegood, Chris Bonts, George Lee, Deborah Morton, Elisha Rimestead. *Not pictured:* Michael O'Neal.

PREFACE

have been a student of the local church for nearly two decades. My research team and I estimate that there are approximately 400,000 churches in the United States. For this work, we have examined more than 50,000 of these churches. My consulting firm, the Rainer Group, has also worked with hundreds of these churches.

Our research projects have looked at some of the most effective evangelistic churches in America. We have studied churches that are reaching the unchurched. We have examined hundreds of churches to discern what they are doing to retain and assimilate members. We took an exciting journey to discover churches that are effectively reaching young people. And we have studied hundreds of other issues in the local church that never made it into the books I have written.

But we have found few "breakout" churches.

I did not plan to assemble a research team and lead a project called "When Good Churches Become Great." Then in November 2002 I received an email from Paul Engle of Zondervan. He had just read Jim Collins's classic *Good to Great* and suggested that a similar project on churches may be of value. When I received that email, a dozen mental bells began to ring. Paul's idea was a good one—*Good to Great* was "the missing piece" of my nearly twenty years of research. I was very familiar with *Good to Great*, having read the book twice in 2001. Later that same year, Albert Mohler, the president of the seminary where I serve as dean, required the executive team of the seminary to read the book. So I digested its pages for a third time.

Good to Great: Why Some Companies Make the Leap . . . and Others Don't by Jim Collins is a masterpiece of research into the business world of America. Collins's team identified eleven Fortune 500 companies that had transitioned from mediocrity to excellence over several years. The book had a profound impact on me. Indeed, as our executive team at the seminary discussed the book, we saw numerous principles that were biblical in their foundations, even though the book has no explicit Christian focus.

I did not delay in assembling a research team for this project. The men and women on the team did an incredible job of locating and studying the

churches in the United States that moved from being good to being great—
what we call "breakout" churches. And as you will see, this research project proved to be the most difficult of any in which I have been involved.

As the data, interviews, and on-site studies of these churches began to
cross my desk, I could see even more clearly why Paul's email resonated
with me. Now I fully understood why my attraction to *Good to Great* was
so profound. In many ways, Collins's research provided the "big picture" to
all of my previous research. I could see my earlier work as components;
now I had a guideline to put all the pieces together.

I wish we had had a way to screen all 400,000 churches to find all the
breakout churches in America. Fortunately, we were able to begin with
over 50,000 churches for which we had data. We added a few thousand
more to the prospect pool through our investigative process.

Let us now begin to look at churches that fought the temptation to be
satisfied with mediocrity. It seems as if, in our interviews with the leaders
of these churches, they all began with a dissatisfaction with the status quo.
Simply stated, good was not enough. To that reality we now turn.

CHAPTER 1

WHY GOOD IS NOT ENOUGH: THE CHRYSALIS FACTOR

The possibility that we may fail in the struggle ought not to deter us from the support of a cause we believe to be just.

—Abraham Lincoln

t is a sin to be good if God has called us to be great.

Christians refer to Matthew 28:18–20 as the *Great* Commission, not the Good Commission. Jesus himself said that the words we read in Matthew 22:37 and 39 are the *Great* Commandments, not the Good Commandments. And the apostle Paul did not call love something that is good; instead, he said "the *greatest* of these is love" (1 Cor. 13:13, emphasis added).

The power of seeking to be great rather than good became clear when I read Jim Collins's book *Good to Great: Why Some Companies Make the Leap . . . and Others Don't*, in which he began with the opening line: "Good is the enemy of great." With the encouragement of my publisher I elected to write a book on churches, modeled on the *Good to Great* framework. This book was inspired by *Good to Great*, and we borrowed the research process, the structure and outline of the book, and the architecture of its ideas as the blueprint for this work.

THE DIFFICULTIES IN FINDING GREAT CHURCHES

Think of some criteria to measure great churches. Attendance increases? Number of conversions? Impact on culture? Transformed lives? If you have settled on one or more criteria, name fifty churches that would meet them. Can you name forty churches? Thirty?

Let's make the search more difficult. Think of churches that meet your "great" criteria after being a so-so church for many years. In other words, discover some churches that have made the leap to greatness.

Let's make the test even more problematic. Name all the churches that have made the transition without changing the senior pastor or senior minister. In other words, the church broke out under the same leadership.

If you are having trouble naming several such churches, you have a taste of the difficulties the research team encountered in this project. We believe, quite simply, that there are very few breakout churches in America. In fact, although we have data on thousands of churches, we found only thirteen churches that survived the rigorous screening.

But the lessons we learned from these churches are priceless.

Figure 1A offers a quick snapshot of the incredible leaps taken by breakout churches. Following the research methodology used by Jim Collins in *Good to Great*, we compared the thirteen churches we found with a carefully selected control group of churches that failed to make the leap. The factors distinguishing one group from the other fascinated our team.

As just one point of comparison, the chart looks at worship attendance of the two groups of churches. The breakout churches had a clearly identified point at which they began to experience significant growth. Drawing upon the *Good to Great* terminology of "transition point," we called this juncture the "breakout point." We then took the five years preceding and the five years following the breakout point and compared the same years with the direct comparison churches.

For the five years prior to breakout, all of the churches were struggling to stay even in worship attendance. Then the difference between the two groups is dramatic. The average worship attendance of the comparison churches declined for the next five years, while in the breakout churches it increased 71 percent.

How did churches with very unremarkable pasts become great churches? What took place in these fellowships that made them so extraordinary? How did these churches make the leap when more than 90 percent of American churches did not come close to doing so?

Can a good but plodding church become a great church? We believe the answer is an unequivocal yes. We hope the stories you are about to read will inspire you to move your church to greatness. Before we get too caught up in the details, let's hear from one church that made the transition—but not without a great sacrifice at great cost.

Figure 1A. Attendance of Breakout Churches and Comparison Churches

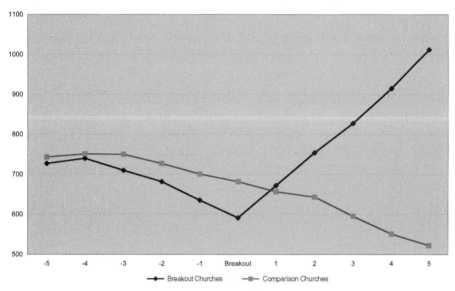

THE TEMPLE CHURCH FACES THE COST OF MAKING THE LEAP

The Temple Church opened its doors for its first worship service at the American Baptist Theological Seminary in Nashville, Tennessee, in 1977. The congregation subsequently met in two other borrowed facilities before constructing its own buildings in 1980. The founding pastor was Bishop Michael Lee Graves.

By most standards, The Temple Church was successful from its inception. Growth was steady, if not spectacular, in the early years. A Christian private school began. An adjunctive ministry, Samaritan's Ministries, reached out to the inner city of North Nashville by providing nutritional support for the hungry, medical assistance, spiritual and psychological counseling, and educational and vocational training. One leader in the community credited The Temple Church with playing a major role in reducing drug and gang violence in the area.

The list of Temple's ministries exceeded fifty and was growing. The church was one of the most respected African-American churches in the early 1980s. A multimillion-dollar facility was complete. The members began to see their identity with the church as a banner of prestige. The Temple Church, by most standards, was making a difference. Then the crash came.

As researcher George P. Lee discovered, not many people recognized that a crash had taken place. True, worship attendance declined from 1,000 in 1984 to 880 in 1985. But Bishop Graves, the only person to sense trouble, felt the decline in attendance was only symptomatic of greater problems.

"There was a sense of apathy growing among the members," Graves reflected. More important, he sensed that God's vision for The Temple Church was for it to be a multiracial, multiethnic church for people of all socioeconomic classes. Yet by 1985 the church was the home largely of middle- and upper-middle-class African Americans.

"The vision of The Temple Church was a vision of encompassing all races, ethnic groups, and nationalities," said Graves. "I never intended for Temple to become a bourgeois congregation of Afrocentric believers. I wanted to affirm our heritage as African Americans while reaching the global community for Christ."

Graves received little comfort from his peers in the ministry. Most of them could not understand why he was so restless. One pastor chastised him, "Graves, if you don't build the rest of your vision, you've achieved more than any of us. Be grateful."

To an outsider, the attendance plateau could be easily explained by the lack of worship space. But Bishop Graves knew the problem went much deeper. He keenly desired to lead in the building of a larger sanctuary, but his suggestions met stiff resistance from many key leaders. They knew that the larger facility would make room for people who were not like them.

A group of 300 church members met with Graves on numerous occasions, hoping to change his mind. This opposition group threatened to withdraw their significant financial support from the church if their demands were not met. After much prayer, Graves decided to hold the course and build the new sanctuary. The entire leadership group left the church.

Graves was devastated. He describes this period as one of "anguish and doubt." He attempted to no avail to reach out to those who left the church. Because of the reduced financial resources in the church, many ministries ceased operation. Even the Temple Academy closed after a decade of ministry.

The bishop internalized his pain and became physically ill. He was hospitalized for weeks at a time. His family physician encouraged him to retire from pastoral ministry, but he refused to stray from the vision God had given him for the church. Eventually his health returned and the church recovered from its losses of members, leaders, and money.

The Temple Church began the transition to greatness. Figure 1B powerfully depicts the transition through the measurement of worship attendance. The crisis in the church reached its peak in 1989 when attendance hit a ten-year low of 710. In 1990 attendance moved up slightly to 750, and a classic breakout point became obvious.

Over the next twelve years the church's membership grew to 3,000, with more than 2,000 in worship attendance, and the number of ministries to the community became greater than ever. A good church became a great church without changing pastoral leadership.

Figure 1B. Average Worship Attendance at The Temple Church

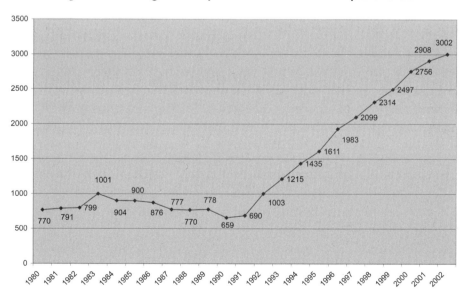

Today the dream of Bishop Michael Graves is a reality. The Temple Church is a multiracial, multiethnic church reaching across all socioeconomic lines. The pastor simply would not be deterred from the vision. This determination and focus came at no small cost to Michael Graves. But as we saw frequently in our research, moving to greatness is never easy. As many of the leaders we interviewed told us, the transition often involves great pain.

WHAT WAS THE PROCESS?

What did we learn from the breakout churches? What can you learn from them? What does it take to move a church to greatness? Those questions became the passion of the research team. So what was the process? Just how did we find these breakout churches?

I have never been satisfied with anecdotal answers or conventional wisdom. When students make a comment like "Research shows . . . ," I demand that they show me the sources of the research and demonstrate the validity of the conclusions. In nearly twenty years of research on the American church, our studies have uncovered some issues that defy the conventional wisdom of the day. Such was definitely the case in the breakout churches project.

The research team will readily agree that this project was one of many lows and only a few highs. We faced monumental challenges as the process unfolded for finding the breakout churches in America.

Stage One: Define the Criteria

What defines a "breakout" church? I am sure we all have different opinions on this question. We do not claim that we have discovered the perfect formulaic approach to defining great churches. We believe, however, that our criteria provide an acceptable screen for the churches in the United States.

1. The church has had at least 26 conversions annually since its breakout year. This number was the minimum we accepted in our previous research on effective evangelistic churches. Simply stated, we believe that any healthy church should be reaching at least one person with the gospel every two weeks.
2. The church has averaged a conversion ratio no higher than 20:1 at least one year since its breakout year. This ratio answers the question, how many members does it take to reach one person for Christ in a year? A ratio of 20:1 suggests that it takes 20 members one year to reach one person.

3. The church had been declining or had plateaued for several years prior to its breakout year, or the church was experiencing some type of stagnation not readily apparent in the statistics.

4. The church broke out of this "slump" and has sustained new growth for several years.

5. The slump, reversal, and breakout all took place under the same pastor. We believe that this criterion, though limiting, was absolutely necessary. We felt compelled to find breakout success stories that took place without a change in leadership. The typical solution to stagnated churches is to replace the pastor. Unfortunately, there are not enough "breakout pastors" to lead even 5 percent of the churches in America. We sought stories of changed leadership values rather than stories of changing leaders.

6. Since the breakout point, the church has made a clear and positive impact on the community, and there are numerous stories that lives have been changed as a direct result of this. While this final criterion is subjective, we wanted more than statistical measures for our breakout churches. You will see that the churches that survived our screens are clear examples of life-changing and community-changing churches.

Stage Two: Find the Churches

We started the project with a great deal of optimism. We received data on some 50,000 churches. We expected to find a number of breakout churches in this mix, but the yield was surprisingly much less than we thought it would be.

Many people warned us that the selection process with churches may prove more difficult than with businesses. Large companies are easy sources of information. Not only are their financial records available for public scrutiny, but many companies are written about in outside sources like magazines and newspapers.[1] The skeptics were right. Rarely did we easily find information on these churches.

We then began the arduous process of contacting key persons around the nation who could assist us in the search. We wrote to well-known pastors, denominational leaders, church leaders selected according to their geographical area, civic leaders, and others. Early on we faced frustration when a few denominational leaders chose not to help us and became protective of their churches' information.

At times I wondered if the research team was ready to throw in the towel. Team member Chris Bonts sent me an email:

> In my work on Breakout Churches, I am sorry to inform you that I found only one church that fit the criteria, a Christian and Missionary Alliance church. I surveyed 1,893 churches and found only one that definitely fit. Several appeared to qualify initially, but further research revealed a change in record keeping, reporting, or an influx of transfer growth. I have already logged over 150 hours on this project, and hope that coming up short does not disqualify me from working for you in the future.

The good news is that we found thirteen churches that clearly met our strict criteria. Some are well known; some are not. The churches in alphabetical order:

Bethel Temple Community Church	Evansville, Indiana
Calvary Memorial Church	Oak Park, Illinois
Central Christian Church	Beloit, Wisconsin
Fairfield New Life Church	Fairfield, California
First Gethsemane Baptist Church	Louisville, Kentucky
Grace Church, CMA	Middleburg Heights, Ohio
Grace Evangelical Free Church	Allen, Texas
Grove City Church of the Nazarene	Grove City, Ohio
Korean Central Presbyterian Church	Vienna, Virginia
Lenexa Baptist Church	Lenexa, Kansas
Southwest Baptist Church	Amarillo, Texas
The Temple Church	Nashville, Tennessee
Xenos Christian Fellowship	Columbus, Ohio

Stage Three: Look for Comparison Churches

Two sets of "great" churches are omitted from this study because of our defined criteria. The first set includes churches that qualify according to our statistical criteria but do not show a period of struggle. Great churches would include Saddleback Valley Community Church in California, under the pastoral leadership of Rick Warren, and Southeast Christian Church in Louisville, Kentucky, led by senior minister Bob Russell. But these are not breakout churches. We were interested in churches that had broken out of a "slump." Some great churches have never experienced a real downturn.

Another group of churches were excluded as "great" because their breakout period took place under a new pastor. St. Stephen Baptist Church in Louisville, Kentucky, met all of our statistical criteria, but its breakout took place when Kevin Cosby became pastor. We were determined to find churches that made the change under the same leadership that had experienced struggles in earlier years.

The largest group of churches left out of the study—about 96 percent of the churches in America—were excluded because they did not meet the criteria based on our previous studies of effective evangelistic churches. These are the "good" churches. Most of them have good pastors and good laypeople, but they have not broken out of their mediocrity.

> **Data drove the selection and exclusion process. We were pleased that our selection screen resulted in geographically, racially, and ethnically diverse churches. However, our criteria did not specifically entail such diversity in the screening process.**

With most of these churches, somewhere in their histories they have become satisfied with the status quo. They resist change and often seek to minister only to those inside the church. They have some or many programs. They may even have large budgets. But they are not making a significant impact on their communities, nor do they see significant numbers of changed lives in their congregations.

These "good" churches became our source for direct comparison with the breakout churches. We carefully selected three good churches to compare with each breakout church. The comparison churches were similar in size at the breakout point of the breakout churches. Their doctrinal positions and demographic compositions were similar. The differences we found in each set of churches became our focal point in better understanding the factors that move churches to greatness. We called these issues the "chrysalis factor."

Stage Four: Discover the Chrysalis Factor

My first high school biology teacher was Mary Carlson. Mrs. Carlson was an outstanding teacher who could make the sciences fascinating. I remember one of her lectures on caterpillars becoming butterflies. While I recall few of the details of the process, I do remember that she called the transition "one of the great miracles of nature."

The chrysalis is the pupa of a butterfly encased in a cocoon. It is the former caterpillar and the future butterfly. It is the stage when that worm-like, slow-moving larva called a caterpillar becomes a beautiful, free-flying butterfly.

We sought to discover the chrysalis factor in the breakout churches. What took place when a church moved from mediocrity to greatness? What factors could we isolate that were unique to the breakout churches?

> The chrysalis factor is analogous to the "black box" in Jim Collins's *Good to Great*. They are both word pictures that describe the factors that led to the transformation of both the churches in our study and the companies in his team's research.

Such was our quest: to identify as clearly as possible the events, patterns, plans, strategies, crises, and other factors that took place when a church made the transition to greatness.

We did not limit the research to mere data. Our research included volumes of interviews with pastors, church staff, and laypeople in the churches. Where we could find outside information, we categorized and sorted the articles or books according to specific areas in the chrysalis factor.

During each step of the process we kept asking, "What is the chrysalis factor?" What is taking place in these breakout churches in the transition? What is taking place in these churches that is *not* taking place in

Figure 1C. The Chrysalis Factor

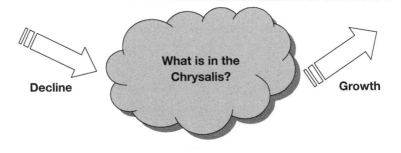

the comparison churches? In an attempt to answer these questions we started with the findings outlined by Jim Collins in *Good to Great,* and in fact, as you will see, the remainder of this book is patterned directly on those ideas.

We had something of an advantage in this search in that we thought the earlier research of Jim Collins would provide some guidelines and insights. Such was the case. The process used by Collins's team was very helpful in our quest.

> **A key difference between our research and Collins's work was our difficulty in getting reliable and objective data. While his team had access to reams of data on Fortune 500 companies, we often had difficulty getting ten years' worth of attendance figures. Also, unlike Collins, we added the requirement that the leadership did not change in the transition to greatness.**

We were particularly struck in chapter 1 of *Good to Great* by how Jim Collins captured readers' interest by highlighting not just what his team found, but also what they *did not* find—which in a tip of the hat to Sherlock Holmes he called "dogs that did not bark." Similarly, we think you may be as fascinated as we were to discover what was *not* present in churches that moved to greatness. Look at a few examples:

- The pastor involved in the transition was not leading by the sheer force of a charismatic personality. Indeed, as we will see, a surprising modesty typified most of these leaders.
- The breakout churches were surprisingly slow in adopting new methodologies and latching on to the latest and hottest trends in the national church scene.
- A deliberately created and clearly articulated vision statement had little or nothing to do with the breakout to greatness. The comparison churches were just as likely to have a vision statement as the others.
- The location of the church, by region of the country or demographic patterns in the community, was not a factor in the breakout process.

- The name of the church and any decision to remove or keep the denominational identity was not a factor in breaking out.
- The development of a strategic plan was just as likely to take place in the comparison churches as in the breakout churches. While we see merit in developing strategies, we do not see this process as part of the chrysalis factor.
- The breakout churches were conservative theologically, but the comparison churches were almost as conservative. Our earlier studies confirmed the importance of clear doctrine in evangelistic churches, but doctrine alone does not move churches to greatness.

Stage Five: Apply What We Learned

The research team was motivated by much more than curiosity and intellectual stimulation. We wanted not only to find out what happens to churches that move to greatness, under the sovereignty of God, but also to apply what we learned for the benefit of the kingdom and other churches.

In the pages that follow, you will see illustrations and explanations of the breakout progression. Nearly all of the principles are very similar at times to Jim Collins's *Good to Great*. We expected similarities since we patterned our research on his work. But there are also some departures from the *Good to Great* conclusions. Churches are quite different from any other kinds of organizations, including other nonprofit entities. Those differences, we believe, account for some of the divergent conclusions.

So before we go on to the various details of our study, let's look at an overview of the breakout framework, which we adapted from page 12 of *Good to Great*. The diagram in figure 1D is linear; that which is on the left precedes that which is on the right. "Acts 6/7 Leadership" comes before "The ABC Moment," which in turn comes before "The Who/What Simultrack."

Figure 1D. The Progression to a Breakout Church

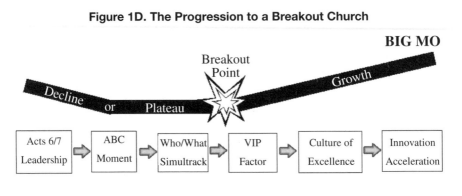

Do the realities of the breakout churches really match the simple linear process shown above? In the strictest sense, no. The churches sometimes were moving on more than one point at a time. Still, the illustration is a close approximation of what took place in the chrysalis factor, the parts of which we will examine now.

THE SIX MAJOR COMPONENTS OF THE CHRYSALIS FACTOR

I do not want to suggest that we have discovered some neat formulaic approach for leading churches to greatness. A sovereign God and the Holy Spirit are not instruments subject to manipulation by humanity. Yet the components of the chrysalis factor may provide insight into *how* God is working in his churches. It is our hope that the stories we tell and the lessons we learned will make a positive difference for you and your church.

> We thought at the onset of the research that we would be able to rank the six components according to importance or priority. After the research concluded, however, we found no such weighting and concluded that they are all so interrelated that one component cannot exist without the others.

Acts 6/7 Legacy Leadership *(patterned after Jim Collins's Level 5 Leadership)*

As we explain in the next two chapters, the breakout pastors all displayed Acts 6/7 leadership. Every other level is important and prerequisite to achieving the Acts 6/7 level.

- *Acts 1: The Called Leader.* In the same way that the early church leaders were called to be witnesses and ministers for Christ (Acts 1), the first step toward Christian leadership today is to receive and respond to the call of God.
- *Acts 2: The Contributing Leader.* On the day of Pentecost (Acts 2), Peter delivered the first sermon in the new church. This action shows that particular functions of the leader, such as prayer and preaching, were foundational for the church and its leadership.

- *Acts 3: The Outwardly-Focused Leader.* Peter and John made the first venture outside the newly formed church as they visited and healed the lame beggar (Acts 3). Only a few leaders achieve this stage of leadership, where they must move beyond the comfort of the church's walls.
- *Acts 4: The Passionate Leader.* The passionate leader is not just outwardly focused, but is also so enthused and sold out on his and the church's mission that his leadership motivates many to follow. Peter and John modeled this type of leadership so much so that it landed them in jail—and then empowered them to be set free (Acts 4). This level of leadership is very rare among pastors and ministers.
- *Acts 5: The Bold Leader.* The bold leader is willing to take incredible steps of faith and make the tough calls that few others will. The bold leader knows the church's mission and purpose and is willing to take whatever steps are necessary to keep the church on track. Peter exemplifies this type of leadership with his bold confrontation of Ananias and Sapphira (Acts 5). Perhaps fewer than 1 percent of church leaders reach this level.
- *Acts 6/7: The Legacy Leader.* While very few church leaders achieve even Acts 3 leadership, an even smaller number become Acts 6/7 leaders. These leaders, like the Twelve in Acts 6, seek to equip others for the work of ministry while deflecting recognition for themselves. Like Stephen in Acts 7, they are not concerned only with the church during their lifetime, but make decisions that will benefit the church after they are gone. They are quick to praise others and equally quick to accept responsibility for anything that may go wrong. All of the breakout church leaders in our findings achieved the Acts 6/7 level.

We are not suggesting that the biblical text of Acts 1–7 is a sequential paradigm through which all leaders progress. We are using highlights of each chapter to exemplify different types of leadership. Our nomenclature is meant to be illustrative rather than normative.

The ABC Moment (patterned after Jim Collins's Confront the Brutal Facts [Yet Never Lose Faith])

All of the breakout churches and their leaders experienced a time we call the ABC moment. The *A* represents an "awareness" that something is not right in the church they serve, that it is not being the church God intended it to be. The *B*, or "belief," stage takes place when the leader becomes willing to seek out and confront the brutal facts about the church's inadequacies. The leader then believes that a wide gap exists between what is and what God intends.

The *C* is the "crisis" that ensues in the leader's heart because of this gap. It typically leads the leader to seek help in understanding the church's purpose and in getting the right people and structures in place so the church can move to greatness.

You will recall that at The Temple Church in Nashville, Bishop Graves came to a point in his ministry where he realized that the church he envisioned God would build was not the church he was leading. His heartfelt desire was to lead a church that reached many ethnic and racial groups across all socioeconomic strata. The "awareness" that took place was his growing dissatisfaction with the church limiting its outreach to middle-class and upper-middle-class African Americans.

Graves believed the church had to face the brutal facts about its failure to accomplish its mission. Yet he met stiff resistance when he confronted key leaders with the need to build a larger sanctuary to reach other ethnic groups. This "belief" that a gap existed between "what is" and "what should be" led to the final stage of the ABC moment, the "crisis."

Bishop Graves never would have known this crisis point if he had given up on his dream to see the church become a true New Testament church. Yet his gentle prodding and persistence ultimately led to many confrontations, the loss of a few hundred key leaders, and his own physical illness and hospitalization.

We are not suggesting that every leader of a breakout church has to find himself in a hospital at some point. Our research shows clearly, though, that the intentional effort to bridge the gap between "what is" and "what should be" comes at some cost to the leader.

The Who/What Simultrack (patterned after Jim Collins's First Who . . . Then What)

The leaders of the breakout churches, seeking to close the gap between what the church is and what God desires it to be, typically responded by addressing three issues simultaneously. First, they asked *what* the purpose of the church really is. Rick Warren's Purpose Driven® model proved immensely helpful to many of the breakout church leaders.[2]

Second, the leaders sought to get the right kind of people on board to move the church to a more purpose-driven posture. Often they brought laypeople and staff to positions of leadership even before they knew exactly what these leaders would be doing. In other words, they were more concerned with *who* the leaders were than with a precise job description for them.

The VIP Factor (patterned after Jim Collins's Hedgehog Concept [Simplicity within Three Circles])

Volumes have been written in both the secular and Christian worlds on the need to discover vision. The leaders of breakout churches did not devise some elaborate process to discover vision. Most of them did not initially have a vision to share with others. To the contrary, as one breakout church leader commented, "Vision discovered me." The researchers found that the leaders discovered vision through intersection of three factors: the passion of the leader; the needs of the community; and the gifts, abilities, talents, and passions of the congregation.

Ray Pritchard became the senior pastor of Calvary Memorial Church in the Chicago suburb of Oak Park, Illinois, in 1989. For three years the church experienced an attendance plateau before breakout growth took place in 1992. Those early years of struggle were the result of several divisive issues in the church.

Pritchard did not go to Calvary clueless about his plans for leadership. He had some definite ideas about the direction the church should take. But he also did not arrive there with a clearly articulated vision summed up in a nice, catchy slogan. Instead, the vision discovered him.

The village of Oak Park has grown increasingly liberal over the past several years. It has one of the nation's largest gay and lesbian communities. Oak Park's village president (similar to a mayor in a small town) is openly lesbian. One of the largest congregations in the area is a Unitarian-Universalist church. Several New Age congregations also call Oak Park home.

Calvary Memorial is one of only two or three churches in this liberal community. The vision for the church is now clear. Calvary believes it can be the very best conservative, evangelical church in Oak Park. The leadership holds strongly to the conviction that the church is vitally needed in such an environment.

But Calvary Memorial's vision did not come out of some strategic planning group or the isolated mind of a senior pastor. Instead, the vision was "discovered" when three factors intersected. This fascinating discovery was made by our team in almost all the breakout churches.

Culture of Excellence (patterned after Jim Collins's Culture of Discipline)

An environment exists in the breakout churches that can best be described as an "environment of excellence." Once the leaders of these churches have become Acts 6/7 leaders, once they have experienced the crucial ABC moment, once they have led the church to discover its purpose and have added the right people and structures, and once the vision develops more clearly, they desire to be certain that such gains are not quickly lost. Everything the church does and is gets measured against a barometer of excellence. From the cleanliness of the nursery to the quality of the preaching, "good" is never enough. The church demands excellence.

Innovation Accelerators (patterned after Jim Collins's Technology Accelerators)

How many church leaders have divided and demoralized congregations by introducing innovative methodologies and approaches before the church was ready to accept them? How many churches are involved in worship wars without clearly understanding the reasons behind the conflict?

Many church leaders attempt to introduce an innovative approach as an end instead of the means. They may see the innovation as "the answer" to their church's woes. But breakout leaders were very balanced in their application of innovations. On the one hand, they were not carried away by the latest concept or church fad. On the other hand, they did not reject innovation outright just because it was something new.

Breakout leaders typically brought on innovative approaches more slowly and with discernment. They did not see the innovation as panacea but as a tool that could enhance an already healthy transition. In other words, innovations were accelerators but not the solutions to all of the church's needs.

David Clark became pastor of Central Christian Church in Beloit, Wisconsin, in 1981. He was not yet thirty years old and, by his own admission, tried to make too many changes too quickly. Some of the dominant leaders opposed Clark and led the church to fire him only six months into his ministry at Central Christian.

One elderly woman, however, led another group in the church to have Clark reinstated. The pastor was restored to his office, and the malcontents eventually left the church. Even so, almost four years would pass before Central Christian Church could recover from the conflict. This time Clark proceeded much more deliberately with regard to change and instead led the congregation to focus on the biblical purposes of the church. Under this leadership the church members began to gauge all of the ministries, programs, and activities by one question: "Does this activity help make fruit-bearing disciples in our church?"

From 1981 to 1989 the church saw little growth, and attendance did not break the 200 barrier. But beginning in 1989, the breakout point, rapid growth ensued. Attendance today exceeds 1,600.

David Clark did not attempt to institute major programmatic and ministry changes after the crisis in 1981. Eventually the church would institute many innovations, such as a Saturday evening service, a Gen X service, the hiring of a full-time children's pastor, and the restructuring of committees into true ministry teams. This time, however, the innovations were not ends to be pursued. The pastor did not seek to bring the latest fad to the church. The innovations that were eventually implemented came because the healthy growth of the church demanded them.

BIBLICAL MODELS OR SECULAR CLONES?

The breakout churches we studied are biblical churches. Their leaders hold a high view of Scripture, and they are intensely obedient to the Great Commission. The churches resemble closely the Jerusalem church in Acts 2:42–47 in their focus on the key purpose to which God has called them. Repeatedly in our interviews and in the published material we studied, we heard it expressed that these churches exist to bring glory to God.

Even the Collins model with which we began our study is not unbiblical. To the contrary, some of his findings have biblical compatibility even though he does not frame his conclusions in a God-centered perspective. For example, this is how Collins describes the leaders of good-to-great companies: "In contrast to the very *I*-centric style of the comparison leaders, we were struck by how the good-to-great leaders *didn't* talk about themselves."[3]

Collins sees these leaders as truly servant leaders. Sometimes his descriptions sound almost biblical: "It wasn't just false modesty. Those who worked with or wrote about the good-to-great leaders continually used words like *quiet, humble, modest, reserved, shy, gracious, mild-mannered, self-effacing, understated, did not believe his own clippings;* and so forth."[4]

Interestingly, Jim Collins does note that some of the good-to-great leaders had strong Christian convictions. "A strong religious belief or conversion might also nurture development of the Level 5 [the highest leadership level] traits," he says. "Colman Mockler, for example, converted to evangelical Christianity while getting his MBA at Harvard, and later, according to the book *Cutting Edge*, became a prime mover in a group of Boston business executives who met frequently over breakfast to discuss the carryover of religious values to corporate life."[5]

AN INCREDIBLE JOURNEY

On a late afternoon in the middle of the summer, I found myself highly frustrated. I knew the research team members were frustrated as well. What had sounded like such a brilliant idea at the outset had led me into the worst research project I have ever been involved in. I was convinced that I would not have entered into the research had I known all the obstacles we would confront.

We discovered along the way how many churches have poor data and records. We could not confirm their growth or lack of growth with any objective measurements. We also discovered that a significant number of churches and denominational entities were unwilling to share their information. Perhaps we would have found a few breakout churches in that pool of undisclosed data.

Our hopes rose when we found several churches that fit the statistical pattern of breakout churches—but then discovered that all of the breakout growth took place when new leadership came to the church. While I am grateful to God for these churches, I did not want to send the message that the only way to experience breakout growth is to fire the pastor.

The research team had written thousands of letters and emails, logged countless hours on the telephone, and delved into church statistics so long that they were ready to take a vow of numerical abstinence. And even I, the leader of this team, had my doubts on that July afternoon.

One would think that a pool of some 400,000 churches would yield hundreds of breakout churches. Our total was thirteen.

Imagine: Begin with 400,000 churches, end with thirteen.

Jim Collins was right. He had warned our team that it would take a long time to get the selection process right and that we would most likely find only a few churches that could meet rigorous criteria.[6]

I thought I could prove Jim Collins wrong. I thought the team and I could find many churches that fit our criteria. But I was wrong. I know that there are more breakout churches in America than we found. But thirteen are all we located. And on that summer afternoon, I questioned my sanity at enduring this project from start to finish.

Then I read again all the research, narratives, interviews, documents, statistics, and other data on the breakout churches. I saw the work of a great God turning around struggling congregations. I read about the impossible becoming possible in God's power.

As I reread this information, I realized that my research team and I had been on an incredible journey. The churches we found had stories that defy human wisdom and power. And I was reminded that the God who led these churches from decline, plateau, and even despair to hope, vitality, and growth is the same God who desires to build his church all over the world.

My team and I desired to show what happens when God takes a struggling congregation and turns it into a thriving congregation. The journey has been incredible. There are thousands of good churches in America, but there are few breakout churches. We have discovered some of them.

It is a sin to be good if God has called us to be great.

I invite you to join me as I share the common principles that moved these churches to greatness.

ACTS 6/7 LEADERSHIP

I am certainly not one of those who needs to be prodded. In fact, if anything, I am the prod.

—Winston Churchill

n *Good to Great,* Jim Collins and his research team uncovered a special type of leadership they called "Level 5 Leadership." The content of this chapter uses Level 5 Leadership as its seed concept. We patterned this chapter on Jim Collins's chapter 2 of *Good to Great.*

When someone writes the history of the American church for the past fifty years, Donald Schaeffer probably will not be remembered as one of the great leaders of this era. Indeed, it is doubtful that any of the pastors of our thirteen breakout churches will be in the annals of contemporary church history.

Donald Schaeffer served for thirty-eight years as senior pastor of Grace Church, a Christian and Missionary Alliance congregation in Middleburg Heights, Ohio. He led the church to grow to an attendance of about 500 by 1980, only to see attendance deteriorate slowly to 400 by 1986. The slow decline continued until 1990, when a breakout took place. By the time Schaeffer's son, Jonathan, assumed the position of senior pastor in 1998, there was a momentum going that would take the church to incredible attendance levels of nearly 1,700 by 2002.

In an interview with researcher Chris Bonts, Donald Schaeffer confessed that his leadership reflected the era in which he started ministry. The pastor was held responsible for virtually every area of ministry, and

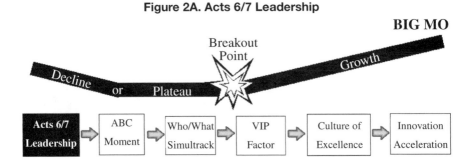

Figure 2A. Acts 6/7 Leadership

the single-staff church was normative. "In seminary, I had never received any training concerning a large staff. I grew up in the era of the single-staffed church," he reflected.[1]

Although the attendance of Grace Church had plateaued around 500 in 1985, the leadership was content with their church. After all, the church was larger than more than 90 percent of the churches in America. But in that same year, Schaeffer was shaken out of his complacency.

A TURNING POINT IN THE CHURCH

The pastor and some elders attended a Church Growth Institute seminar led by Bill Orr. They returned from the seminar with a new desire and vision to reach greater Cleveland with the gospel. Bill Orr told them that churches do not remain plateaued. They either begin to grow again or they begin to die. Schaeffer could no longer be content with business as usual.

"By the time we went to that conference," Schaeffer recalls, "I had gotten comfortable in ministry. We had a self-sustaining ministry, and I was working very hard every week raising my family of nine children and pastoring a church running between 400 and 500 in worship. I enjoyed my job, and I worked diligently in my preaching and pastoral ministry, but at that conference I realized that we had to begin to grow again."

Schaeffer experienced an inner turmoil that he realized was a blessing from God. "That conference was used by God to spark an emotional and philosophical change in my ministry," he said. "It was a dramatic change in attitude toward the church and our responsibility to proclaim the gospel and reach a lost world for Christ."

He admitted that he was guilty of smugness and complacency to this point. "Prior to that point in my ministry, there was a certain amount of self-satisfaction with the job I had done. God used that conference to create dissatisfaction."

Those who served with Schaeffer noted a change in his attitude and approach to ministry. Humility replaced self-satisfaction. The team approach to ministry replaced a loner approach. An outward focus replaced an inward focus.

The Donald Schaeffer story is a remarkable tale of transformed leadership. Though numbers never tell the full story, the worship attendance patterns in figure 2B are insightful. The first twenty years of his ministry were times of significant numerical growth. Unlike many leaders we know, Schaeffer was able to lead a church to more than 400 in attendance with little staff support. We have dubbed that period the "Loner Growth Phase."

But the cost of a loner ministry began to manifest itself over the next ten years as attendance plateaued and then declined to 397 in average worship attendance. We have labeled this period simply the "Plateau and Decline Phase." It was during this phase (1985) that Schaeffer attended the Church Growth Institute seminar.

The next stage of Schaeffer's ministry, the "Breakout Phase," represents the exciting period following the transformational years after the seminar. But note that numerical results were not immediate. The seminar took place in 1985, but breakout growth did not occur until 1990. Nevertheless, the pastor persevered as he communicated his vision to the church.

That perseverance is typical of the leaders we studied in this project. They stay with a church during the difficult times even though there may be numerous temptations to move to a greener pasture. Schaeffer notes, "I had several opportunities to leave, but I knew God had called me here and I wanted to stay and see the work through. I never sensed or felt God calling me away from here."

While we see many common characteristics of breakout church leaders, one trait that manifests itself repeatedly is persistence. These leaders see a clear goal, and though it may take years to reach the goal, they do not see giving up as an option.

Figure 2B. Grace Church, CMA, Loner Growth Phase

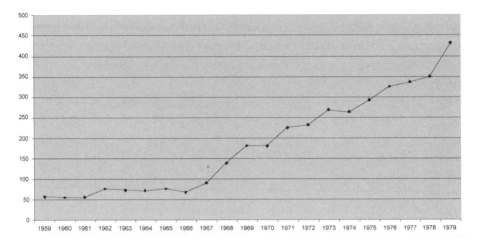

Figure 2C. Grace Church, CMA, Plateau and Decline Phase

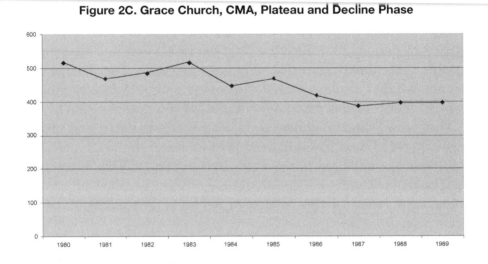

Schaeffer was passionate about the ministry and health of Grace Church beyond his own ministry and lifetime. By the time he became the senior pastor in 1998, the church had moved into another phase, this time a fast-growth era we call the "Momentum Phase."

Figure 2D. Grace Church, CMA, Breakout Growth Phase

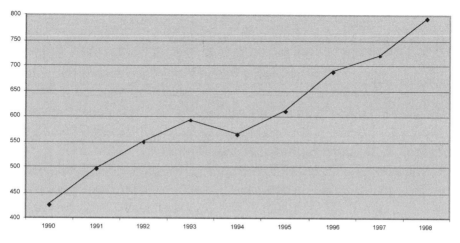

Figure 2E. Grace Church, CMA, Momentum Phase

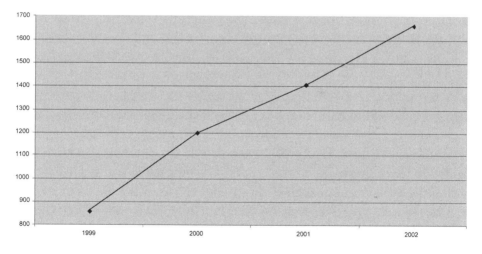

A COMPELLING MODESTY

In chapter 2 of *Good to Great*, Jim Collins elaborates on the attributes of the Level 5 Leader in a section titled "A Compelling Modesty." We liked that title so much that we decided to use it here, for it also is an apt description of the Acts 6/7 Leader. Donald Schaeffer's "compelling modesty" defies the stereotype of large-church leaders.

On page 27 of *Good to Great*, Jim Collins writes that "those who worked with or wrote about the good-to-great leaders continually used words like *quiet, humble, modest, reserved, shy, gracious, mild-mannered, self-effacing, understated, did not believe his own clippings;* and so forth."[2] Similarly, in interviewing people about Schaeffer and the other pastors of the breakout churches, we heard words like *modest, humble, quiet, others-centered, deflects accolades,* and *open to criticism*. In fact, the combined characteristics of the breakout leaders formed the pattern we call "Acts 6/7 Leadership." Let's look at our term and the meanings behind it.

When Jim Collins led the research for *Good to Great*, he insisted that his team avoid the trap of crediting or blaming a company's performance solely on leadership. He writes, "I gave the research team explicit instructions to *downplay* the role of top executives so that we could avoid the simplistic 'credit the leader' or 'blame the leader' thinking common today."[3]

Collins's research team could not rest with that mandate. They kept finding the critical role of leadership as these companies moved from good to great. Collins mused, "I kept insisting, 'Ignore the executives.' But the research team kept pushing back, 'No! There is something consistently unusual about them. We can't ignore them.'" How did the debate resolve? Collins admits, "Finally—as should always be the case—the data won." Good-to-great leaders "were all cut from the same cloth."[4]

I did not ask my research team to ignore factors of leadership in the turnaround of these churches. But I did fear that leadership traits would be such a major factor that most pastors would think, "It's no use. I can never be that kind of leader." Our project, however, had a different approach from Collins's. Our criteria demanded that the senior pastor must have been a part of the decline and plateau of the church as well as the breakout growth. In other words, the process of breakout included more than the transformation of a church; it included the transformation of a leader.

That is the reason you do not see the names of most well-known pastors in this book. You will not find Rick Warren, John MacArthur, James Merritt, Roger Spradlin, Phil Neighbors, Buddy Gray, Bill Hybels, or Jack Graham. Nor will you find Andy Stanley, Ed Young, Jerry Vines, Bob Russell, Fred Luter, Kevin Ezell, Kevin Cosby, or Robert Lewis. As far as we could tell, these leaders did not experience a period of plateau or decline in their churches. Some of them started churches and saw growth at the outset. Others came into churches that were struggling and led them to immediate turnarounds.

While I admire the ministries of these "great" leaders, I grieve for pastors who read about these men, attend their conferences, study their books, but seldom see any similar results in their own churches.

> **One of the great passions of this project is to provide hope for struggling leaders and churches. While we admittedly found very few churches that met our breakout criteria, the few we found told us that, in God's power, transformation can and does take place.**

AM I DOOMED TO MEDIOCRITY?

When I had a speaking engagement in Visalia, California, a pastor from the area spoke to me with bluntness. "Dr. Rainer," he began, "I really do want to have a ministry that makes a difference. But I just don't have the same leadership skills as some of the megachurch pastors. Is it possible to learn how to be a better leader? Or am I doomed for mediocrity the rest of my ministry?"

This book is the story of churches *and* leaders that broke from the shackles of mediocrity to become great churches and great leaders. What does a breakout church leader look like? Figure 2F provides a picture of the Acts 6/7 Leader. View the graphic from bottom to top, realizing that a leader cannot reach a particular level until he or she has attained all previous levels.

Figure 2F. The Leader Pyramid

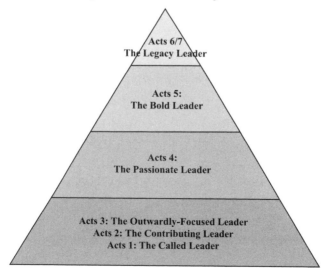

Acts 6/7
The Legacy Leader

Acts 5:
The Bold Leader

Acts 4:
The Passionate Leader

Acts 3: The Outwardly-Focused Leader
Acts 2: The Contributing Leader
Acts 1: The Called Leader

Acts 1: The Called Leader

The early church leaders were called to be witnesses of and for Christ (Acts 1:8). The Twelve were called to be the leaders of the church, including the calling of Matthias to replace Judas (Acts 1:21–26). All the breakout leaders whom we researched have a definitive testimony of God's call in their lives for vocational ministry, particularly in the local church.

In reading about the called leader, you might question why this first stage is even mentioned. After all, are not all church leaders called by God? The answer is an unequivocal no. We have worked with and interviewed a number of church leaders who see their ministries as no different from a secular job. But we have never come across a breakout leader who does not have a clear sense of being called into ministry by God.

Acts 2: The Contributing Leader

Most of the second chapter of Acts is devoted to Peter's sermon. We see leader Peter carrying forth the basic and essential elements of preaching (Acts 2:14–39) and prayer (v. 42). Glimpses of the first church are evident in verses 42–47.

Again, one may wonder if all church leaders are contributing leaders. Do not all pastors preach? Do not all pray? The answer is that only a minority spend significant time in these foundational ministries. In our research on effective evangelistic churches, we found that the leaders spent approximately twenty hours per week in sermon preparation and prayer. The leaders of the comparison (less evangelistic) churches spent only five hours per week in sermon preparation and prayer. And only 4 percent of churches in America met our criteria to be an effective evangelistic church.[5]

Acts 3: The Outwardly-Focused Leader

In the third chapter of Acts, Peter and John venture beyond the gathering of the church described at the end of chapter 2. The message of Christ and its healing power were delivered to the beggar who sat at the temple gate that was called Beautiful (Acts 3:1–10).

The third stage of leadership is found in leaders who consistently and persistently move the church to look beyond itself. These leaders give evangelism a priority, and they lead the congregation to other types of ministries beyond the walls of the church.

Acts 4: The Passionate Leader

When John Ewart joined my consulting team, the Rainer Group, in 2001, one of his key roles was to provide an assessment of leadership issues in the churches with which we worked. After a year, he began to articulate an issue that I have observed over my twenty years of consultation: Leaders of healthy churches have an obvious passion for their ministries. The passion is evident in their preaching, their conversations, and their numerous leadership roles.

This passion is not a personality trait. We see it in both quiet leaders and gregarious leaders. They exude an obvious energy and love for the work and ministry God has called them to do. Ewart says it well: "Passion is hard to define, but I know it when I see it."

Acts 4 relates how Peter and John were arrested and then, upon their release, were ordered by the Jewish religious council not to speak or teach about Jesus. But the two men responded, "Whether it is right in the sight of God to give heed to you rather than to God, you be the judge; for we cannot stop speaking about what we have seen and heard" (Acts 4:19–20 NASB).

The passion for these apostles' ministry is evident to us today even as their opponents acknowledged two thousand years ago: "Now as they observed the confidence of Peter and John and understood that they were uneducated and untrained men, they were amazed, and began to recognize them as having been with Jesus" (Acts 4:13 NASB). Perhaps the last words the writer Luke uses in that verse describe passion best: "they . . . began to recognize them as having been with Jesus."

Acts 5: The Bold Leader

The bold leader is willing to take incredible steps of faith, to make tough calls that few other leaders will make. The bold leader knows the mission and purpose of the church and is willing to take whatever steps are necessary to keep the church focused and on track.

Many of the highly visible pastors of churches today are Acts 5 leaders. They have led their churches to relocate, to undertake massive stewardship campaigns, to begin intensive ministries in the community, and to feel a discomfort with the status quo. They are determined and focused. And they are willing to pay the price when they perceive a certain course is best for the church.

Peter exemplifies this type of leadership in Acts 5 with his bold confrontation of Ananias and Sapphira. The couple threatened to derail the church from its forward movement with their deceitfulness over the sale of some property (Acts 5:1–11). God's judgment—the death penalty—may seem harsh to some people today, but the fact is that the church was able to move forward after this issue was resolved (Acts 5:12–16).

Acts 6/7: The Legacy Leader

Acts 6/7 leaders are hard to find. They have all the attributes of the previous stages plus more. These leaders, such as the Twelve mentioned in Acts 6:1–7, are quick to give ministry to others and let them take the credit for their work. Indeed, they desire to deflect recognition to others. They are quick to praise others and equally quick to accept responsibility for anything that may go wrong.

But Acts 6/7 leaders, like Stephen, are not merely concerned about the church during their lifetime; they seek to make decisions that will benefit the church after they are gone. This kind of leader is rare. We found very few within the thousands of churches we researched.

WHAT WE FOUND WHEN LOOKING AT TODAY'S LEADERS

What is the status of leadership in the church today? We looked at 427 churches where we have consulted or done fairly extensive research. We then looked at the leadership and made a determination of their level of leadership according to the Acts 6/7 progression.[6] We were surprised at the results.

Figure 2G. Levels of Leadership

Level of Leadership	Description	Percentage of Senior Pastors Who Have Attained This Level
Acts 1 The Called Leader	Knows of God's call to ministry and has responded to that call	98%
Acts 2 The Contributing Leader	Takes time to do well the basics of Christian ministry such as preaching, teaching, and prayer	22%
Acts 3 The Outwardly-Focused Leader	Seeks to lead church and self to ministry beyond the walls of the church	14%

Acts 4 The Passionate Leader	Exudes a contagious enthusiasm for ministry; others gladly follow	6%
Acts 5 The Bold Leader	Is willing to take risks, where success is only possible in God's power	3%
Acts 6/7 The Legacy Leader	Has a burden for a successful ministry beyond his own lifetime	Less than 1%

Fewer than 1 percent of the senior pastors we studied have attained this level of leadership. Yet we believe that this type of leadership is needed for the long-term health of churches. Eight out of ten of the approximately 400,000 churches in the United States are declining or have plateaued.[7] Acts 6/7 leadership is desperately needed. Is there any hope for the American church?

We noticed in the leadership styles of pastors we studied a significant difference when a leader moves from one level to the next. A church inevitably experiences noticeable gains if its leader moves just one level. Perhaps a goal leaders should establish immediately is to move from their present level to the next.

I would not have led this research project, nor would I have written this book unless I believed there is hope. It is my passion to communicate to church leaders the characteristics of breakout churches and their leaders. My motive is not merely descriptive but also prescriptive.

SOME SURPRISES WE FOUND IN BREAKOUT CHURCH LEADERS

The fourteen pastors who lead the thirteen breakout churches we studied (two are copastors) are a diverse group of leaders—racially, geographically, ethnically, and socioeconomically. Yet we observed many commonalities among them. When we aligned these common features with the comparison group of pastors, many characteristics appeared to be unique to the breakout group.

As the research team assimilated the leadership information, we often found ourselves discussing some of the surprises we uncovered. Most of the leaders fit all of the descriptions below.

Slow Progress Is Fine

When T. Vaughn Walker became pastor of the First Gethsemane Baptist Church in Louisville, Kentucky, the church's budget was under the influence and control of the deacons and trustees. There was a critical need for significant input from other ministry leadership in a more comprehensive budgeting process. Walker himself did not want budgetary control, but he did need the process changed so that the church would have the resources to carry forth the vision. Budget priorities offer insight into the heartbeat of ministry foci. The process was more focused on maintenance and survival rather than on vision and growth.

Our surprise is not that Walker succeeded in getting this change accomplished. Rather, we were surprised that it took him seven years to do so. "It was not a life or death need for the church," Walker commented. "I knew I could finally lead the change if I was patient, loving, and persistent."

When we looked at some of the leaders of comparison churches, we noticed two broad approaches to leading change. One group was dubbed by the research team "the peacemakers." Because change inevitably leads to some level of conflict, they helped defend the status quo to avoid pain.

The other group was called "my way or the highway leaders." These leaders tended to be autocratic in their decision making. It was not uncommon during our interviews to hear statements like this one from a pastor in the Midwest: "I've told the people in my church that the vision is clear. And if they can't get on board with the vision, then they can find another church."

We noticed that these autocratic pastors tend to have a pattern of conflict in the churches they serve. They may see short-term or even mid-term numerical gains in their churches, but any positive result of their ministry is seldom long-lasting. Some have been fired from their churches; others have left under pressure. And they have left a trail of hurting and angry members in many of the churches they served.

> **Our studies found that the damage wrought by an autocratic leadership style is often swift and deep and sometimes irreversible. The "peacemakers," by contrast, tend to lead churches downward slowly and even imperceptibly, yet at the end of the day, what remains is a hurting, unhealthy, and usually smaller church.**

The breakout pastors, however, tended to approach the role of leadership for change with three levels of awareness. These three patterns seem to be consistent in all of these leaders.

- They desired to communicate clearly their love for the members of the congregation. They did not feel that people should be readily discarded if they disagreed with the vision.
- They recognized that the established church is often entrenched in tradition and therefore change is difficult and often takes time.
- They knew that change must ultimately take place and that goals must be achieved if the church is to move forward. Unlike the peacemakers, they moved persistently and patiently toward their goals.

More Breakout Church Leaders Are Thin-Skinned Than Thick-Skinned

A mentor pastor once advised me that if I wanted to survive in local church ministry, I would have to learn to ignore most of the criticisms I received. After serving as pastor in four churches in four states, I found that I was just as sensitive to criticism then as at the beginning of my ministry.

I guess I had some level of relief when our team discovered that breakout church leaders tend to be more thin-skinned than thick-skinned. Xenos Christian Fellowship in Columbus, Ohio, began as a college Bible study at Ohio State University in 1970. Xenos experienced rapid growth in the 1970s and the early 1980s. But the body still did not look like an institutional church until 1982, when it took on its present name and hired the first of its paid staff.

Although Xenos clearly has a more institutional flavor today than it used to have, it is still not your typical congregation. So when the leadership started buying property and constructing buildings in the early 1990s, some of the congregants thought the church was becoming too "worldly." Further conflict took place when the church leaders confronted a "hypercharismatic" group in the church and when they began to question the biblical validity of the counseling ministries.

From 1991 to 1994 the church experienced a mass exodus of 1,200 to 1,500 people. Attendance declined from 3,800 to 2,400. The perception of some pundits of megachurch pastors is that they let the critics have their say and then they move on with little personal suffering. Such is not the case with the leadership of Xenos.

Dennis McCallum, who serves as lead pastor along with Gary DeLashmutt, describes the pain he endured during this time of attrition and criticism: "Many of the people asked the leaders to leave. It took a church vote to keep us here. We lost a third of the church. It was very depressing. There was a lingering sense of defeat."

We were impressed with the honesty and openness of these leaders as they shared the pain they experienced. In all of the breakout church leaders, we saw very caring men. They said that most of the struggles they experienced were necessary, but the loss of members and the constant criticisms hurt them deeply. Criticisms did not just roll off them. They dealt with the critics and persevered but often at great personal cost.

Many of the Breakout Leaders Are Reluctant Leaders

It is fascinating to hear many of the leaders talk about their current positions. They did not plan to be a leader of a great church; some specifically said they did not, at one point, even want to serve in their current leadership role.

The parallel between the breakout church leaders and the good-to-great leaders in Collins's research is striking. Collins could have been describing the pastors when he wrote, "The good-to-great leaders never wanted to become larger than life heroes. They never aspired to be put on a pedestal or become unreachable icons. They were seemingly ordinary people quietly producing extraordinary results."[8]

Stephen Schwambach found himself in a difficult position in 1981. His father, pastor of Bethel Temple Community Church for thirty years, wanted to step down as head pastor. But he wasn't ready to retire. Instead, he proposed that he and his son switch roles. From now on, the son would lead the church as pastor. The father would simply be a member of his son's pastoral staff—but retain the honorary title of Senior Pastor until his retirement, ten years in the future.

> When we compared the breakout church leaders with the comparison church leaders, we saw three distinct groups in our understanding of their ambitions. One group frankly seemed to have no ambition. They were either in a survival or coasting mode. A second group was personally ambitious. They tended to speak in the first person singular. The third group, our breakout leaders, did have personal ambitions, but they more often spoke of their ambitions for the churches they served.

After lengthy discussions, the deacons, elders, board of trustees, and congregation voted in favor of the proposal. But privately, few members believed the arrangement would last. It almost didn't.

At first, the young pastor was thrilled with the opportunity to lead his home church. Burning with the vision to build a church of passionately committed believers who would reach the unchurched, he eagerly embraced what he believed was a once-in-a-lifetime opportunity from God.

But his optimistic dreams soon turned into a long-running nightmare. "These were precious Christian people whom the Lord loved very much," he says. "Unfortunately, my leadership style was long on zeal and short on wisdom." Consequently, many of the important changes the young pastor proposed were met with firm resistance. Families that preferred his father's approach began to leave the church. Attendance fell. Budgets grew tight. Criticism of Schwambach's pastoral leadership grew.

Through it all, God graciously brought in a steady stream of new people who responded to the new pastor's leadership. Yet a significant core of the church continued to resist the changes their pastor sought to implement. The painful internal battles continued. When one dearly loved pastoral staff member had to be let go, 200 members left with him.

At the height of the turmoil, one of the embattled pastor's mentors frankly advised him, "It's easier to give birth than to raise the dead."[9] That made sense. Convinced he was the wrong fit for this congregation, Schwambach began to beg God to release him from Bethel Temple and allow him to start a church in a city that might be more receptive to the methods he felt were essential to reaching the unchurched.

In early 1993, more than a decade after being named pastor, Schwambach embarked on a protracted time of prayer and fasting. During this period he felt God further clarifying the vision that had so far failed to be fulfilled. Schwambach felt boxed in. "I don't have the *right* to force these saints of yours to change!" he cried to the Lord in frustration.

"No, you don't," he sensed the Lord saying within him. "But I do—and I intend to use *you* to do it."

Weary of the battle but now convinced that God wanted him to stay, Schwambach submitted—and went back to work. Little did he realize, however, that it would take almost another decade—a total of nearly twenty years—before the church would begin to experience breakout growth.

Breakout church leaders are willing, and sometimes even want, to make slow progress. They tend to be more thin-skinned than thick-skinned. And they are often reluctant leaders. These are three of the discoveries we made in our research that seem to go contrary to conventional wisdom. But the burning question remains, "What are the characteristics of a breakout church leader?" When this massive project concluded, our team felt as though we had made significant progress in answering that question. We turn to those answers in the next chapter.

IN ESSENCE, IN SUMMARY
ACTS 6/7 LEADERSHIP

- Keep in mind throughout this book that the criteria to qualify as a breakout church included the church experiencing both a period of struggle and a time of breakout growth under the same pastor's leadership.

- We place church leaders in six different levels of leadership. Only 14 percent were Acts 3 or higher; only 6 percent were Acts 4 or higher; and only 3 percent were Acts 5 or higher. Leaders in the Acts 6/7 level, the highest category, account for less than one percent of all pastors.

- Acts 6/7 leaders tend to accept slow progress. They are sensitive to criticism, but they do not let their critics deter them from the goals and visions they sense God has given them.

- An Acts 6/7 leader consistently finds ways to communicate the love they have for their congregations.

- Many of the Acts 6/7 leaders are reluctant leaders. They neither planned nor desired to serve in their present position.

- One of the surprises that surfaced in our research was that the Acts 6/7 leaders are sensitive to criticism. We assumed that they would be more thick-skinned rather than thin-skinned.

- We found no autocratic leaders in the breakout churches. While they were strong leaders, their humility precluded them from being dictatorial leaders. Yet some of these leaders admitted that they were autocratic in the past. One of the major transformations that took place in their lives personally was the move away from dictatorial leadership.

CHAPTER 3

EIGHT KEYS TO ACTS 6/7 LEADERSHIP

Do what you can, with what you have, where you are.

—Theodore Roosevelt

I am reluctant to articulate the characteristics of breakout church leaders in step-by-step fashion for fear that some may take the information and reduce it to a neat, quick-fix formula and that others may see this approach as human-centered, denying the reality of a sovereign God. Neither of these potential concerns reflects our intent. Nevertheless, a very clear pattern did develop when we lined up the several qualities present in all of our breakout church leaders with the qualities of the leaders in the comparison churches.

Keep in mind that it is the total and the composition of these traits that distinguish the breakout church leaders from the leaders of the comparison churches. One of the keys, for example, a long-tenured pastorate, could be found in a number of the comparison churches. But that quality alone did not make a good or mediocre leader into a great leader. Indeed, we found several pastors who led their churches in long-term declines.

Figure 3A. Acts 6/7 Leadership

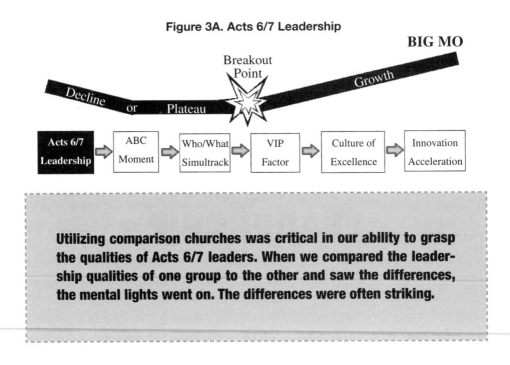

Utilizing comparison churches was critical in our ability to grasp the qualities of Acts 6/7 leaders. When we compared the leadership qualities of one group to the other and saw the differences, the mental lights went on. The differences were often striking.

I was tempted to list these qualities in some order of importance or priority, but I quickly realized that I had no data support for doing so; I would just be reflecting my own biases. The order is therefore more logical than a ranking showing importance.

FIERCE BIBLICAL FAITHFULNESS

All of the Acts 6/7 leaders are evangelicals who hold a high view of Scripture. If we had not utilized comparison churches, we probably would have concluded that a conservative view of Scripture was a distinctive characteristic of breakout church leaders. Our problem with this conclusion, however, is that many of the comparison church leaders were conservative as well. What then distinguished the two groups in their views of Scripture?

This study, as many of our previous studies, affirms the importance of leadership holding a high view of Scripture.[1] But the Acts 6/7 leaders do far more than merely believe the truth claims of Scripture; they also passionately live out their beliefs. We can find, for example, hundreds of churches where senior pastors say they believe in an inerrant Scripture. But in many of those churches, we see little evangelistic fruit and low levels of ministry to the community. They say they believe the Bible commands Christians to reach people for Christ, but their churches have little evangelistic fruit. They say they believe they are to be salt and light, but their churches have nominal ministries in the communities they are supposed to serve.

> **In many of the comparison churches we studied, the community ministries they cited were often poorly resourced food and clothes closets and the dedication of a minuscule portion of their budgets for "benevolence." Little intentional ministry was obvious.**

Calvary Memorial Church is located in Oak Park, Illinois, an older suburb of Chicago with a significant number of homosexuals in the community. The church was once almost all Anglo, but Pastor Ray Pritchard led the church to reach out in the racially and ethnically diverse community. Today one-third of the church's congregants are in the non-Anglo category, and that number is increasing.

One of the few evangelical congregations in the community, Calvary Memorial often receives criticism for its biblical stands. If one of our comparison churches was located in Oak Park, you might very well hear its leaders preach and teach against the homosexual lifestyle. Calvary Memorial Church takes the same biblical position as many of the comparison churches, but the congregation is not content to deride those with lifestyles contrary to Scripture.

In the late 1990s, Oak Park elected a homosexual mayor. The political victory put the spotlight on Calvary, one of the few churches to voice publicly its biblical opposition to the homosexual lifestyle. But Calvary leadership did more. At one point Pritchard had a much-publicized dialogue with an openly gay pastor in the community (which began somewhat tense but ended amicably). This discussion served to open doors of ministry to people the church would not otherwise be able to reach. Calvary began a counseling ministry with a significant portion of its time dedicated to reaching homosexuals in the community in a redemptive fashion.

Belief in the authority of Scripture is requisite for church leaders. But Acts 6/7 leaders both believe and act upon their belief.

THE TENURE ISSUE

Acts 6/7 leaders are willing and even want to have long-term ministries at one church. The church in America is mired in unhealthy structures and traditions that cannot be reversed in a short period. These leaders have a long-term view of ministry and are ever persistent in moving the church forward. But they know that three steps forward are often followed by two steps backward.

The chart below puts the tenure issue in perspective. We have three bodies of data from which to draw our conclusions. One group, of course, includes the Acts 6/7 leaders. We show the tenure of each of those pastors. The next group is the comparison group of thirty-nine pastors. The final group is our most recent survey of 553 churches and the pastoral tenure of those pastors.[2] The latter group is our closest approximation to a national average.

We have noted for years in our research that a direct correlation is present between pastoral tenure and evangelistic effectiveness in churches.[3]

Breakout Church and Location	Tenure of Acts 6/7 Pastor
Bethel Temple Community Church Evansville, Indiana	24 Years*
Calvary Memorial Church Oak Park, Illinois	15 Years*
Central Christian Church Beloit, Wisconsin	23 Years*
Fairfield New Life Church Fairfield, California	12 Years*
First Gethsemane Baptist Church Louisville, Kentucky	20 Years*
Korean Central Presbyterian Church Vienna, Virginia	26 Years
Grace Church, Christian and Missionary Alliance Middleburg Heights, Ohio	38 Years
Grace Evangelical Free Church Allen, Texas	12 Years*

Grove City Church of the Nazarene Grove City, Ohio	7 Years
Lenexa Baptist Church Lenexa, Kansas	14 Years*
Southwest Baptist Church Amarillo, Texas	28 Years*
The Temple Church Nashville, Texas	27 Years*
Xenos Christian Fellowship Columbus, Ohio	28 Years*# 28 Years*#
Average Tenure Acts 6/7 Pastors	21.6 Years
Average Tenure Comparison Church Pastors	4.2 Years
Average Tenure National Survey of Pastors	3.6 Years

*Still active. Years through 2004.
#Xenos has two lead pastors who were not designated in that role until the early 1990s. The years shown represent their entire tenure as elders at the church.

But this contrast is striking. The average tenure of a breakout church leader exceeds twenty-one years, while the other pastors in our study have been at their churches only about four years.

The obvious question asks how these leaders have remained at one place for such a long period. After studying thousands of churches for two decades, I have come to the conclusion that long tenure should be normative, but that several factors are creating abnormally short tenures. Indeed, our research indicates that the problem of the short-term pastor is a relatively recent phenomenon from the past fifty years.[4] Both churches and their leaders are responsible for this new development.

On the one hand, pastors are often quick to leave a church when a seemingly better, sometimes bigger, opportunity comes their way. While we cannot and will not question God's call on any one pastor when it comes to moves, we cannot help but be concerned about the overall trend .in quick moves. A pastor of one of our comparison churches said: "I have made five moves to what I thought were greener pastures. If I had stayed at my first or even second church, I believe that church would be very healthy today, and I would be more content. I just wish somehow I could communicate this message to younger pastors."

On the other hand, churches and their lay leaders can be incredibly demanding of, if not vicious to, pastors. In my consulting ministry with the Rainer Group, I often deal with lay leaders who treat pastors like CEOs and expect immediate results of them. And ironically, while these lay leaders demand quick results, they can be reluctant to give the pastor any authority to carry out the initiatives they expect to take place. The result is frustration for both parties. No wonder it is not uncommon to see pastors leave under pressure or even be forcefully terminated in such situations.

Long pastoral tenure is not a panacea or the single answer to struggling churches across America, but I believe that long tenure is *one* of the key requisites for churches to move from mediocrity to goodness to greatness.

> **All of our breakout church leaders have or had long pastoral tenure. Similarly, all of our church leaders experienced some level of conflict in their ministries. The two issues are closely related. Many of the pastors of the comparison churches left the churches they served at the early signs of conflict. The breakout church leaders endured the pain and did not leave. They were tenacious. Their short-term pain brought long-term gains.**

CONFIDENT HUMILITY

Grace Evangelical Free Church in Allen, Texas, sits in the shadows of megachurches in the Dallas–Fort Worth metroplex. With an attendance of approximately 300, the church gets none of the recognition of the larger churches. Indeed, if the vision of the church becomes a reality, Grace will never be a megachurch. The plans call for the planting of new churches every time attendance reaches 500.

During Senior Pastor Joel Walters's twelve years at Grace, he led the church slowly but persistently to realize that all ministries cannot be the responsibility of one person. "We realized that one person cannot care for all people in a 200-plus worship service," Walters told researcher Elisha Rimestead. Most of the ministry responsibility now takes place in small groups that meet in homes.

Like all of our breakout church pastors, Walters realized that any change in this established church would take time. "The church went through five pastors in ten years and experienced difficult times," he told us. This pastor began to lead change with a methodical quiet confidence. Eventually the church broke the 200 barrier and is now poised to exceed 300 in attendance.

When our researcher interviewed laypeople at Grace, he found an amazing consistency in the descriptions of Walters. "He has consistently and confidently communicated the vision of planting new churches and equipping people to do ministry," one member noted. Another member observed, "His confidence is contagious, but he is very humble too. He loves and cares for the flock immensely."

As our team examined the characteristics of church leaders in the Acts 6/7 progression, we noticed a distinct break between Acts 3 leaders and Acts 4 leaders. Leaders at Acts 4 and higher displayed an unmistakable confidence in their leadership abilities. They had a focus, determination, and unswerving faith in what could be accomplished. The laypeople in the churches spoke of this confidence often. Indeed, this confident leadership seemed to be a requisite to attract followers to the ministry of the church.

Yet we noticed another distinct break between Acts 5 leaders and Acts 6/7 leaders. Confidence is evident in both groups. But the Acts 6/7 leaders displayed an unpretentious humility with their confidence. We would often hear phrases such as, "When I came to this church . . ." among the Level 4 and Level 5 leaders. They were eager to tell us of *their* accomplishments. While we would not accuse all of these leaders of being egotistical in their ministries, many were happy to tell us of their leadership abilities.

We saw no less confidence in the Acts 6/7 leaders, but their confidence centered more on what God was doing in their lives and less on their own inherent abilities. They were often reluctant to attribute any of the church's accomplishments to themselves. Their modesty was compelling and sincere. Because most of our breakout church leaders had experienced difficult times in their ministries, any sense of self-importance had been tempered over the years. While they confidently believed their leadership was critical to the health of the church, they also believed their leadership abilities were a gift from a God upon whom they were totally dependent.

Researcher Michael O'Neal interviewed Don Green, vice president of development at Lincoln Christian College and Seminary in Lincoln, Illinois.

He is very familiar with the ministry of David Clark, pastor of Central Christian Church in Beloit, Wisconsin. His description of Clark describes the essence of an Acts 6/7 leader well. "David is at the same time a very ambitious yet unassuming leader," Don Green told us. "He is a catalyst for change and growth without seeking the spotlight. He leads with single-minded direction without being self-centered. He has openly and publicly shared the credit for the church's success with a superb staff and lay leaders while being very self-effacing and taking very little credit for himself."

Don Green's closing comments about David Clark were telling: "I personally know several megachurch pastors, but few demonstrate the depth of humility and the servant's heart that David does."

> Confident humility may at first seem to be an oxymoron. But this phrase is incredibly descriptive of Acts 6/7 leaders. The vast majority of the leaders of our comparison churches were woefully lacking in confidence of their leadership abilities. But among the relatively few leaders we researched who *did* demonstrate clear confidence, only a very small number of them exhibited the trait of humility.

ACCEPTANCE OF RESPONSIBILITY

In writing about Level 5 Leadership, Jim Collins noted that comparison (non-Level 5) leaders pointed "out the window" to factors other than themselves when things went poorly or they experienced difficulty. Level 5 leaders, by contrast, pointed "into the mirror" and accepted full responsibility.[5]

Our interviews with the pastors of the comparison churches turned out to be draining experiences. These leaders would often demonstrate a victim's mentality. Indeed, we could compile a small book just quoting the many explanations we have heard for the ineffectiveness of their ministries. The quotes below are representative of this issue.

- "The members in my church just don't want to follow my leadership."
- "There is no growth in this area. We don't have the opportunity to reach many people."
- "The board in my church resists any changes."

- "We are mostly an older congregation. Most of the people in my church are set in their ways."
- "I've tried everything I know to help this church. They just like things the way they are."
- "We have an ugly, old building for a worship center. It's just not attractive to prospects coming to the church."
- "I'll have to go to another church if I am ever to have an effective ministry. It will never happen here."
- "The larger churches in this area are stealing the members of my church and other smaller churches."

I have no desire to be critical of the leaders of these comparison churches. I realize that many of these pastors are facing difficult situations and dealing with difficult people. But the contrast was stark in our interviews with these leaders compared to the breakout church leaders.

We simply did not hear the excuses for ineffective ministry from the Acts 6/7 leaders even though many of them had prolonged periods of struggles. Others face difficult demographic opportunities. A few find their churches in the shadows of megachurches. But they refuse to blame others. They accept the responsibility that comes with being a leader.

> **In one case a comparison church was located in the same community as our breakout church. The pastor of the breakout church told us of "the hundreds of lost and unchurched people that could be reached" in that community. The pastor of the comparison church insisted that the community was "almost completely churched," with no people left to reach.**

A contagious optimism exudes from the Acts 6/7 leaders. They see no obstacle as being so great that the church, in God's power, cannot overcome. Our interviews with these leaders energized us. I remember when researcher Laura Cruse returned from her interviews with the leaders of Xenos Christian Fellowship in Columbus, Ohio. For days she could not stop talking about the God-centered enthusiasm that was clearly evident at the church.

Weak leaders of churches blame people and circumstances. Breakout church leaders accept responsibility and see God's possibilities in even difficult situations.

UNCONDITIONAL LOVE OF THE PEOPLE

Keep in mind that most of our breakout church leaders experienced tremendous pain and heartache as they led their churches. One was fired and rehired. Many considered quitting. Others were urged to step down. Many members left their churches. Won Sang Lee saw one-third of Korean Central Presbyterian Church's membership leave early in his ministry at the Washington, D.C.,–area congregation.

Despite the pains and trials they experienced, the breakout church leaders still express an intense love for the members of their congregations. Some of the leaders viewed the model of Jesus to be emblematic for their own ministries. Christ's death on the cross was an unconditional act of love for people who did not deserve his love. Some of these leaders said they have prayed for this unconditional love for their congregants. And although they cannot match the love of Christ in its depth, they can demonstrate it in their unconditional acceptance of all of their members.

One of the breakout church leaders told us his story in anonymity, since the offending party was still at the church. "Max" was initially one of the pastor's greatest adversaries. Indeed, on one occasion he led an unsuccessful movement to have the pastor dismissed. Though the pastor would confront Max and disagree with him, he always did so in a spirit of love.

When Max went through a very painful personal problem, the pastor stood by him and ministered to him and his family. Max's attitude toward the pastor changed quickly. He is now one of his biggest supporters.

"I admit that I went home on some days ready to kill Max. He was the biggest pain I have ever known in ministry," the pastor told us. "But my godly wife kept reminding me to love him as Christ loved me. Through prayer I eventually began really feeling love toward Max, even when he was my biggest critic. God even showed me some things I could learn from Max's criticisms. It was not the most fun experience of my ministry, but I did learn a lot."

The comparison church leaders often told us of the many problem people in their churches. We rarely heard those stories from the Acts 6/7 leaders. Breakout church leaders love their flock unconditionally.

PERSISTENCE

Because these leaders have a long-term perspective of their ministries at the churches they serve, they are able to lead toward progress one incremental step at a time. That is not to say that they have a laissez-faire attitude; to the contrary, the Acts 6/7 leaders are incredibly persistent.

> **An obvious parallel exists between persistence and long tenure. Our definition of persistence, however, is broader than tenure. For example, it includes the fulfillment of goals regardless of the time needed to complete the task.**

The story of J. Alan Ford and Southwest Baptist Church in Amarillo, Texas, is a classic story of persistent leadership. Ford became the pastor of Southwest at the young age of twenty-eight in 1976. The church struggled for a number of years as he led the congregation to reach the community. No outreach plan seemed to work. Still the pastor persisted.

Ford admitted that he was considering leaving the church until he attended a leadership seminar led by John Maxwell. He gleaned some insights from the conference to help the members take responsibility for reaching the community. Ford endured an economic slowdown in the community and the loss of some key financial supporters, but still he persisted.

The church has experienced several attendance plateaus, but it broke out of those plateaus as the pastor provided leadership to move the church to the next level. After the church's struggles in Ford's early years of ministry, breakout growth finally took place. That growth would soon be stymied by facility barriers, but the pastor led the church to buy land and build new facilities.

After moving to the new facilities, the church again hit a plateau. This time the pastor saw the need to reorganize the church so that all members would receive ministry and care. He led the church to organize Sunday school classes into small groups where small-group leaders would be responsible for ministry. Once again the church broke out of its plateau and moved into a growth mode. Today the church averages over 1,300 in worship attendance. But Alan Ford had days when he wondered if he would even stay at the church.

> **Most of the breakout churches in our study did not experience explosive overnight growth. For most, the path of growth was slow, methodical, and strewn with obstacles. Persistent, never-say-die leadership was a key instrument that God used to grow these churches to the next level. Giving up was always a temptation but never an option.**

The combination of pastoral tenure and persistence seems to be a powerful combination that God has used to move these churches to greatness. While many of our comparison church leaders had a pattern of leaving churches at the early signs of difficulties and obstacles, the Acts 6/7 leaders recognize that the greatest days for the church may lie just beyond the latest struggle.

THE OUTWARDLY-FOCUSED VISION

The concept of vision seems to be elusive for many leaders. The breakout church leaders, however, grasp this issue as well as anyone we have studied. In chapter 6 I provide a thorough examination of vision in breakout churches. However, one matter is worthy of note at this point in the book. The Acts 6/7 leaders did not just grasp vision, communicate vision, and implement vision. They consistently had a vision that was outwardly focused. In other words, a key component of their vision was to reach those who were not yet part of the church. To say that these leaders were evangelistically focused would be an understatement. They were *passionate* about reaching the lost and unchurched, and the visions they communicated inevitably reflected this priority.

A DESIRE FOR A LASTING LEGACY

On page 26 of *Good to Great*, in a section titled "Ambition for the Company: Setting Up Successors for Success," Jim Collins writes, "Level 5 leaders want to see the company even more successful in the next generation, comfortable with the idea that most people won't even know that the roots of that success trace back to their efforts."

Similarly, one of the key distinguishing marks of an Acts 6/7 leader is the desire to see the church do well and to make a difference well beyond the ministry of the current leadership. In none of our interviews with the leaders of the comparison churches did we hear any discussion of the church beyond their current ministries.

Rather than highlighting any one pastor, I would like you to listen to the comments of several of the Acts 6/7 leaders. You will certainly get a clear message of their legacy perspective.

- "I am working with the leadership of the church to make certain a good plan is in place to call my successor on or before my retirement."
- "I pray that God will allow me to look at this church from heaven fifty years from now and find out that the fruit of what we did is lasting."
- "Every time we look at doing something new or making some change, we ask how this might affect the church twenty-five years from now."
- "Some of the ideas we have may be quick fixes. We are asking God what will work for the long haul."
- "I pray that the church I leave one day will be a better church for my successor."

The ambition and drive of these leaders cannot be denied. And that ambition is not limited to their personal successes. They are ambitious for the church to be thriving and healthy well beyond their ministries and even their lifetimes.

ACTS 6/7 LEADERS: MADE OR BORN?

Some of us are born with gifts and characteristics that would make us more likely to be Acts 6/7 leaders than others. In that sense, some are more likely to attain this level of leadership than others. But I am also convinced, after hearing from these breakout church leaders, that many of the traits can be learned and sharply honed.

Readers of this book inevitably are concerned with their ability to reach the Acts 6/7 leader level. The leaders of the breakout churches would likely respond that their pilgrimage in leadership has often been arduous and painful, but that the journey has been worth it. Most of the leaders also told us that their leadership skills are God-powered rather than human-centered.

In fact, we heard many times of the intense prayer lives of these pastors who sought to be the type of leaders God called them to be.

At the end of the Level 5 Leadership chapter in *Good to Great*, Jim Collins writes, "We cannot say for sure what percentage of people have the seed [of Level 5] within, or how many of those can nurture it."[6]

In the final analysis, we cannot know what "portion" of Acts 6/7 leadership is inborn and what portion is acquired. The leaders will tell you, however, that you can make significant strides in becoming a better leader. Such are their own testimonies. Indeed, as you read the characteristics of breakout leaders, I hope you saw the possibility for those same characteristics in your life.

In none of our breakout churches did the pastor tell us that he began exercising Acts 6/7 leadership at the onset of his ministry. To the contrary, we discovered that the leaders and the churches often experienced some intense wake-up call to move them in a new direction. We dubbed those wake-up calls "ABC moments." To that fascinating discovery we now turn.

IN ESSENCE, IN SUMMARY
EIGHT KEYS TO ACTS 6/7 LEADERSHIP

- In noting characteristics of the breakout leaders in contrast to the comparison church leaders, we noted eight key characteristics that differentiated the two groups.

- These leaders display fierce biblical faithfulness. They not only give mental assent to key doctrinal truths, but they also practice these beliefs in their preaching, teaching, leadership, and ministry.

- Acts 6/7 leaders have an average tenure at their churches of 21.6 years, compared to the national average of 3.6 years. The issue of long tenure is critical, because much of the transition to greatness is a long-term process.

- "Confident humility" describes well the attitude of Acts 6/7 leaders. They have a high level of confidence but no appearance of arrogance or haughtiness.

- Our comparison church leaders were quick to place blame on people and circumstances. The Acts 6/7 leaders accepted the responsibility for their ministry and did not blame others when things did not go well.

- Acts 6/7 leaders have and show an unconditional love for the congregants they serve.

- Acts 6/7 leaders are persistent. They never consider a setback a failure.

- The visions cast by Acts 6/7 leaders always include an evangelistic passion.

- Acts 6/7 leaders are concerned about their ministries well beyond their own tenure or even lifetime. That is why we call them legacy leaders.

- We believe that many of the characteristics of Acts 6/7 leaders can be learned and applied by others.

THE ABC MOMENT

Get the facts, or the facts will get you. And when you get them, get them right, or they will get you wrong. All things are difficult before they are easy.

—Thomas Fuller

I n *Good to Great,* Jim Collins and his research team uncovered a pattern of leadership behavior that he called "Confront the Brutal Facts (Yet Never Lose Faith)." We patterned this chapter on Jim Collins's chapter 4 of *Good to Great.*

Good churches do not become breakout churches until the leaders confront reality. And most church leaders are unable or unwilling to confront reality.

In the spring of 2001, I led my consultation team, the Rainer Group, to conduct a thorough analysis of a church with a proud heritage and established reputation in the community. The pastor, who had just marked the one-year point at the church, called me for advice and consultation. "I think we need your team to take a look at our church," he said.

"Why? Why do you think you need an outside perspective?" I asked.

He paused and then responded. "I'm not sure. Something just doesn't seem right here. I was led to believe that this church was one of the strongest in the area. Frankly, after one year at this place, I just can't see where we are making any difference."

Figure 4A. The ABC Moment

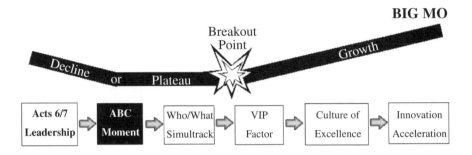

I accepted the assignment and gathered my consultation team. We made the journey to the mid-size city and began our work. We had already assembled a plethora of information on the church prior to arrival. We conducted dozens of interviews. We took our top facility experts and looked over the land and the buildings. With our demographic information in hand, we did a thorough analysis of the community in which the church was located.

Our initial work took three days. When we returned to Louisville, our team met to assimilate and compare information. My approach in leading a consultation team is to begin with the larger perspective and then focus on the supporting details. This time was no different.

WHAT'S THE BIG PICTURE?

"Okay, what's the big picture?" I asked. My team members always anticipate that first question. "This time," I said, "take two minutes and write your answers on a piece of paper." I then collected the six pieces of paper. I have kept them to this day as a reminder of where many churches are and where they are going. The consulting team members' responses were:

- "The church is slowly dying and the members think the church is still in its greatest days."
- "This will be a difficult consult. The people are unwilling to face the reality of the slow erosion taking place in the church."
- "My interviews don't match the reality of the research we did on the church. The people are living in another world."

- "The church thinks it's growing. The numbers say they are dying."
- "The church refuses to believe that this is not 1977."
- "It seems like possible suggestions of correction will be met with hostility. I wonder if we can help a church that refuses to see that it needs help."

The team members' assessments were accurate and prophetic. I had the dubious honor of presenting our findings to more than 500 members on a Sunday evening. Such was the venue the leadership had chosen. I began with some introductory comments and then presented my first PowerPoint slide. The chart showed the church's worship attendance for the past ten years: a decline from 1,100 to 900.

Presuming that such basic information would need little discussion, I prepared to move to the next slide but stopped when I saw two dozen hands go up. I did not even know it was question-and-answer time.

The first person told me that my numbers were wrong. My gentle response was a reminder that the church office provided me the numbers. The second person insisted that the church was growing: "People join our church every week." My suggestion that the losses were greater than the additions met with deaf ears.

By the time the third member voiced her opinion, I knew the night would be long. "We are one of the best churches in the denomination; I think this whole consulting thing is silly." Three hours later my worst-case prophecy was reality. I went home dejected and despondent. The church continues its slow erosion to this day.

WAKE-UP CALLS AND THE BRUTAL FACTS

When I first read the chapter "Confront the Brutal Facts" in *Good to Great*, I guessed that this issue would be critical in churches that made the transition to greatness. My main error was underestimating how critical this factor would be. One of the key reasons many churches today are in a slow but deadly path of erosion is the failure of the people to accept that the church is in trouble and that immediate changes are needed.

Though the cold facts can be depressing, I still remain an obnoxious optimist about the American church. And though the vast majority of churches with which I consult and study are addicted to mediocrity, I have seen enough great churches to have hope. Indeed, the purpose of our research and this book was to demonstrate those few churches that have made that difficult transition to greatness. All of the churches that made the cut with our strict criteria experienced an "ABC moment."

Readers familiar with Jim Collins's *Good to Great* will notice that in his progression "confronting the brutal facts" was the third major step in moving to greatness. In our study of breakout churches, the ABC moment preceded every other step except Acts 6/7 leadership. Unlike the corporate world, churches rarely review their "reality." They do not take time to see their progress or, in most cases, their declines. They move slowly toward death, but no one is willing to admit the patient is sick.

An ABC (awareness/belief/crisis) moment is a wake-up call, a realization that something is not right and that business as usual is no longer an option. Typically this wake-up call comes in a progression of three steps. Our breakout churches clearly fit this pattern.

Figure 4B. The A-B-Cs of the ABC Moment

Awareness	Leadership and key persons become aware that the church is not nearly all God intended it to be. At this stage it is common for church leaders to seek some type of outside perspective, such as attending a conference, zealously reading about issues related to the church, or hiring outside consultants. There is a keen desire to learn and improve.
Belief	The leadership confronts the brutal facts of the church's reality. This stage is often a wake-up call to make necessary changes. The leaders do not despair over the needed changes, but instead have a strong belief that God can use them to make a less-than-desirable situation good.
Crisis	Once change has begun, a crisis takes place in the heart of the leader, in the members of the church, or even in the attitudes of the members toward the leader. This often painful stage is the time when many pastors leave.

Before we look at the ABC moments in breakout churches, let's take a quick look at where most churches are today. The news is not very good.

THE AMERICAN CHURCH: MIRED IN MEDIOCRITY

Though I do remain an obnoxious optimist about the church, I still have grave concerns about U.S. congregations. I hope the following information is not too depressing; my desire is not to depress but to provide a wake-up call to church leaders and members who have become comfortable or complacent.

Doctrinal Ignorance

Perhaps one of my greatest concerns about the church in America is the well-documented ignorance that many Christians have about the doctrines of the faith. Without a clear understanding of what we believe, we lose our distinction, our reason for existence, our direction, and our purpose. George Barna is a leader in documenting the frightening slide in holding to basic beliefs among Christians.[1]

When our team does a consultation in a church, we typically ask a representative sampling of the membership to respond to a 160-item Church Health Survey™. The last ten questions are basic doctrinal questions of which we would normally suppose most Christians would be in agreement. Item number 154 says, "The only way to heaven is through Christ." Five years ago the average percentage of congregants who agreed or strongly agreed with this statement was 97 percent. The average for our most recent year was 83 percent.[2]

Most of our consulting assignments are in evangelical churches where supposedly a conservative view of Scripture is espoused. But our most recent data indicate that as many as 1 in 5 evangelicals believes there are ways to heaven outside Jesus. Certainly Jesus himself did not believe in multiple ways of salvation (John 14:6). Perhaps the problem is more than doctrinal ignorance; perhaps it is doctrinal disbelief as well.

Evangelistic Apathy

The American church is not growing. From 1990 to 2000 the U.S. population grew from 248 million to 281 million, a 13 percent increase.[3] In that same period, worship attendance in American churches grew by slightly less than 1 percent.[4] The church is a long way from keeping pace with the population growth.

It now takes 85 church members a year to reach one person for Christ.[5] And fewer than 15 percent of church members indicated that they had shared with someone how to become a Christian in the past twelve months.[6] And more than 8 of 10 churches are either declining or growing less than their community's population growth rate.[7] A growing number of Christians tell us that they are reluctant to be evangelistic because they do not want to impose their beliefs on others.

Ministry Irrelevance

One commonality among many of the breakout churches was their passion to make a difference in their communities. We will look at that issue in detail in chapter 6. In most of our comparison churches, however, the leadership could not name one significant ministry to the communities in which the church was located.

Unfortunately, the comparison churches are normative in America. Most of the ministry in the church is focused on the membership. From the community's perspective, the church is irrelevant. Indeed, it is not uncommon for us to find that the majority of people in a community do not even know that the church in question exists.

Fellowship Fractures

My consulting firm prefers not to get involved in conflict management and resolution in churches. There are other firms that specialize in that specific area. Part of my reason for avoiding these types of consultations is my own personality. I become emotionally drained dealing with the barbs and accusations that are common in conflicts.

In several of our consults over the past twelve months, our consulting team became involved in church conflicts unintentionally. We were called to provide consultation for other reasons but found that we could not address those issues until we dealt with the conflict in the church.

I guess we should not be surprised at the level of conflict in churches. When congregants focus inwardly, they become self-serving and begin to ask what the church is doing for them. And when these inwardly-focused members do not get their way in worship styles, pastoral attention, music choices, and carpet colors, they pitch holy temper tantrums. A divided church is inevitably an inwardly-focused church.

I could continue this line of reasoning for pages and provide you reams of data that show the plight of the American church, but that is not the purpose of this book. The purpose of this book is to show you churches that have broken out to greatness. I hope, however, that this basic amount of disconcerting information will help you, the reader, to understand why wake-up calls or ABC moments are in order.

Before we move to the specifics of the breakout churches in our study, we need to address one more question: Why are churches not aware of the plight many are experiencing? That is, why don't more church leaders have ABC moments? We believe Satan has a weapon even more lethal than church splits and the moral failures of church leaders. We call it slow erosion.

SLOW EROSION: THE DEADLY PATH

The information in figure 4C is telling. The numbers represent the average worship attendance for the thirty-nine comparison churches in our study for the most recent ten years for which we have data. Look at the slow erosion in attendance.

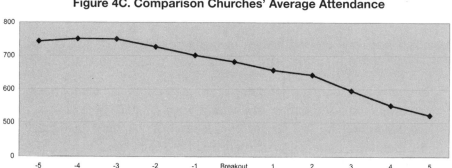

Figure 4C. Comparison Churches' Average Attendance

Though we can clearly see the attendance decline in the comparison churches, we find quite often that members in these churches have little awareness of any negative trends. From our perspective of an eleven-year chart, we see a decrease in attendance of 221 persons in eleven years, a 30 percent decline. From the perspective of the faithful church member who attends each week, the decline in attendance is only one person every two and one-half weeks and is not noticeable to those on the inside.

It is in such situations that a wake-up call or ABC moment is most problematic. And tens of thousands of churches across America show attendance patterns similar to that of the comparison churches.

Churches rarely print annual reports as corporations do. Some send in their statistical information each year to a denomination, but few people pay any attention to the slowly declining attendence. When the erosion is so slow, it is incredibly easy to be oblivious to negative trends.

Why did we have such difficulty finding breakout churches for our study? One of the major reasons is that few church leaders are in touch with the reality of what is taking place in their congregations. And even fewer are willing to confront those brutal facts and do something about it. But thirteen churches in our study did not deny reality. They were willing to look at the bad news because they believed they served a God who could do anything. The ABC moments in our breakout churches are stories of courage, inspiration, and perseverance.

AWARENESS: WAKING UP TO REALITY

The ministry of David Clark at Central Christian Church has been like the proverbial roller-coaster ride. When Clark first came to the Beloit, Wisconsin, church in 1981, he was ready to make changes, and to make them rapidly. The church was small and the decision-making power was in the hands of a few people in the church.

> We quickly discerned that many of the pastors of our comparison churches did not want to face reality. They, by their own volition, were avoiding the first step of awareness. Why? In their more candid moments, many of the pastors admitted they knew that if they faced reality, they would feel compelled to lead their churches to make changes. But many had already been burned in ministry, and they did not want to face the inevitable conflict change brings. The pain was just too great for potential gain, some told us.

By his own admission, Clark did not try to win the confidence and trust of these power brokers. He moved full-steam ahead with his plans for change. And the power group quickly fired him only six months into his ministry at Central.

Clark did have his supporters. An elderly woman led a petition drive to have the young pastor reinstated. The drive was successful, but the ministry did not improve that much for Clark. For the next four years the pastor found himself trying to help the congregation heal from the conflict. The time was emotionally draining, and Clark confessed that many times he was "ready to throw in the towel."

From 1981 to 1988 the church's attendance remained in the low to mid 200s. But what is unique about David Clark, at least compared to most church leaders we have studied, is that he never has been satisfied with the status quo. He actually seeks to confront the brutal facts of his church's situation. As a result, he regularly has times of "awareness" when he realizes the church is not where it should be.

Clark's openness to outside influences is notable. Some of the leaders at Central Christian Church told us of a Church Growth Institute seminar that became a wake-up call of awareness for them. The pastor speaks openly about the influence of Rick Warren's Purpose Driven Church model in his ministry.

One key point of awareness for Clark took place in 1986 when he realized that Central Christian Church was not reaching lost people, and that the people in the congregation perceived their fellowship to be a small neighborhood church. The pastor did not sit idly and have a pity party for himself and the church. He led the church to focus on a vision to reach lost and unchurched persons throughout all of southern Wisconsin.

When researcher Michael O'Neal interviewed church leaders and members years after the 1986 wake-up call, he was amazed to see how deeply this vision had impacted many in the congregation. Listen to some of the comments from these interviews:

- "Our main focus is on reaching the unchurched for Christ."
- "Our vision is to be light to the community."
- "Everything that we do is trying to touch the community."
- "We focus on the unsaved and do whatever it takes to reach them."
- "Our church has a gift at attracting the unchurched."

Central Christian Church struggled for years under Clark's leadership. From 1981 to 1988 the church average worship attendance ranged from 227 to 257, a classic plateau pattern. By 2002 attendance exceeded 1,400. The church had become aware of its need to change, to move forward, and their leader had determined that the status quo was unacceptable. The difference in just a few years is incredible, if not miraculous.

I often interact with consultants in the corporate world. It is not unusual for them to tell me that they do not know how I work with non-profit organizations, particularly churches. They perceive them to be organizations entrenched in tradition with fierce resistance to the change a consultant should bring to the table.

In many ways, their critiques have several elements of truth. We screened several thousand churches to find only thirteen breakout churches. How, then, did the thirteen churches break out of the crowd? How did they take a different path that led to growth and effectiveness when most churches would slide down the slippery slope of slow erosion?

We cannot overstate the critical importance of *awareness*. Many, if not most, church leaders do not move their churches out of slow erosion because they are unwilling or unable to see the facts and discern what is taking place. I mentioned earlier a conversation I had with a struggling pastor in Visalia, California. When I told him that awareness was the first step to change, he responded with an unlikely question. "How can I become aware?" He helped me to realize that often it is not enough for us to tell church leaders to become aware; we need to help them understand *how* to become aware.

> In the thirteen breakout churches, we were able to find clear indicators that most of the leaders followed the three steps that you will read next. All thirteen churches had leaders who engaged in the first step, "Accept Painful Reality." All of the leaders also followed the second step, "Is/Should Be Discernment." And at least eleven of the thirteen breakout churches had leaders who indicated the impact of the third step, "Positive Outside Influences," in the turnaround in their churches.

As we examined closely the process by which our breakout church leaders developed an awareness of their churches' situations, we saw three distinct stages in their attempts to see reality more clearly. These three components are critical if leaders really desire to learn the truth about their churches.

Accept Painful Reality
⇓
Is/Should Be Discernment
⇓
Positive Outside Influences

Accept Painful Reality

A fascinating parallel exists between a person who is struggling and a church that is struggling. When a person is unwilling to admit that a physical or emotional problem exists, that problem will worsen until he or she admits everything is not all right. Similarly, slow erosion in a church takes place over a period of years, and until the leaders and members are willing to admit that a problem exists, no remedial effort is taken. Thus further erosion and even death of the church are likely.

This failure of church leaders and members to take the first step of accepting painful reality is epidemic in the American church. Sometimes I am surprised that more than 40,000 churches in the United States are growing. I am not surprised that more than 300,000 churches are not growing.

> **Numerical measures of baptism are not ultimate indicators of evangelistic health. There can be good reasons for baptismal declines. For example, some churches may baptize anyone and everyone just to get their numbers higher. A decline in baptisms could then represent a more accurate reading of true conversion.**

Our research included a comparison church that I will call Mountain Community Church. The church was started in 1990 with great hope and a positive beginning. By 1993 average worship attendance was 550, remarkable growth in such a short period. The last data we have on the church indicate that the worship attendance is 410 in 2003. The church's attendance has declined, albeit slightly, every year since the peak of 550 in 1993. Additionally, our study of the church during the ten-year period 1993 to 2003 indicates that four key community ministries have been discontinued. The number of conversions in the church, measured by baptisms, has declined from 88 in 1993 to 21 in 2003.

We interviewed seven laypeople and three ministerial staff in the church. Without giving them any indication that we had an awareness of any of the issues above, we asked a general question: How do you think the church is doing today? Listen to seven of the responses:

- "We are on an incredible ride. Our impact in the community is great, and the members in the church are truly growing as disciples."
- "I would have to say that our strength is really in evangelism. That is the focus in the church, and we are really doing a good job there."
- "The growth of our church is incredible. We were just started in 1990, and look where we are today."
- "We are a real friendly church. That's why we continue to see people come to our church, join our church, and invite other people to our church. You can see the growth of our church as people join each week."
- "Mountain Community Church is a miraculous story. You won't find many churches that have seen the growth that we have."
- "I couldn't imagine being at any other church. I am really close to the people in my small group."
- "The church is doing great because we are being fed the Word of God each week. That's the real strength of our church."

I don't doubt the integrity of these respondents or the perceived truthfulness of their answers. But the reality is that the church has declined more than 20 percent in ten years, and the major community ministries have been discontinued. The number of people reached for Christ each year has also declined precipitously.

The leaders of breakout churches do not hesitate to look at the statistics of their churches, even if the reality of the numbers is painful. They insist on having a clear awareness of the state of the church. They do not want any punches pulled. They are insistent that ministries to the community be evaluated regularly. They attempt in various ways to discern the spiritual growth of their members and the evangelistic successes and failures toward the lost and the unchurched. They attempt to discover the efficacy of their preaching and teaching in the doctrinal awareness of their congregants. Awareness can be uncomfortable since the picture painted by the facts may not be pretty. That's why so few church leaders today are willing to take the first step of accepting painful reality.

Some of the breakout church leaders told us they were often criticized for focusing on numbers. One of the leaders responded by
saying that numbers were never a goal for them, but they are one
helpful indicator of health or lack of health. He quoted Charles
Spurgeon, who said, "It has been noted that those who object to
[numbers] are often brethren whose unsatisfactory reports should
somewhat humiliate them."[8]

Is/Should Be Discernment

The second stage of awareness we noted in many of these leaders
was their clear understanding that the present state of their churches
was not that of a healthy church. The leaders not only faced the painful
reality of where they were. They had some clear idea of where the
church should be.

"I woke up one morning and entertained some pretty negative
thoughts," one of the leaders confided in anonymity. "I really wondered if
my life was worth living. I can't say I was suicidal, but I was really down."

The impetus behind these thoughts was a long night of tossing and
turning. He continued, "I talked to a pastor friend who was in a community a whole lot like mine. His church had almost doubled in seven
years. My church was slightly smaller than it was seven years ago. What
a wake-up call! I saw where the church was, and I saw where the church
should be."

Though the wake-up call can be alarming, leaders should be encouraged when it takes place. It is an indication that help is on the way.

This "Is/Should Be Discernment" phase was sometimes the result of an
inner conviction. Other times this phase was precipitated by some outside
influence that was used by God to convict the leader of necessary changes.
We called that third phase "Positive Outside Influences."

Positive Outside Influences

Southwest Baptist Church of Amarillo was an independent congregation from its inception in 1973 until 2003, when the church voted to

dual-align with the Southern Baptist Convention. J. Alan Ford has served as senior pastor since 1976.

The early days of Ford's pastoral ministry were shaky. Generally accepted in his original role as associate pastor and worship leader, Ford's youthfulness was an issue when he assumed the role of senior pastor in 1976. The twenty-eight-year-old pastor found himself in a confrontation with a power group in the church. Concurrent to that church conflict was a serious economic downturn in the community, and attendance and budget-level giving began to decline. Ford seriously considered leaving the church.

But one characteristic we noted of Ford and the other breakout leaders was their insatiable appetite to learn and their persistent drive to improve. The young pastor regularly sought outside help for his ministry in various forms.

> **What are some of the key differences between an Acts 5 leader and an Acts 6/7 leader? One clear difference was "confident humility" (see page 58). A second key difference was the Acts 6/7 leaders' desire for positive outside influences. The Acts 5 leaders, to the contrary, rarely sought outside counsel in conferences, books, consultations, or other similar influences.**

At about the time he was entertaining thoughts of leaving Southwest Baptist Church, Ford attended a John Maxwell seminar. "Because I came from an independent Baptist background," he explained, "my model of ministry was for the pastor to do all the work. The Maxwell seminar opened my eyes to the need to develop lay leadership to do the ministry in the church."

A second positive influence on the pastor's life and ministry was the Purpose Driven paradigm articulated by Rick Warren. He began to see clearly the need to lead the church forward with intentionality, rather than the old paradigm of church-as-usual.

But the influences did not end there. He noted to our researcher Deborah Morton the impact of the book *High Expectations*. "Dr. Rainer's book really kick-started me," he told us. "When I first read it, I thought it was ignorant, so I threw it in the backseat of the car and forgot about it."

But God had other plans for Ford and the book. He continued, "My wife and I went on vacation, and I didn't have anything to read, so I pulled it out of the backseat and reread it. This time a light went on. The message was clear. You get what you expect from people. It changed my life and the way I looked at my church and what I began to expect from my church and the people."

Eleven of the thirteen breakout churches had leaders who could articulate some major positive outside influence in their ministries. But what about the comparison church leaders? Did they not mention outside influences as well?

Over one-half of the thirty-nine comparison church leaders did indicate a positive outside influence in their ministries. Is it accurate then to conclude that this factor is unique to our breakout leaders? The research team helped me to see the difference between the two groups. Perhaps the visual representation below clarifies the differences.

<u>**Comparison Church Leaders**</u>   <u>**Breakout Church Leaders**</u>

Outside Influences   **Accept Painful Reality**
⇓   ⇓
Implement Changes   **Is/Should Be Discernment**
                                    ⇓
                         Positive Outside Influences
                                    ⇓
                         Influence Change

The comparison church leaders would often attend conferences or read books and see the outside influence as the next great initiative for the church. They would do so without taking a realistic assessment of their current situation or their church members' ability to handle immediate and sometimes radical change. These leaders would often fail to understand their own cultural context and how a new initiative might work in their area.

Therefore the consequences were often disastrous. Major church conflicts and not a few church splits were the painful results of these changes. The leaders became excited about the latest and newest ideas and introduced them to their churches with little forethought to the congregation's response or to the culture of the community.

The breakout leaders, however, did not seek outside influences until they saw the need. That need would be apparent as they went first through the Accept Painful Reality and Is/Should Be Discernment phases. They did not implement some new initiative blindly. The leaders knew clearly the less-than-perfect reality of their churches. They also could see the place where the church should be. Only then did they accept some positive outside influences, and even at that point they moved with caution and discernment.

The ABC moment is first a moment of awareness. I hope in these several pages you have better understood what these wake-up calls look like in the practical application. But please understand, these breakout church leaders did not dwell on the negative once they became aware of their church's situation. Their attitudes were anything but hopeless. To the contrary, their attitudes exemplified unswerving faith. We called that part of the ABC moment "Belief."

BELIEF: FAITH DURING DIFFICULTIES

In *Good to Great*, chapter 4, Jim Collins and his team identified a powerful idea they call "The Stockdale Paradox," named after a former POW, Admiral James Stockdale. The Stockdale Paradox consists of two sides of a coin: "Retain faith that you will prevail in the end, regardless of the difficulties and at the same time confront the most brutal facts of your current reality, whatever they might be."[9]

Do you remember the story of The Temple Church in Nashville, Tennessee, in chapter 1? Michael Graves came to the painful awareness that the church he led was not the church God intended it to be. The vision called for a multiethnic and multiracial congregation of all economic strata. But the young pastor realized that almost all of the members of the growing church were middle-class and upper-middle-class African Americans.

Attempts to lead change proved futile for the pastor. Indeed, a group of some 300 members, major contributors to the church, attempted to thwart Graves's attempts to reach other groups. This power group confronted the pastor on numerous occasions with threats of leaving and withholding financial support. The conflict sent the pastor to the hospital for an extended period.

Many of Graves's friends and colaborers in ministry urged the pastor to give up his dream. They chastised him for not being satisfied with the blessings God had already given him. Graves's physician suggested that he leave the ministry altogether. But the pastor would not be deterred from the vision God had given him for The Temple Church.

A few of the pastors in the comparison group did take the first step of awareness in the ABC moment progression. But these few were so distressed by the reality of their situation that they retreated into denial and business as usual. The breakout church leaders, however, believed that better days were ahead. In the face of overwhelming bad news, they refused to abandon the dream and vision God had given them for their churches.

This strange paradox of unswerving faith in the midst of bad news typified these leaders. It is not that they were thick-skinned or insensitive tyrants who cared little for the feelings of those who might oppose them. These leaders told us many stories of great hurt and deep wounds in their ministries. Still they persevered.

> **If I could make one recommendation to hurting and struggling leaders, it would be to immerse themselves in the stories of great faith in the church. Read Hebrews 11 again and again. Read Paul's letters and his missionary journeys in the book of Acts. Read historical accounts of Christian men and women who believed that God had better days for them in the midst of some of the most troubling and painful times. Bad news and conflict are common in all of the churches we studied. The difference in the breakout church leaders, however, is their unshakable faith that God will bring victory.**

Very few of the comparison leaders took the first step of awareness. Of the few who did, none expressed belief that better days were ahead. None believed that God would take their struggles and turn them into victories.

The breakout church leaders, however, never used the word *impossible* to describe even their direst moments. When tough times came to them and to their churches, they acknowledged their pain but soon began anticipating how God would give them the next victory. They moved forward. And it was the step of moving forward that inevitably ushered in the next phase, "Crisis."

CRISIS: THE COST OF VICTORIES

By this point in the book, you may be greatly inspired by the numerous stories of leaders who persevered in the midst of significant trials. On the other hand, you may be scared to death by the high cost these leaders paid to move their churches to new levels of excellence. You have already read of leaders who were dismissed, stressed-out leaders who found themselves in the hospital, and leaders who faced the wrath of those who were once supporters. Unfortunately, difficulties are commonplace in churches that move to greatness. Sometimes moments of crisis are sensed internally by those who lead the change in the church. Inevitably the crisis also takes place with many of the members. And more often than not, the members who experience the crisis blame the pastor for the difficulties they encounter.

The Cost of Breakout Leadership

Lenexa Baptist Church is located in the largest county in Kansas. When nearby Emmanuel Baptist Church started Lenexa Baptist, many had high hopes that the new church would reach a number of people in the fast-growing area. In 1990 the church called its first and only pastor, Steve Dighton. Lenexa already had an attendance of 160 the year the pastor arrived.

Pastor Dighton is a highly motivated and evangelistic leader. He led the church to start new ministries and to reach out in the community with aggressive evangelistic methodologies. Worship attendance grew to almost 200 in 1992, just two years after the pastor began his ministry at Lenexa. The growth of the church and the aggressive approaches of the ministries engendered two definitive and opposite reactions. One group was thrilled with the positive gains in membership and attendance. Another group decried the aggressive outreach efforts and deeply desired to get "our church" back.

The latter group began meeting in secret, closed-door meetings. In 1993 they began openly calling for Steve Dighton to resign as pastor. Dighton seriously considered resigning for the good of the church. On numerous occasions during the conflict, he wondered if another church opportunity might avail itself. Any opportunity, the pastor thought, might be better than his present situation. But God just would not release the pastor from the church. He stayed and persevered even when families began leaving. He held on when attendance dropped to about 100 in 1994, one-half its highest level just two years earlier. The church split was very painful, both to those who stayed and those who left.

Dighton spent the next two years helping the church recover from the traumatic split. He met with leaders of the church in restaurants, homes, and coffee shops for very open and candid discussions. It was also a time of introspection for the pastor. He learned even more the importance of loving the members of the church he served.

The church eventually recovered emotionally, spiritually, and numerically. By 1996 the worship attendance finally surpassed the previous highs set in 1992. The church that wondered if it would survive became a congregation of about 1,400 by the end of 2003. The gain has been significant, but the pain has been great as well.

Are the Crises and the Pain Necessary?

I must admit that I did not expect crises to be a part of the stories of all the breakout churches. I also admit that my bias caused me not to want to convey this information in this book. Frankly, I fear that many leaders may be dissuaded from leading churches to greatness once they read these stories of conflict and pain. If you are one of those who has reacted in the way I feared, please hear two important responses.

First, most of the churches that made the breakout cut were congregations that had become mired in mediocrity and in clear patterns of decline. Any changes that put these churches on paths of growth and health would bring major institutional disruption. These changes could very well precipitate spiritual warfare as well. Change is difficult. Major systemic change often engenders a battle cry.

Second, virtually every leader in Scripture endured some type of conflict in his or her life. The cost of following Christ is great. We cannot become complacent with the status quo just to avoid conflict. We must lead. Yes, we must love the people, and we must console them when change becomes increasingly painful to them. But we must lead. We cannot be content with a life and a ministry that could be described in the epitaph: "This leader avoided conflict well."

Remember the Paradox of "Confident Humility"

At the risk of being redundant, let me remind you of one of the key characteristics of breakout church leaders. While they were clearly confident in their God-given leadership abilities, they were also very humble.

I mention the issue of humility at this point lest someone think that conflict is a method to lead a church to greatness. None of the leaders in our study desired conflict. They all weighed a plethora of options to avoid the conflict. But in the final analysis, they did not avoid conflict if no other options were available.

If you could hear the words from each of the leaders of these churches personally, you would probably better understand their hearts. They are truly humble leaders. They do not proclaim "my way or the highway" to the church members they serve. There is no arrogance in their approaches to ministry. They hurt deeply every time a member leaves the church in disagreement.

I have heard too many other church leaders boast of their "back door revivals." I have sensed that these leaders wear the exodus of the dissidents like a badge of honor. Such is not the case with the breakout church leaders. They all had an exodus of members, but each loss inflicted wounds that they mention years later.

THE ABC MOMENT AND THE CONGREGATION

Throughout most of this chapter you have heard about the ABC moment from the perspective of the leadership of the church. But in most of our breakout churches, a significant number of the laity experienced similar wake-up calls. The ABC moment was not limited to a single person; it often included a large portion of the congregation.

> **Our research for this book included many interviews with laity in the thirteen breakout churches. Their insights were invaluable. In almost every interview, we could hear these church members speak of a key ABC moment for them in the church. In fact, in three of our churches, laypeople experienced a wake-up call prior to the senior pastor.**

About six months prior to writing this book, I was consulting with a large church in the Midwest. My team presented our preliminary report to a group that included the ministry staff and a number of lay leaders. Part of our report included the rather dismal number of young people reached by the church during the past several years.

A sixty-seven-year-old man who had been at this church for more than forty years asked us to repeat the data about the dearth of young people reached. He was quiet for a moment, and then, much to everyone's surprise, he began to weep. "We are not even reaching my grandchildren," he sobbed. "I never realized how complacent we have become."

I have heard that this man is now leading a charge in the church to do whatever it takes to reach young people. He is forcing people out of their comfort zones and has become a key ally with the pastor in moving the church to greatness.

A similar story could be told in many of the thirteen churches. The ABC moment cannot be limited to one person if a church is to break out.

ABC MOMENT, THEN WHAT?

The breakout churches were not content to have a moment of revelation and then continue business as usual. Neither staff nor lay leaders could any longer be content with the status quo. Change was inevitable and necessary.

These wake-up calls were often life changing to those who received them. Their lives and ministries would never be the same.

The remainder of this book shows what took place after the ABC moment. The stories are incredible even though the challenges were daunting. Join me as we look at the first critical steps that were made after the wake-up call took place. We call those first steps the "Who/What Simultrack."

IN ESSENCE, IN SUMMARY
THE ABC MOMENT

- The ABC moment is a wake-up call for church leaders typified by the breakout leaders in our study. It consists of three stages: Awareness, Belief, and Crisis.

- Because the American church is mired in mediocrity, change is difficult and often wrought with conflict.

- The pastors of the comparison churches often avoided the Awareness stage because they feared they might have to lead their churches in change. The pain was just too great for the potential gain.

- In the breakout churches, leaders of all thirteen churches engaged in both the first and second steps, "Accept Painful Awareness" and "Is/Should Be Discernment." Eleven of the leaders indicated the impact of the third step, "Positive Outside Influences."

- Comparison church leaders often utilized outside resources to implement change. Breakout leaders, however, attempted to understand the reality of their context fully before embracing outside influences.

- Breakout church leaders exemplified the strange paradox of unswerving faith in the midst of bad news.

- The cost of moving a church to greatness is often measured in crises, sometimes severe crises.

CHAPTER 5

THE WHO/WHAT SIMULTRACK

Mediocrity knows nothing higher than itself, but talent immediately recognizes genius.

—Sir Arthur Conan Doyle

In *Good to Great*, Jim Collins and his research team identified a principle they called "First Who . . . Then What." The idea for this chapter came from chapter 3 of *Good to Great*, where Collins discusses the importance of getting "the right people on the bus, the wrong people off the bus, and the right people in the right seats" and then figuring out where to drive the bus.[1]

The calls or emails come almost daily: "Dr. Rainer, we are in desperate need of a youth pastor. Can you recommend someone?" "We need a person to lead our evangelism ministries. Please send any resumes you may have." "We are looking for the best worship leader there is. Money is no object."

I have noticed a growing frustration among church leaders, both lay and staff, in filling openings for personnel. Very few of these leaders are satisfied with the process of finding the right person, and even fewer are satisfied that they found the right persons, for paid or volunteer positions.

Figure 5A. The Who/What Simultrack

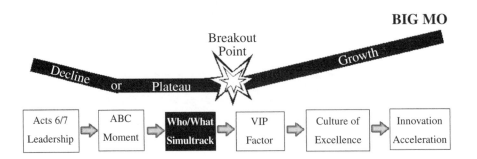

The breakout churches, however, seem to have little problem finding people of excellence to be a part of their ministry teams. The reasons are twofold. First, these churches tend to attract the best people because of their clear and compelling vision. Second, the breakout church leaders often do not wait for an opening before bringing a person on staff or providing a place for a lay leader to serve. If they come across a promising individual, they invite him or her to join the team even if there is no clear place for the person at the time. It typically does not take long before that capable and motivated person is making a difference in the church using his or her God-given gifts and abilities.

We found that our breakout churches were often finding the right people and developing the right structures very soon after their wake-up call, or ABC moment. Within a short time of becoming aware of the great need for the church to make significant changes, the leaders were pursuing both the right people and the right infrastructure for the church. We called that phenomenon the "Who/What Simultrack."

WHAT EXACTLY IS A SIMULTRACK?

A simultrack is one or more tracks being pursued at the same time. The leaders in our breakout churches discovered that they had to move quickly to lead their churches out of mediocrity. Not only were personnel needs immediately apparent, but the structures of the church were in need of a major overhaul as well. The leaders, therefore, multitasked and began tackling both projects simultaneously. A schematic of their approach looks something like a railroad track. One rail is the search for the right people; the other rail is the quest for the right structures.

Figure 5B. The Who/What Simultrack

A TALE OF TWO APPROACHES

In contrast to the breakout churches, the comparison churches rarely attempted significant structural change. And only three of the thirty-nine comparison churches took a path that came close to the "right people" approach.

Bethel Temple Community Church in Evansville, Indiana, was one of the breakout churches that understood clearly the need to find the right people. The leaders in the church had already been influenced by Collins's *Good to Great* when we began studying the congregation. We heard several leaders cite Collins's principle: "The executives who ignited the transformation from good to great did not first figure out where to drive the bus and then get the people to take it there. No, they *first* got the right people on the bus (and the wrong people off the bus) and *then* figured out where to drive it."[2]

These "bus" issues played an important role in Bethel Temple's chrysalis factor. One of the pastors noted that they have seen the wisdom of getting the right people, and they have placed many "homegrown" persons in places of ministry leadership.

Senior Pastor Stephen Schwambach reported sadly that the church lost 200 people over the "bus" issue. "It created a loss of momentum, confidence, and income," he told us. But the decisions made, as much as it grieved him, were for the good of the church. Still, Schwambach laments that the difficulty of the decision created a situation in which it was prolonged for entirely too long.

Collins addresses this very issue in *Good to Great:* "To let people languish in uncertainty for months or years, stealing precious time in their lives that they could use to move on to something else, when in the end they aren't going to make it anyway—*that* would be ruthless. To deal with it up front and let people get on with their lives—that is *rigorous*."[3]

Schwambach credits his leadership team with much of the God-given success at Bethel Temple. Executive Pastor Bret Nicholson has been particularly valuable. Nicholson was a longtime member of the church brought to his current position by Schwambach. "Bret's appointment was huge," the pastor proclaimed. "Bret has the patience to work through all the nitty-gritty details. He is able to translate the visions I cast and implement them," Schwambach told us.

In contrast, the three churches we selected as comparison churches to Bethel Temple Community Church followed the traditional and often unsuccessful formula for finding staff. When a position was vacated, they sought to fill it with a person who would have the same job description. They never asked if the current position was the best for the church at that point in its history. If an education position was vacated, they looked for an education minister. If an associate pastor position was open, they sought an associate pastor to fill it.

Furthermore, none of the three comparison churches was proactive in bringing people on staff ahead of growth or adding a person to the ministry staff just because he or she was the "right" person. They dared not bring a person on the team if an official position was not vacant at the time. They conducted business as usual, and as a result, they are on a clear path of slow erosion.

THE STRUCTURE ISSUE

The other track of the Who/What Simultrack is structure. I use the terms *structure* and *infrastructure* synonymously in this book to refer to the basic facilities, programs, and organizational systems needed to keep the church running day by day.

> **Readers familiar with *Good to Great* might think that Jim Collins's "First Who ... Then What" analysis contradicts the breakout churches' Who/What Simultrack approach. This is not the case. Collins's "what" is the vision of the organization. The "what" in this book refers to structures. Many churches are woefully lacking in their structures, and leadership must deal with this issue at the same time they are dealing with people issues. If both issues are not remedied, the church cannot move to greater health and growth.**

Pastor Won Sang Lee had a host of structural issues to handle when he became pastor of Korean Central Presbyterian Church in the Washington, D.C., area in 1977. The elder board, for example, was not functioning as biblical elders, so Lee introduced changes. These changes essentially took the responsibilities of micromanagement away from the elders. As a consequence, several of the elders left the church (Who and What working simultaneously).

The church initially met in the facilities of Trinity Presbyterian Church in Arlington, Virginia, but by 1981 Korean Central had outgrown its borrowed facilities. It took four years for the church to find land and construct buildings. In November 1985 the church had its first worship services in its new buildings. The church would continue to acquire land and add buildings as attendance approached 4,000 by 2003.

Another structural change was precipitated by the influx of different generations of Korean Americans. Those who were born in the United States typically preferred an English-speaking worship service. The immigrants from Korea, however, preferred the Korean-speaking services. When the demand for a new English- or Korean-speaking service was obvious, the pastor would lead the church to meet the need. By 2003 the Korean Central Presbyterian Church had seven services on Sunday: 7:45 a.m., 9:15 a.m. (two meeting simultaneously), 10:45 a.m., 12:30 p.m., 2:00 p.m., and 3:30 p.m.

When Korean Central Presbyterian Church made structural changes, the impetus behind the moves was to follow the vision of the church. The comparison churches, however, approached infrastructure change differently. Thirty of the thirty-nine comparison churches decided against much-needed structural changes because of the conflict or perceived conflict the decision would engender. One comparison church refused to relocate even though the four acres it owns can hardly accommodate the 500 persons in worship attendance today. Attempts to acquire more land have proved unsuccessful.

Why is the church refusing to make such an obvious move? Key members in the church have strong emotional and sentimental attachment to the 115-year-old sanctuary. They have threatened to leave or withhold money if any such attempt is made. The church has already shown signs of slow erosion. Attendance has dropped by almost 100 in the past three years.

Other comparison churches have made structural changes that seem to have little relationship to the true needs of the church. One built a new sanctuary even though the older sanctuary was more than adequate in space and utility. Why? Because some key influencers in the church thought a new worship center "would make a statement about the church." We were not sure what that statement was, but attendance has declined six of the past seven years.

> In many of the comparison churches, structural changes are made with little thought about the vision of the church and its needs for the future. One church refuses to let any new deacons serve on the deacon body and has kept the same eight deacons on a nonrotating system for the past fifteen years. The few new members who do come to the church eventually leave because of their correct perception that the church is controlled by a few people. The church has had twelve consecutive years of declining attendance.

ACTS 5 LEADERS AND ACTS 6/7 LEADERS ON THE WHO/WHAT SIMULTRACK

We were particularly interested in discerning any differences between the two highest categories of leaders in our studies. Did the Acts 6/7 legacy leader approach the who/what issue differently than the Acts 5 bold leader? First, we must acknowledge that more similarities exist than differences.

On issues of structural change, an Acts 5 leader is just as quick to move as an Acts 6/7 leader. Indeed, the decision to make rapid and bold moves structurally often typified the Acts 5 leader. While both types of leaders were willing and even eager to make the needed changes, the leaders responded differently to the members of the congregation as changes were made.

From our interviews with each set of leaders, we saw clearly that the Acts 6/7 leader was much more likely to voice concerns about any church members who felt left behind in a major structural move in the church. Just a few pages back, for example, we noted the grieving process Stephen Schwambach experienced over a loss of members due to major changes. Likewise, we told the story in chapter 1 of Michael Graves at The Temple Church in Nashville. This senior pastor met repeatedly with the dissident group in his congregation and made multiple attempts to get them on board with the changes that were being made.

> **A note of clarification is in order at this point. The Acts 5 leader and the comparison church leaders are not the same people. Indeed, none of the comparison churches had Acts 5 leaders. Remember, only 3 percent of all the pastors we studied qualified for this level. It is rare to see someone attain this level of leadership even though it is not the highest level. Acts 6/7 leadership was limited to less than 1 percent of all the pastors we studied.[4] When we compare an Acts 5 leader with an Acts 6/7 leader, we are essentially comparing a very good leader with an excellent leader.**

To the contrary, we did not see such efforts at reconciliation among the Acts 5 leaders. None of the researchers would describe these leaders as uncaring or insensitive. They did, however, make conscious decisions *not* to attempt to hold on to any opposition group in the church. Their philosophy of ministry was clear. They could not spend significant time on detractors when so much positive work had to be done.

We on the research team had to admit that the attitudes of the other group, the Acts 6/7 leaders, seemed counterintuitive. Why would they expend limited resources of time and energy on people who were unlikely to change? Why did they hold on tenaciously to detractors until they saw absolutely no hope in reclamation?

The answers to these questions cannot be produced from a ready database. Anecdotally, however, the crises these leaders experienced seemed to impact their hearts to reach out to even the most vocal of critics. Noted one breakout leader, "I know it sounds unrealistic, but I don't want to leave one person behind." Our immediate response to his statement was a simple "Why?"

"Because," he said, "I have been through the fire at this church. I know what it's like to be hurt in a place that's supposed to be a place of healing and hope. I can't stand the thought of someone experiencing the pain I felt."

Similar issues manifested themselves as the Acts 6/7 leaders and Acts 5 leaders dealt with people issues. For example, the staff of the breakout churches had an average tenure of 12.5 years. The staff of the churches with an Acts 5 leader, however, had been at the church an average of only 6.8 years.[5]

The ministry staff of the breakout churches typically asserted three factors that held them at their churches. First, they spoke of the compelling and clear vision of the churches they served. Second, they inevitably mentioned the dynamic leadership skills of the senior pastors with whom they served. Third, almost all of the staff with whom we spoke told us of the great caring attitude of the pastor.

The staff of the churches with Acts 5 leaders typically affirmed the first two issues as factors that kept them at the church. But we rarely heard them mention the issue of a caring pastor as one of the draws of the church. Again, we did not sense that Acts 5 leaders were uncaring. They simply did not give the personal time to staff that we saw in the lives of the Acts 6/7 leaders.

> Keep in mind as you read this information about the "who" in breakout churches that the average pastoral tenure was 21.6 years at the point of our study. Many of the Acts 6/7 leaders felt that the long stay at their churches has allowed them to make many mistakes and, hopefully, to correct them. They all freely admit that they are much better at dealing with the "who" issues today than they were in the early years of their ministries.

KEY LESSONS LEARNED ABOUT THE "WHO" IN BREAKOUT CHURCHES

We could distinguish no discernible pattern indicating whether the breakout churches gave greater priority to the "who" or to the "what." Such is the reason we concluded that the churches were operating on a simultrack, focusing on both issues at the same time.

But as we looked at the unique issues concerning people and structure, we were able to make some definitive conclusions. Let's look first at the lessons we learned about the "who" in breakout churches.

On pages 54–60 of *Good to Great,* Jim Collins identified three practical disciplines: when in doubt, don't hire; when you need to make a people change, act; put your best people on your biggest opportunities, not your biggest problems. We adopted the first two of these practical disciplines in the pages that follow.

When in Doubt, Wait

Breakout churches often learned lessons the hard way. Their past experiences were horror tales of filling a slot as quickly as possible. Not only did they fail in the past to discern if the position they were seeking was best for the church, they often were impatient in filling the positions. The important lesson they have learned is that it is better to have an unfilled position than to fill it with the wrong person. One breakout senior pastor shared with request of anonymity a painful lesson learned early in his ministry.

"I had been at the church two years, and we had an opening for an associate pastor," he told us. "Leaders in the church said we needed to fill the position because the church always had an associate pastor. I never really questioned if we needed an associate pastor or what the best job description for one might be."

When a church member told the pastor she knew a "fine man who has just been down on his luck," the pastor quickly sought and received church approval to bring the new pastor to the ministry team.

"It was a disaster waiting to happen," the pastor lamented. "I called his former church (where he had abruptly resigned), and their pastor told me he was just not a good fit, although he was a fine man. That should have sent bells ringing in my head. If he is such a fine man, why did the pastor recommend him to our church instead of keeping him at his church?"

The pastor continued the story: "It took me about three weeks to learn why he was not a good fit in the other church. He was a lazy bum! And he never did any of the things on his job description. All he wanted to do was counsel people. That's where he got his ego fulfillment. But counseling was not supposed to be a part of his job description."

The breakout churches have learned that it is better to wait than to bring the wrong person on the team. They have also learned some important lessons about dealing with personnel problems once they are discovered.

Act Quickly and Compassionately

The pastor's story, of course, does not end with the discovery that the wrong person had been added to the ministry team. The pastor and other leaders were now confronted with the problem of how to respond to this ministry mismatch.

"Our response was like most churches," he recalled. "We did nothing. Oh, we talked about it, fussed about it, and met about it. But we still did nothing. We just didn't want to deal with the conflict we knew we would have. I guess we thought we would have some kind of magical solution when we woke up one morning."

But the situation deteriorated instead. The associate pastor still did not do his basic assignments, and he spent more and more time counseling despite the fact that his job description did not mention counseling.

"By the time we decided we had to do something, we had a real mess," the pastor said. "This associate pastor had built quite a following with his counselees and their families. When we made the painful decision to terminate him, we lost many families. I'll bet it took us two years to recover from that fiasco."

The breakout churches have learned to act quickly and compassionately when a personnel issue becomes negative. If termination seems to be the only solution, the person terminated often receives generous severance pay. Some of the churches even provide a job or ministry or counseling to the person well beyond the point of termination.

"We've learned this lesson the hard way too," the senior pastor told us. "If you let a situation that needs attention continue, it will only get worse. But you have to handle everything you do in a Christlike manner."

Does the same philosophy apply to laypeople in mismatched positions in the church? We learned in the breakout churches, the answer is yes with some qualifications. Typically the church leadership did not deal with every situation in which a layperson was in a mismatched ministry situation. They did, however, deal with those situations in which the layperson was in a key and influential position. The cost was often high, but the cost of doing nothing was greater. After hearing from various leaders in the breakout churches, the research team noticed a very similar pattern in dealing with people who were mismatched with positions. We called the approach of the churches the "three Cs": *closure, compassion,* and *communication.*

Closure   **Compassion**

Communication

First, breakout churches refused to let troublesome people issues continue. Despite the difficulties in making such decisions, they did so and brought *closure*. But they dealt with the individuals involved with *compassion*. Unlike some of the corporate world decision makers (and those in many churches for that matter), leaders in the breakout churches attempted to discern how Christ would handle the situation. There is no doubt that he would have responded with love and compassion.

Perhaps the most unique characteristic displayed by the breakout churches was their insistence that any decision affecting people in key positions in the church would entail clear *communication*. The rumor mill could not start if the reasons behind a dismissal or a transfer were stated clearly and quickly. Of course, confidential matters were not revealed, but the members of the congregation had sufficient information to understand why a difficult decision was made.

Compatibility Is as Important as Competency

The breakout churches did not just look for the best qualified people to be a part of the ministry team. They sought people who would be the right fit with their personalities and philosophies of ministry. The "team" concept is vital in these churches. In the athletic world, we sometimes see a team of extraordinary athletes who perform poorly in competition because they don't work well together. The same thing can happen in the church. Our breakout churches know how critical it is to have highly competent people on their ministry team who work well together. In fact, the lay and staff leaders in these churches used the word *chemistry* more than a dozen times to describe the teamwork of their ministries. Look at just a few of their comments:

- "Our pastors have an incredible chemistry. It's as if we can almost anticipate what each other's next move will be."
- "No one tries to take credit for the way God blesses our church. It's all a team effort."
- "The chemistry of our staff is remarkable. Most of us have been together for over ten years. Serving at this church is both joy and fun."
- "I don't think any one of us is a superstar. We're all just a bunch of unknowns that work together in an incredible way."
- "I have had dozens of offers to go to other churches. But I can't find any place where everyone works together like they do at this church. I just don't think there's a better place on earth for me."

> **Surprisingly, in our interviews with ministers in the comparison churches, we heard more discussion about competent staff than we heard in the breakout churches. We suspect that the breakout church staff are every bit as competent as those in the comparison churches, if not more so. But the breakout church leaders consistently placed the same value, and often a higher value, on the need for staff compatibility.**

Micromanagement of Staff Is a Formula for Failure

I recently completed an initial interview with a leadership group from a church that requested the Rainer Group to provide consultation services. In the course of our discussions, my consulting team and I heard on several occasions the lay members refer to the Pastor Liaison Committee (PLC). After about five comments about the PLC, John Ewart, the lead consultant for this particular assignment, asked the obvious question: "Why do you have a PLC?"

Some of the church leaders seemed surprised that we would ask such a question. One lay leader spoke up: "The PLC is the group to whom the pastor is accountable. He meets with us every week to keep us updated on what he is doing. And we tell him what we are hearing among church members. We are able to tell of his negative talk so he can deal with it right away."

John Ewart and I, who together have pastored in seven churches, looked at each other with a one-word response: "Ugh!" We couldn't imagine having to report to a group every week. And we would be driven crazy by hearing every little criticism each week.

The leaders of the breakout churches don't mind accountability. But they detest micromanagement. If micromanagement is deemed necessary, then the person who is receiving this oversight is probably not capable of doing the job. Senior pastors of the breakout churches are not micromanaged. And they don't micromanage the people who work with them. The pattern of people management in these churches is consistent.

Figure 5C. The Pattern of People Management

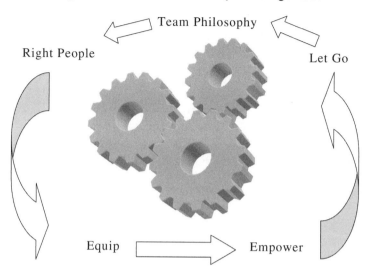

The compelling culture in these churches exudes teamwork and compatibility among staff and key lay leaders. That culture seeks and finds the right people who are then equipped to accomplish the roles of ministry for which they have been given responsibility. Once equipped, they are given authority to carry out their responsibilities. They are thus let go to do the work of ministry without worry of some micromanaging body or individual.

This climate of trust and freedom attracts even more of the right people to the church. David Cobb is Pastor for Worship and Arts at the Fairfield New Life Church, a Nazarene congregation near Sacramento, California. Pastor Cobb is effusive with compliments for Senior Pastor Jon Harris: "It was the pastor's vision that was such a draw to this church. It was a bit unusual for me to come to this Anglo church since I am an African American."

What has been Pastor Cobb's experience at Fairfield New Life? "I have full responsibility for overseeing the program for everything in the morning services, which includes media, music, and drama," he responded. The church clearly has an environment of trust and freedom for the pastors to do the work to which they have been called. Pastor Cobb continued, "I have also been entrusted with the responsibility to lead the small-group ministry and the adult ministry."

In this culture of freedom and trust, the staff has grown in their ministries. The church also has grown. When Harris arrived in 1992, worship attendance was 94. For the next five years the church showed no growth until a breakout occurred in 1997. By 2003 attendance was 712.

Needless to say, the research team was very impressed with all the "people" decisions of the breakout churches. Recall, however, that these churches worked on both "who" and "what" simultaneously. We learned some important lessons about the "what" as well.

KEY LESSONS LEARNED ABOUT THE "WHAT" IN BREAKOUT CHURCHES

Grace Church, a Christian and Missionary Alliance church in the Cleveland, Ohio, area, was led by Senior Pastor Donald Schaeffer for thirty-eight years. He was succeeded by his son, Jonathan Schaeffer, in 1998. Average worship attendance has grown from 58 to 1,663 under the leadership of the two Schaeffers. But the church experienced a prolonged period of no growth from 1979 to 1990.

Donald Schaeffer experienced an ABC moment while attending a Church Growth Institute in 1985. The business-as-usual philosophy was no longer acceptable. The "who" issue would continue to emphasize finding gifted staff who did not require close supervision. The pastor's hiring approach was straightforward: "When building my staff, I have always sought to hire wild horses that had to be tamed rather than tame horses that had to be prodded." The difference Pastor Schaeffer would make this time would be to equip them and work more closely with them early in their ministries so they could work unhindered for the long haul.

The "what" issues of structure were more problematic because there were so many areas of need. The small-group ministry was lacking, so the leadership began increased emphasis on and greater allocation of resources for this area. Formal structures of leadership development were established. New means of assimilation were considered and implemented. For example, Grace Church raised the expectation level for new members and leaders alike, which in turn increased the assimilation rate. Currently the church requires a twelve-week assimilation course called "In Touch" for all new members.

The structural changes also included numerous physical facility improvements. The most dramatic of the improvements was a total relocation to a new facility in 1996. The leadership of the church still believes, however, that they should have done more. Researcher Chris Bonts expressed their sentiments this way: "One mistake or regret expressed by all the staff was that they all wished they had erected bigger facilities the first time they built. Even though they relocated to a new facility in 1996, they are currently in the middle of an eight-million-dollar building program because they are rapidly running out of space."

Grace Church, like all of the breakout churches, immediately pursued both "who" and "what" changes after their ABC moment. The path of the simultrack was the only option because so much had to be done. We've already discussed several important "who" lessons; now let's look at some key "what" lessons.

The Church Must Learn What Its Purposes Are

Though it might sound simplistic, a church must know why it exists to know what it is supposed to do. Any structural decisions must be based on the purposes of the church.

From a biblical perspective, the clear purpose of the church is to bring glory to God. What the breakout churches discovered, however, were the "how" factors. How do we in the course of daily ministry do those things that will bring glory to God?

It is in the answer to this question that the influence and the genius of the Purpose Driven model become evident. The articulator of this model, Rick Warren, seems to engender opinions to one extreme or the other.[6] What many of the critics do not seem to grasp, however, is that the Purpose Driven model is not a new program or fad; it is rather a philosophy of ministry that begins with the question, "What is the church supposed to do?"[7]

Structural issues must begin with an understanding of the reasons structures are needed. We have seen countless churches spend millions of dollars on buildings with no real grasp of what they are trying to accomplish with the new facilities. We have seen even more churches adopt programs and ministries just because it was the latest offering of a denomination or some well-known ministry.

While some churches adopt the Purpose Driven paradigm to articulate their reasons for existence,[8] others often cite the Great Commission, particularly Matthew 28:18–20, as their framework for ministry.[9] The essential issue, however, is not the adoption of a slogan or a program. The essential issue is for churches to understand why they do what they do.

Structural changes are meaningless, if not harmful, unless churches grasp this reality.

Facilities and Location Are Means and Not Ends, But They Are Very Important

The breakout churches understood that a certain location or well-constructed facilities are not a panacea to a church's needs. But they also understood that poor location, limited acreage, and poor facilities could be a hindrance to church health.[10]

The comparison churches tended to make facility and location decisions based on the inward needs of the congregation. If influential people in the church desired to have a nicer fellowship hall to meet their desires, a fellowship hall would be constructed. The breakout churches did not ignore the desires of the church members, but they persistently evaluated if a facility decision would have a positive impact on reaching the lost and the unchurched.

Because the comparison church members often saw facilities and location as issues of their own needs and desires, any other rationale for change frequently met stiff resistance. We conducted interviews with lay leaders in a comparison church that had an obvious and serious need to relocate. One's words were telling: "We will move to another location over my dead body." The church recently voted down a relocation proposal.

Breakout churches see facilities and location as means—very important means. Comparison churches often see these factors as ends in themselves.

Small Groups Are Essential to the Health of Churches

Breakout churches understand that church members must get connected with a small group for them to grow in spiritual health and to remain connected with the church. Members who are involved in worship services alone tend to drift toward inactivity.[11]

The breakout churches placed great emphasis on small groups, whether in a Sunday school model or a more nontraditional model. They understood the importance of relationship connections that are made at the small-group level.

All of the comparison churches had some type of small-group structure in their congregations as well. But only eight of the thirty-nine comparison churches were strategic and clear in their purposes of the small groups. And only those eight placed any type of ongoing emphasis on small groups.

> When we examined the small-group structures in the churches, we were particularly focusing on open-ended small groups as opposed to closed-ended small groups. The closed-ended groups have a definitive termination point and often have closed enrollment. The open-ended groups are ongoing, and entry into them is always open to new persons. These are the groups that typically engender lasting relationships.

Leadership Groups Are Clearly Defined

In the breakout churches, we were able to discern quickly the roles of key leadership groups such as staff, deacons, and elders. In twenty-four of the thirty-nine comparison churches, confusion abounded on the specific roles of the groups.

In our research in one of the comparison churches, an elder and a deacon were interviewed together. When we asked them what their specific roles were, they began to cite similar responsibilities. They then began to disagree vociferously with each other. We had to intervene as a shouting match ensued. This church has declined 37 percent in the past five years.

A FINAL OBSERVATION ON WHO AND WHAT: A CULTURE OF SERIOUS FUN

On page 62 of *Good to Great*, Jim Collins notes that "it was striking to hear [the good-to-great leaders] talk about the transition era, for no matter how dark the days or how big the tasks, these people had fun!" Amazingly, we found the exact same thing. A consistent observation noted by the research team was the obvious joy present in both the staff and the laity of the breakout churches. Indeed, one of the researchers commented, "These people just seem to have fun."

We would not suggest for a moment that they did not take their ministries seriously. To the contrary, we will see in the next chapter that these leaders were passionately serious about the work to which God has called them. But they did not believe that serious ministry and fun were mutually exclusive. They told us repeatedly that ministry is a joy when you understand what you're supposed to do and why you're supposed to do it. Purpose in their lives and ministries engendered joy, fun, and laughter.

This structure or culture of serious fun was a primary attraction for other prospective staff members and church members. The "what" attracted the "who." People want to have purpose in their lives. They want their churches to have purpose as well. Life is just too short to wander and go through the motions every day. Thus playing church is not an option for those who are a part of these great congregations.

In this culture, the environment is perfect for churches to understand more clearly the specific vision God has called them to accomplish. The Who/What Simultrack thus leads to clarity of vision. We will see how that takes place in the next chapter.

IN ESSENCE, IN SUMMARY
THE WHO/WHAT SIMULTRACK

- Breakout churches pursued simultaneously the paths of getting the right infrastructure and getting the right people after they experienced their ABC moment.

- Our definition of infrastructure included such elements as facilities, location, leadership groups, organizational methods, and small groups.

- The breakout churches would often leave a position unfilled for a long period of time rather than get the wrong person. When in doubt, they told us, it is better to wait.

- When "people" mistakes were made, or when personnel mismatches became obvious, the breakout churches would act quickly and compassionately. Comparison churches tended to fail to act quickly in such situations, usually resulting in a bad situation becoming worse.

- The process of acting quickly and compassionately we described as the "three Cs": closure, compassion, and communication. The element of communication was what particularly stood out among the breakout churches. When a personnel decision of termination or reassignment was made, the leadership communicated clearly the reasons for such a decision to the congregation. Comparison churches, in contrast, often kept the congregation in the dark over the move.

- Compatibility was more important than competency as the churches selected ministry leaders.

- The breakout churches considered micromanagement of the senior pastor and staff to be a formula for failure.

- The first key issue in implementing a healthy infrastructure in the breakout churches was understanding the church's purposes. The Purpose Driven paradigm articulated by Rick Warren was highly influential in some of the churches. Facilities and location are means — not ends — in breakout churches, but they are very important means.

- Breakout churches focused significant resources on small groups for assimilation and outreach health.

- The breakout churches, unlike the majority of the comparison churches, understood clearly the roles of key leadership groups such as elders, deacons, and staff.

- A culture of "serious fun" typified most of the breakout churches.

THE VIP FACTOR

I don't know the key to success, but the key to failure is to try to please everyone.

—Bill Cosby

n *Good to Great*, Jim Collins included a pivotal chapter entitled "The Hedgehog Concept (Simplicity within the Three Circles)." The idea for this chapter was ignited by chapter 5 of *Good to Great*. Just as Jim Collins's Hedgehog Concept was built around three intersecting circles, so we have built this chapter around three intersecting circles.

Breakout churches have little concern about discovering the vision for their congregations.

In view of the enormous amount of resources available for helping churches and leaders discover vision, such a statement may seem ludicrous. But breakout churches simply do not seek to discover their vision.

Please read and hear these words carefully. The thirteen churches in our study do care about a vision for their congregations. And they do think that vision is important. They just don't seek to *discover* their vision.

In working with pastors and church leaders all over the world, I have seen that a common frustration is their perceived inability to discover a vision for their churches and then communicate and lead by that vision. Noted a senior pastor in one of the comparison churches: "I have spent the past five years of my ministry trying to get this vision thing down. I have

Figure 6A. The VIP Factor

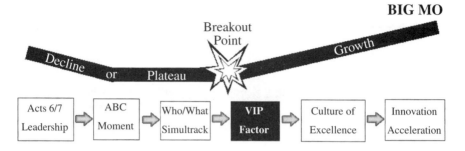

read books, attended seminars, and prayed to God to give me clarity. But I don't know any more today than I did five years ago. I am so frustrated and confused."

Our research team did not hear those same cries from the leaders of the breakout churches. To the contrary, we didn't hear any of them mention *any* efforts to discover vision. Yet they all have a clear and compelling vision today. How did they do it?

NOT EVEN A VISION TO BE A CHURCH

Xenos Christian Fellowship in Columbus, Ohio, is a church with an edge. I don't mean the edge of replacing the traditional with the contemporary. Rather, this church has leaders and members who embrace a radical Christianity that distinguishes them from the world.

In 1970 a group of Ohio State University students began printing an underground newspaper in the basement of their boardinghouse. Knowing that the Greek word for fish, *Ichthus*, was also an acronym used by early Christians meaning "Jesus Christ, God's Son, the Savior," they decided to call their newspaper *The Fish*.

Students began gathering in the basement of the house, which soon became a center for regular Bible studies. The Fish House Fellowship, as it soon became known, attracted students searching for answers during the turbulent times of the early 1970s. From its inception, this gathering was a magnet, drawing people to a Christian faith that is distinctive in its approach to the unchurched and the hurting.

The gathering did not become a church until 1982. When the church that same year took on the name Xenos Christian Fellowship, it was articulating its vision by its very name. This nondenominational, evangelical church is now a 4,000-attendance congregation with 150 persons on staff. They state in their history: "The name *Xenos* encompasses much of what we strive to be as a church. In the Greek language, *xenos* refers primarily to one who is a sojourner in a foreign land, a biblical description of Christians whose ultimate home is heaven. The word also applies to one who provides hospitality to sojourners. While we want to identify with the world we live in, we also strive to be distinctive in our love and sacrifice."

The words above are a clear and compelling vision. But Xenos Christian Fellowship did not agonize in search of this vision. Neither did the other breakout churches, most of which were a bit more traditional than Xenos. What these thirteen churches had in common was a vision that "discovered" them rather than a painful search to find out God's specific plan.[1] Our research uncovered a fascinating parallel in the breakout churches on this enigmatic issue of vision.

THE DISCOVERY OF THE VIP FACTOR

One of the amazing features of the breakout churches is their ability to discern and communicate essential matters simply. By contrast, one of the comparison churches had a brochure explaining their vision that looked like a manual from an engineering school. For the breakout churches, simple and straightforward is better.

The breakout churches did not develop some elaborate plan to discover and communicate vision. But we did discern a common pattern among these churches that we named the "VIP factor," with the acronym representing the words "Vision Intersection Profile." If you think the VIP sounds like Jim Collins's Hedgehog Concept, the similarity is not coincidental. We found Collins's explanation of the three intersecting circles of the Hedgehog Concept to be ingenious and applicable to churches. We essentially used his three circles as he lays them out, but substituted "Community Needs" for the "Economic Engine" of his Hedgehog Concept.

Figure 6B depicts the simplicity of the vision concept in the breakout churches. One circle represents the passion of the leadership. Remember, all of the breakout leaders were persons of obvious and intense passion for their ministry. In the six levels of leadership detailed in chapter 2, passion was the key factor in Acts 4 leadership. A second circle shows the passions, gifts, and talents of the congregation. I will elaborate on this issue shortly. The third circle represents the community in which the congregation is located. But more than an awareness of the presence of the community, the church has keen insights into the needs, desires, and hurts of the community.

Figure 6B. The Vision Intersection Profile

When the churches were clear on all three areas of the Vision Intersection Profile, vision became equally clear. Not all of the leader's passions are the same as the congregation's gifts and passions, but some are. Not all of the community's needs are the same as the intersection of the leader's and congregation's passions, but some are. When all three points intersect, the church knows its vision.

On page 95 of *Good to Great*, Jim Collins writes, "The essential strategic difference between the good-to-great and comparison companies lay in two fundamental distictions. First, the good-to-great companies founded their strategies on deep understanding along three key dimensions—what we came to call the three circles. Second, the good-to-great companies translated that understanding into a simple, crystalline concept that guided all their efforts."[2] Remarkably, the simplicity of understanding three intersecting points stands out as a characteristic of the breakout churches. Since I began this chapter highlighting Xenos Christian Fellowship, let's walk through the process of grasping how that church has such a clear vision today.

> We found a dearth of written vision statements among the break-out churches. Conversely, we found written vision statements in more than 70 percent of the comparison churches. The leaders of the comparison churches seem to think that, if they could just get an idea in writing before the congregation, the people would follow. The breakout leaders discovered vision long before any statements were written, if they were ever written.

THE VIP FACTOR AND XENOS CHRISTIAN FELLOWSHIP

Xenos Christian Fellowship, you may recall from chapter 2, went through an agonizing process to be the church it is today. From 1991 to 1994 attendance dropped from 3,800 to 2,400. While it might be an oversimplification to analyze the conflict this way, the problem was essentially one of conflicting visions.

One significant segment of the congregation felt that the church was becoming too institutionalized and too worldly. They longed for the informal days of the Fish House Fellowship. They objected to the leadership's moves to purchase property, build facilities, and of course, raise the funds to do so.

Another large portion of the membership saw the church as a counseling church. The counseling ministry by the early 1990s was huge at Xenos. But many in the church were concerned that this ministry was becoming unwieldy, less biblical, and more secular-oriented.

A weak attempt was also made to develop the church into a Willow Creek model, particularly moving toward ministry networking. While the leadership affirms much of the ministry of Willow Creek Community Church, they did not believe that such a model was the right fit for Xenos.

Another faction felt that the vision of the church could best be expressed in the manifestation of sign gifts.[3] These more charismatic groups seemed to be developing as autonomous units within the home groups.

You can well imagine how these disparate and often conflicting visions led to many struggles within the church. Nevertheless, the leadership of the church went forward with the purchase of land and construction of facilities. The growing counseling ministry, which was rapidly becoming a dominating force and ministry within the church, was halted. The extreme charismatic groups were publicly criticized. When the dissident groups attempted to remove the leadership in a congregational vote, they failed. Between 1,200 and 1,500 people left the church in a mass exodus.

Xenos Christian Fellowship was reeling from the conflict. Yet they were certainly not alone in facing this kind of conflict. In many churches the leaders leave when a congregation reaches such a point of tension and hurt. Many, perhaps most, churches never fully recover from a loss of as many as one-third of the members. Xenos not only recovered, but today the church is very healthy and vibrant.

REDISCOVERING THE VISION

Like many churches, Xenos Christian Fellowship has a mission statement. And like many churches, it is broad enough that it could be applied to a large number of churches:

> The church exists as an extension of Christ's ministry to reconcile the world to God (2 Corinthians 5:19). Therefore, Xenos Christian Fellowship exists to help people learn how to draw close to God. This work begins by inviting people to receive the gift of forgiveness offered through Jesus Christ. We are committed to fostering spiritual growth by encouraging all people to respond to God's love through loving service toward God and all people. Specifically, we direct our resources to serving the family, the non-Christian community locally and internationally, and the broader Christian community.

This broad statement could be used by any church. It does not recognize the unique history and the unique context of Xenos Christian Fellowship in Columbus, Ohio. The church does, however, have a clear vision that is uniquely its own. While we could find no specific written statements in our research of the church, our team did discern a clear and compelling vision of the church. We called this vision "Evangelistic Disciples."

> **Keep in mind that we are defining "mission" as a general statement of *any* church's purposes. "Vision," however, refers to God's specific plan for a specific church at a specific time in its history.**

We believe that this vision is embedded in both the church's history and in its present. Let's return to the Vision Intersection Profile to see how this vision developed at Xenos.

VIP: Leadership Passions

One of the three critical components of vision is a clear grasp by the leadership of their ministry passions. Dennis McCallum and Gary DeLashmutt are the lead pastors of Xenos. McCallum was one of the original Ohio State University students who began with Xenos when it was only a Christian underground newspaper called *The Fish*. When the boardinghouse where the newspaper was published became an attraction to students searching for answers in turbulent times, McCallum was among those who had a passion to evangelize and disciple these students. One of those non-Christian students who journeyed to the boardinghouse was DeLashmutt. As he was evangelized and discipled, he too became passionate about reaching the lost and discipling new Christians.

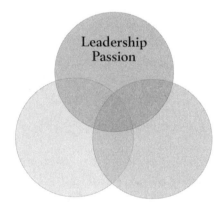

This passion was evident in our time with Xenos. In researcher Laura Cruse's interview with staff and laity, she asked Pastor McCallum directly to state his passion in ministry. He responded without hesitation: "Personal discipleship and personal character. If we raise up Christian disciples, they will naturally evangelize and bring growth to the church." McCallum has been with Xenos and its predecessor groups since 1970. In the course of more than three decades his passion to make evangelizing disciples has not waned.

Pastor DeLashmutt exudes that same passion. Among his many leadership responsibilities, he is responsible for the central teaching and preaching time on the weekend. When we asked him about the church conflict of 1991 to 1994, he responded that the key to recovery was to get focused on the vision: mentoring Christians who will become evangelists themselves.

In almost every area we researched in the church, and particularly among the leadership of the church, we heard the recurring theme: If you disciple Christians in a biblical manner, they will develop into believers for whom evangelism is a regular part of their lives and ministries.

VIP: Congregation's Gifts and Passions

Sometimes I lament the idiocy of my own leadership when I served as pastor of four different churches before coming to Southern Seminary as dean in 1994. In my last pastorate, I led a significant portion of the church membership to discover and understand their spiritual gifts.[4]

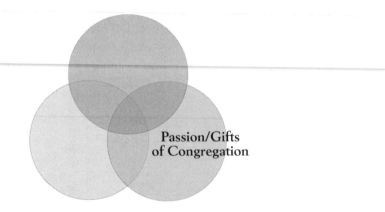

Passion/Gifts of Congregation

After an extensive and prolonged process, and after many members had a good grasp of their own spiritual gifts, I then declared that it was time for them to begin using their gifts in ministry. I had no plan or process in place for them to do so, nor did I direct them in a way that would complement my own passions for ministry articulated often from the pulpit and other venues. I could have learned much from Xenos.

A second key factor in vision discovery among the breakout churches is their grasp of the passions and gifts of the congregation. This factor is depicted in the second circle of the VIP factor.

When Xenos Christian Fellowship experienced its tumultuous period in the early 1990s, the issue was basically aligning the gifts and the passions of the congregants with the passions of the leadership, passions that had been evident since 1970. But some of the members were more passionate about counseling ministries. Others were passionate about ministries of a more extreme charismatic bent.

The leadership of the church knew, however, that a significant majority of the members, probably about two-thirds, were passionate about evangelizing lost persons and mentoring new Christians.[5] For a season, the leaders of the church let these disparate groups go their own directions. Their 20/20 hindsight sees that early confrontation of this issue may have limited the severity of the crisis.

> When leaders in a church are passionately clear about their vision, two inevitable results transpire. First, some will not be attracted to such a vision and will not join the congregation. If they are members, they will probably leave to find a church that is a better fit for their gifts and passions. Second, others will be attracted to the church because it reflects at least an aspect of their gifts and passions. The result is a congregation that is very unified in its vision and ministries.

After the exodus of one-third of the Xenos fellowship, the elders asked Pastor McCallum to write a paper about the direction and vision of the church. The paper was a refocus of the original vision that the church was to develop disciples who would become evangelistic in their daily walk with Christ. That recasting of the vision was the impetus behind discontinuing the ministry networking structure the church had adopted from Willow Creek.[6] They stayed with home groups as the key structure for evangelism and discipleship.

The church also developed the Xenos Servant Team, an incredible structure to recognize and equip adults who are clearly passionate about the vision of the church and are willing and desirous to become mentors and examples to others. Again, the vision is apparent in the development of this group. The Servant Team is made up of mature Christians who disciple others to become more obedient followers of Christ, including fulfilling the very natural process of sharing their faith with others.

The qualifications to become a part of the Servant Team are many. Look at just a summary of the requirements.[7]

- Maintain personal times of prayer and Bible study.
- Attend and contribute to a Xenos home fellowship group over a period of years.
- Attend and contribute to one of the ministries at the Central Teaching.
- Provide regular and substantial financial giving to the church's general fund.
- Serve in a defined ministry or leadership role.
- Undertake yearly self-equipping projects.
- Practice mature management of interpersonal conflict and dissent in the congregation.
- Live up to the character qualifications for deacon as given in 1 Timothy 3.
- Complete extensive coursework (a minimum of six defined courses).
- Be nominated by an existing Servant Team member and endorsed by others.
- Be willing to undergo a background check and be interviewed by leaders of the church.
- Avoid discrediting behavior.
- Submit to an annual follow-up interview if requested.

> **The Xenos leadership team leaves little doubt about what they expect of the Servant Team. The Xenos website states: "The Xenos Servant Team is no casual organization, like a garden club. It is a high commitment association of dedicated Christian workers— men and women resolved to give their all for Christ. Qualifying for the team normally takes years of work and growth. Yet, even with these restrictions, more members join each month."[8]**

Despite these lengthy and arduous requirements, some 850 adults are part of this team and an integral part of the vision to see Christians grow into mature evangelizing Christians. The leadership passion has intersected with the passion and gifts of the congregation.

VIP: Community Needs

Any church that is obedient to God's command to make disciples (Matt. 28:19) and to be his witnesses (Acts 1:8) must have a vision that includes the world. The world may be next door or it may be another continent, but the church has clear and pressing responsibilities beyond its doors. The third circle in the VIP factor is community needs.

When the gatherings that were precursors to Xenos started meeting, the "world" was coming to them. College students from homes all over the world began gathering at the Fish House Fellowship. They had deep needs, particularly the need to receive the forgiving grace of our Lord Jesus Christ.

Though over three decades have passed since those early gatherings, the vision of the church remains clearly evangelistic. Xenos believes that a truly mature follower of Christ will have a passion for the world. The counseling ministries in the early 1990s had become inwardly focused. In many ways the charismatic groups had become self-focused as well. Their ministry foci simply did not complement the original outward focus of the church. The ensuing conflict was inevitable.

More than thirty years later, the church still has a passion to reach and meet the needs of the community. At the end of each year, Xenos issues an annual report on the state of the church. The report is a thorough review of the congregation's ministries, and at numerous points in the report, the elders assess the impact of the church on the community.

A fascinating initiative again reflects the VIP factor. Xenos elders started Urban Concern. The mission of Urban Concern is "to work with individuals in the inner city to break the cycle of poverty and hopelessness. We are committed to raising up leaders who play an active role in restoring their own community."[9]

As this ministry has grown and made a difference in the inner-city areas of Columbus, Ohio, it has become both locally and nationally recognized.

Recognition of this ministry includes impressive accolades: White House Thousand Points of Light Award, World Vision Mustard Seed Award, and Columbus *Dispatch* Community Service Award.

Consistent with its vision, the church has discerned that one of the greatest needs in the community is to impact the lives of inner-city youth and reach them with Christ's love. Figure 6C illustrates how the VIP factor comes together for Xenos Christian Fellowship.

Figure 6C. The VIP Factor at Xenos Christian Fellowship

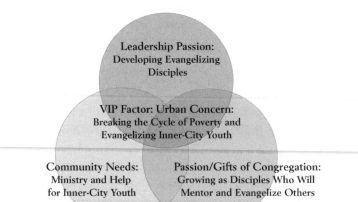

WHEN VISION DISCOVERS THE CHURCH

The ministry of Urban Concern is only a part of the Xenos Christian Fellowship vision. Indeed, the unique utilization of home groups involves many more people than Urban Concern. I highlighted this inner-city ministry, however, because I see very few churches, particularly churches that are predominately Anglo, developing a major ministry to inner-city youth.

The leadership did not declare one day that the church would start an initiative in the inner city in a few years. Instead, the leaders pursued their passion of developing disciples who would have an outreach passion. Unfortunately, many churches today consider discipleship as something totally separate from evangelism. Xenos leadership, however, built into the "DNA" of the church a passion to reach others as one grows as a disciple in Christ. Congregation members had these same passions and desires.

Ultimately the church discovered a great community need in the South Linden area of Columbus. The youth of this community were in a vicious cycle of poverty. Jim Swearingen, who serves as executive director of Urban

Concern, noted: "One of the biggest factors in poor educational outcomes is family incomes. If we can help families in poverty to succeed educationally, then we hold a key to overall success in the educational system."[10]

After consulting with and researching thousands of churches, I am convinced that this ministry never would have come to fruition in most churches. Either the leadership does not have the passion, or the members of the church are not equipped in their own areas of passion and gifts to see such a need in the community. Nevertheless, this dire situation does not have to be permanent. Xenos and other churches have made successful transitions; so can your church.

Xenos Christian Fellowship did not agonize and utilize multiple instruments to discover this aspect of the vision for their church. Instead, Urban Concern was a natural outgrowth of the VIP factor. The ministry is a clear example of the vision to make evangelizing disciples.

> **Many of the specific ministries of the breakout churches could hardly have been conceived by a vision committee in a church. Some are just too unique to have their origins in the collective wisdom of a group. Grove City Church of the Nazarene in Grove City, Ohio, for example, has a biker ministry that reaches thousands each year. Steve Combs, associate pastor, says that "passionate leaders drive the ministries at Grove City." In 1999 the church baptized 100 persons in one service alone.**

IMPLICATIONS OF THE VIP FACTOR

The Vision Intersection Profile provided the research team with a clear picture of the process by which the breakout churches discover vision. As we reviewed each of the thirteen churches and their own issues related to the VIP factor, several implications became evident to our team.

Choose What You Can Do Best (But You Can't Do Everything)

In chapter 5 of *Good to Great*, Jim Collins highlights the importance of a company understanding what it can (and cannot) be the best at. We incorporated Collins's insight as the basis for the text of this section.

One of the comparison churches in our study seemed to be involved in more ministries than was humanly possible. We asked one of the laypeople about our observation, and she replied, "Oh yeah, we start a new ministry every two or three weeks. It depends on what the pastor heard from some of his buddies, or the latest church growth fad."

But how do you keep all those ministries staffed and functional? "We don't," she deadpanned. "The staff loses their enthusiasm about them even though they remain on paper as a ministry in the church."

The breakout churches focused on doing a few things and doing those few things well. They did not attempt to carry out all of the passions of the leadership. Nor did they attempt to implement all of the passions and desires of the congregation. And they certainly did not try to meet all of the needs of the communities where they served. But in those cases where all three areas intersected, the Vision Intersection Profile, the churches were laser-focused in doing these relatively few ministries well.

The VIP Factor Assumes Leadership Passion

Without passion there is no vision. We found no churches that had anything resembling a true vision unless the leadership, particularly the pastor, was clearly passionate about something.

This issue alone could explain the dearth of vision in many churches today. Recall our study of leaders in chapter 2. Of the 427 churches we examined, only 6 percent of those congregations had a leader who was clearly passionate.[11] Vision begins with God who gives his direction to those who are passionate about the work of ministry.

If 94 percent of leaders lack passion, what drives them in ministry? The answers are varied, but none is encouraging. Some of the leaders in our comparison churches were clearly driven by survival. They made decisions based on their best chance of creating the least resistance. Similarly, some leaders were driven by conflict avoidance. Their jobs may not have been on the line, but they still had a strong aversion to any conflict.

Sadly, some leaders seemed to be driven by self-promotion. Many of the decisions they made seemed to be the result of determining the amount of recognition they would get. Still others were driven by tradition; they did not want to do anything that got them out of their routines and comfort. Some leaders were driven by fear and made decisions that took the least amount of faith. Fearing failure, they never took God-given risks.

A Clear and Compelling Vision Must Include the Congregation

The breakout leaders understood the clear meaning of Acts 6. If ministry is left in the hands of only a select few believers (the Twelve in the case of Acts 6), there will always be shortfalls and incomplete ministries. But the breakout churches did not see the members as mere spectators of the leadership's performance. Their gifts and passions were a vital part of the church's vision.

How do breakout churches make certain they include the congregation in the vision? Although some of the comparison churches made spiritual gift inventories available and had ministry fairs so that members could sign up for a particular ministry, the breakout churches simply created an atmosphere of permission that allowed members to follow their passions and desires in ministries. These churches weren't adverse to programs and tools, but their primary approach was to have a climate of openness to members' involvement in and development of ministries in the church.

You Must Be Passionate about Your Community

Many of the comparison churches just did not seem to get it. A congregation cannot be an island in a community of needs. In the majority of comparison churches in our study, merchants within a half-mile radius of the church could not tell us where the church was located. The church was irrelevant to the community.

There can be no vision without a clear discernment of the community's needs. And there can be no discernment of the community's needs without a passion for the community. Frankly, some of the leaders of the comparison churches viewed the community as a means to their ends—increase attendance, add to the budget, lead the area churches in baptisms. The breakout churches, however, had a passion to reach and minister to the community. They did not first ask how the community might benefit the church. As best as the research team could tell, the motives of the breakout church leaders were selfless.

The Korean Central Presbyterian Church in Vienna, Virginia, is a clear example of selfless motives in reaching the community. As the name of the church indicates, almost all of the members are Koreans; in this case, first- and second-generation Koreans. The vision of the church is amazingly similar to that of Xenos Christian Fellowship: "Training the Saints to Transform the World."

These "maturing saints" began to see needs in the community far beyond the Korean-American population. In 1994 they opened a senior adult center to meet the needs of an aging population. This effort resulted in recognition by the governor of Virginia.[12]

In 2000 the church purchased the Community Service Center of Washington, D.C., to minister to the indigent population, to alcoholics, and to drug addicts in the downtown area. Most of the beneficiaries of this ministry are African Americans. Korean Central Presbyterian Church is passionate about its community, and that passion has led to a clear and compelling vision for the church.

Vision Is Dynamic

The Vision Intersection Profile has three major components, and any one of those components can experience change over the course of time. When one component changes significantly, the vision changes as well.

Two implications are worth noting on this issue. First, the church should continually be sensitive to the possibility that what it is doing today may not be what God would have it do tomorrow. The leader's passion may change. The congregation's passions and gifts may change, especially as the makeup of the church shifts. The community's needs will probably change over time as well. Therefore the church must be sensitive to God's new directions and paths.

Nevertheless, we did not see in the breakout churches a chaotic and random shifting of vision from year to year. Indeed, we were amazed at the consistency of the vision over time. It seems that when change in the vision takes place, it is a gradual and incremental change. In the example of Xenos Christian Fellowship, many of the ministries they are doing today are dramatically different than those of several years ago. But the essence of the vision, evangelizing disciples, is as true today as it was in 1970.

BREAKING OUT . . . AND VISIONARY

Perhaps at times as you are reading this book, you have become discouraged, even disillusioned, with the church. I understand. Such attitudes have been mine on more than one occasion. But when we on the research team did our final work on these churches, we left the process more optimistic than ever.

You see, we spent time with visionaries. We hung out with people of great faith. Yes, they are fallible and sometimes sinful persons, but God has used them in extraordinary ways. Some of the visionaries served on the staff. Some were senior pastors. Some were laypeople. But all were visionaries. They believed in a God of miracles. They attempted things that would be impossible without a supernatural God. They went into the promised land of God's possibilities, and they will never be the same. And we on the breakout churches research team were inspired, even changed, by their faith.

As our team met together one evening, one of the researchers commented, "It seems like the leaders in these churches understand how short life is, and they want to make a difference for God in the short time they have. They don't want to waste their time doing things that don't matter. They have vision because they stay in touch with God."

His words were well spoken and accurate. And they explained much about breakout churches and their leaders. These leaders understand the incredible brevity of life. They desire to make a difference for the glory of God in this short period. And they trust in a God of miracles for whom all things are possible. That distinction makes all the difference. It is a distinction embraced by those who have broken out and one never realized by those who fail to grasp this supernatural reality.

IN ESSENCE, IN SUMMARY
THE VIP FACTOR

- Attempts at vision discovery were rare in breakout churches but common in comparison churches. An often-heard comment in the breakout churches was "Vision discovered us."

- The VIP factor stands for Vision Intersection Profile. Three different factors merge, and their overlapping point is the vision of the church.

- The first of the three VIP factors is the passion of the church's leadership. Our studies indicate that only 6 percent of church leaders indicate even a modest level of passion for their ministries.

- The second of the three VIP factors is the passion and gifts of the congregation. In breakout churches, a climate of ministry freedom encourages members to pursue ministry according to their own passions and gifts.

- The third of the VIP factors is community needs. The breakout churches were passionate about discovering the needs of the community and then meeting those needs. Unlike the comparison churches, the breakout churches moved into a community ministry with no thought of reciprocation. They sought to provide for the community even if they received nothing in return.

- A clear implication of the VIP factor is that visionary churches choose only to pursue a few areas where they can excel. They do not attempt to do everything.

- Another implication of the VIP factor is that vision is dynamic. Because vision consists of three components, any of which may change, the entire vision is never constant. Our breakout churches, however, were amazingly consistent in their visions year by year. They were open to changing the vision, but they were very careful not to chase the latest fad, the latest methodology, or the presumed most pressing need.

CHAPTER 7

A CULTURE OF EXCELLENCE

It takes discipline to say, "No, thank you" to big opportunities. The fact that something is a "once-in-a-lifetime opportunity" is irrelevant if it doesn't fit within the three circles.

—*Jim Collins*, Good to Great

Chapter 6 of *Good to Great* is entitled "A Culture of Discipline." We imported that concept here in this chapter, changing the terminology slightly to "A Culture of Excellence."

First Gethsemane Baptist Church sits in the shadow of several great churches in Louisville, Kentucky: Southeast Christian Church, Highview Baptist Church, and St. Stephen Baptist Church, to name a few. When pundits are asked to name the outstanding churches in the area, the latter three are typically mentioned first.

Like most of our breakout churches, First Gethsemane is mentioned rarely in books and articles. And like most of our breakout churches, First Gethsemane has made strides that were often plodding and imperceptible to most students of the American church.

T. Vaughn Walker became pastor of this predominately African-American church in 1984. Worship attendance reached 200 that year, with a beginning membership of about 135, but growth began to take place

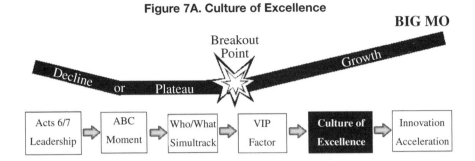

Figure 7A. Culture of Excellence

immediately. By 1990 attendance was 375, nearly double the level of six years earlier. Then the church plateaued, and for the next several years, attendance remained around the level of 350 to 375, although membership continued to grow modestly. Not only did Walker lead the church out of its plateau, but by 2003 the active membership roll reached 2,100, with attendance ranging between 1,000 and 1,300. The congregation had become one of the fastest-growing churches in the region.

> **Remember that one key qualifier for the breakout churches was that they had to experience a decline or plateau and then break out of the decline and sustain growth for a number of years. Both the decline and the breakout growth had to take place under the same pastor. The three great churches mentioned above, for example, did not meet one or both of these criteria.**

HOW DID THEY DO IT?

How did First Gethsemane Baptist Church break out and grow? Certainly no one factor explains this phenomenal breakout growth. Vaughn Walker and his wife, Cheryl, are prayer warriors. Not only do they pray and fast for the church regularly themselves, but they have also led the members to times of intensive corporate prayer.

Perhaps persistence could explain some of First Gethsemane's growth. Walker was tempted toward and even offered opportunities to move elsewhere, especially when times were tough and growth had plateaued. But he persevered and stayed with the church. God obviously used Walker's leadership skills in this breakout transition. He is a determined leader who is willing to wait until opportunities avail themselves.

Furthermore, Walker and the other leaders at First Gethsemane believe that anything attempted for God should be done with excellence. For instance, Walker insists on excellence in music and worship. He is leading the church to excellence in facilities. His preaching reflects hours of labor and prayer that could only be described as excellent. Walker has also led the members of his congregation to do ministry with excellence. Recognizing that the paid staff cannot meet all ministry needs in a large and rapidly growing congregation, he has led church members to develop a remarkable ministry organization.

The ministries of First Gethsemane are divided into ten divisions with more than sixty areas of member involvement. While four paid full-time, three paid part-time, and three volunteer part-time staff members oversee the ten divisions, the vast majority of the more than sixty ministries are led by lay volunteers. Their efforts are making an astounding impact both within the church and in the community.

"By allowing the laity to become an integral part of the ministry," notes Walker, "they become empowered and become owners of the overall vision and ministry of First Gethsemane." Vaughn Walker could not be satisfied with the typical hit-and-miss ministries and programs of many churches across America. You can hear the passion in his descriptions of the work God is doing at the church. And you can sense his drive for excellence in all that takes place through the ministry of First Gethsemane Baptist Church. It is this excellence in all things that is also a clear characteristic of the breakout churches. Chapter 6 of *Good to Great* is entitled "A Culture of Discipline." We have imported that concept here and call it "A Culture of Excellence."

EXCELLENCE IN ALL THINGS

The breakout churches all have experienced some difficult times. None of the leaders has any desire to return to the days of struggle and, in many cases, conflict. This attitude was discerned easily by the research team. The leaders' quest for excellence thus can be partially explained by their disdain for events of days past.

In one of our team meetings, I asked the researchers what common element was emerging in our finalists for the breakout churches. "Excellence in all things," replied Elisha Rimestead. "They don't want to do anything unless they are doing their best." The other team members concurred.

As we evaluated our findings further, another consensus emerged. The breakout churches were not fanatical about excellence in the same way a Fortune 500 corporation might emphasize excellence. The church leaders all spoke about a drive to glorify God, to please the Savior, or to do their best in his power for his sake. In other words, we found the drive for a culture of excellence to be theologically and biblically driven.

> **The breakout churches were all evangelical churches, and many of the comparison churches were conservative and evangelical in their theology as well. The breakout churches, however, were consistently trying to practice their theology. One good example took place in a comparison church where I noted how they had posted their clearly stated beliefs and expectations in a frame on a foyer wall. When I complimented the church lay leader on their clear statement of faith and expectations, he responded. "Oh, that thing has been up there forever. No one pays any attention to it." In many of the comparison churches, "no one paid attention to it."**

A STORY OF EXCELLENCE IN EVANGELISM

The written history of Central Christian Church in Beloit, Wisconsin, states: "Central Christian Church has never been satisfied with 'being satisfied.'" Such an attitude was common in the breakout churches but nonexistent in the comparison churches.[1]

For many years Central Christian lost its focus and its drive for excellence. By the mid-1980s Pastor David Clark began to preach, teach, and exhort the church to pursue the biblical purposes to which God had called the church.[2] The leadership of the church realized that Central Christian was falling short in many areas. Nowhere was this inadequacy more evident than in the area of local evangelism.

The critical turning point took place in 1986 when the church began to dream of being more than just a neighborhood church. The leadership sensed God's direction for Central Christian to become a major evangelistic force in the entire region of Southern Wisconsin.

This drive for evangelistic excellence led the church to secure the help of Church Growth Services of South Bend, Indiana, to develop a plan for future outreach and growth. Like all of the other breakout churches, the impact of a "positive outside influence" was instrumental in moving the church to greatness.[3]

The new focus and the new quest for excellence led to stunning numerical results. From 1911 to 1985, Central Christian Church worship attendance grew from 59 to 200. But from 1986 to 2003 attendance grew from 200 to 1,600. More important, the church is truly living up to its own expectations of evangelistic excellence. Total conversions to Christ, reported as baptisms, now approach nearly 200 per year.[4]

EXCELLENCE IN MINISTRY TOO

Like First Gethsemane Baptist Church, Central Christian was not content to see the 80/20 Pareto Principle in ministry.[5] In other words, the church was ready to break the normative pattern of 20 percent of the members doing 80 percent of the ministry. Several steps were taken to engender more member involvement in ministry, but the most important step took place in 2000.

One of the amazing stories of the breakout churches is the story of the "before and after." When these churches were "good," programs took place as usual and the church had no discernible focus or energy. But when the churches became "great," business as usual was never acceptable. Indeed, the research team noted that the greatest potential weakness of the breakout churches was their reticence in celebrating victories. The churches seem to believe that a celebration may imply satisfaction with the current status of the church.

In that year, Central Christian Church doubled its number of lay ministers. At the beginning of 2000, Pastor Clark preached seven consecutive sermons on "every member ministry." He challenged every member to be a "one-hour hero," a person who ministers at least one hour every week. Some clean the nursery; some wash windows; some clean toilets; some participate in evangelism ministries. One woman comes to church every Wednesday to make certain that pencils are in the pews. In just one year the number of "one-hour heroes" grew from 300 to 600. Appropriately, the church sets aside a special day each year to honor and recognize these volunteer lay ministers.

EXCELLENCE IN MANY PLACES

The breakout stories of excellence seem endless. Many have to do with facilities. Indeed, the leaders of breakout churches often chide themselves for failing to build sufficient space or to construct quality space. A clear and discernible difference is apparent when one drives to or walks onto the campus of a breakout church versus a comparison church. A culture of excellence is evident in the facilities and grounds.

My favorite city in the world is Naples, Florida. I have traveled to hundreds of places, so I believe my assessment is a fair comparison. The moment you enter the city limits, you are immediately impressed with the neatness of this southwest Florida town. Even the landscaping in the medians is a work of art. Walk in the downtown area around Fifth Avenue South, and you are awestruck by the beauty and the cleanliness of one of the world's most attractive downtown areas. Walk the pristine beaches, such as Vanderbilt Beach, and you will not see one item of trash. Attend one of the outdoor theater productions. Spend hours in the tropical zoo. Wherever you go, whatever you do, Naples, Florida, is an obvious and powerful testimony of excellence. The first time my wife and I visited Naples, we had amazingly similar reactions: "Somebody really cares about this place."

Such was the reaction of our research team in their interaction with the breakout churches. When a researcher visited a church, he or she was impressed with the facilities, with the ministries, with the evangelistic outreach, with the commitment of the ministry staff, and with the obvious commitment of the laity. The same word was repeated in many of the reports from the researchers: *excellence*.

But we must be careful to qualify what we mean by excellence. The breakout churches were not churches of excellence in every conceivable area. They chose the areas in which they could be excellent and did not attempt to do everything else. Quite often the area in which the focus of excellence was most obvious was the Vision Intersection Profile.

THE VIP FACTOR AND EXCELLENCE

In chapter 6 I used the VIP factor as a graphic way to picture and understand a church's vision. The vision, of course, is the current focus of the breakout churches. Our research revealed an amazing correlation between the culture of excellence and the VIP factor.

The VIP factor, you will recall, is the intersection of three important variables in the life of a church: leadership passion, the congregation's gifts and passions, and the community's needs. I illustrated the intersections with three circles.

Figure 7B. The Vision Intersection Profile

On page 134 of *Good to Great*, Jim Collins writes, "The good-to-great companies at their best followed a simple mantra: *Anything that does not fit with our [three circles], we will not do.*"[6] Breakout churches learned that they could not do everything with excellence. One of the major changes the thirteen churches made in their transition to greatness was their near fanatical focus on those few areas where they could excel. This devotion manifested itself most clearly in the churches' pursuit of excellence in the VIP factor.

A VISION FOR "THOSE WHO ARE NOT YET HERE"

When researcher Doug Whitaker shared his report on Grove City Church of the Nazarene in Grove City, Ohio, I was impressed by his concise description of the congregation: "It seemed to me, as I interviewed people in this church, that everything they did revolved around those who were not there yet."[7] The VIP factor seemed clear at Grove City. The intersection of the three circles is a vision for the lost and the unchurched, "those who are not yet here."

Figure 7C. The VIP Factor at Grove City Church of the Nazarene

The leadership of Grove City Church of the Nazarene has many passions for their church. The congregation is gifted in many ways other than those directly related to evangelism. And the people of the community obviously have physical and emotional needs in addition to their greatest need of salvation through Christ. But the church cannot do everything well. Therefore they have determined to place much of their focus on being a church of excellence that will reach the lost and the unchurched.

The move to do a few things with excellence meant that everything the church did had to be evaluated ruthlessly. "Sacred cows" were handled with care, but the church had to move forward. A few critics within the church and within the denomination could have caused the church to lose its focus. But the church remained fanatically focused on doing a few things with excellence.

The church started a biker ministry with one major focus: reach the lost bikers with the gospel of Christ. They were clearly "those who are not yet here." Steve Combs, associate pastor, noted that "passionate leaders drive the ministries at Grove City, and most of those are driven to reach the lost." The biker ministry reaches thousands each year. In 1999 Grove City baptized 100 persons in one service.

All decisions at Grove City seem to revolve around the VIP factor. All efforts at excellence are focused on just a few areas. Many of the leaders spoke often about "the barn experience." The board and staff were at a retreat and met in a barn for free time and fellowship. They sensed a powerful presence of the Holy Spirit that ultimately led the group to recommend the building of a new worship center.

The key to this story is not the construction of a new building. The real story is the leaders' awareness that they would have little to no room for new people if they did not build soon. Simply stated, what drove the decision was a focus on "those who are not yet here."

> We tried to discern why the quest for excellence was not taking place in the comparison churches. Though we would be hesitant to isolate explanations to a single reason, we had little doubt that at least a partial explanation could be found in the churches' failure to pursue fanatically just a few areas of ministry. The comparison churches had much longer lists of programs and ministries than the breakout churches and often followed the crowd after the latest fad. To the contrary, breakout churches were extremely careful in their evaluations of new opportunities. They typically asked two questions: Does it fit our vision? Can we take on this new responsibility and do it with excellence?

THE FREEDOM/EXPECTATION PARADOX

The church is the paradigmatic volunteer organization. Paid staff comprises a very small portion of the "workforce." Yet the breakout churches consistently had both staff and lay workers who demonstrated excellence in their ministries. To the contrary, the comparison church leaders consistently complained about their inability to attract workers for the plethora of ministries offered by the churches. How did the breakout churches attract workers in both quantity and quality?

On pages 124–26 of *Good to Great,* Jim Collins has a section entitled "Freedom (and Responsibility) within a Framework" wherein he describes how the good-to-great companies gave their people freedom to determine the best path to achieving company objectives while also holding them rigorously accountable for achieving the objectives. People within the good-to-great companies had freedom, but freedom within the contraints of a framework. In our interviews with lay and staff leaders, we consistently heard two themes that were a magnet for them in their work in the breakout churches. These two themes seemed to be paradoxical. On the one hand, these quality workers relished the freedom given to them to carry out their work. They were clear that any attempts to micromanage them would be met with stiff resistance. On the other hand, they were equally clear that they cherished the high-expectation environment of their churches. They wanted freedom, but they wanted clear boundaries of high expectations. We dubbed this reality the "Freedom/Expectation Paradox" as illustrated in figure 7D. A similar matrix and idea are introduced in the "Good to Great Matrix of Creative Discipline" that appears on page 122 of *Good to Great.*

Figure 7D. The Freedom/Expectation Paradox

Quadrant 1	Quadrant 2
High Expectation/ Low Freedom	High Expectation/ High Freedom
7 Comparison Churches	13 Breakout Churches
Quadrant 3	**Quadrant 4**
Low Expectation/ Low Freedom	Low Expectation/ High Freedom
25 Comparison Churches	7 Comparison Churches

THE QUADRANT 2 CHURCH

One early emerging pattern our team discovered as we researched the breakout churches was an attitude of joy and the expression of fulfillment of being in a church that gave great freedom in ministry while establishing high expectations.

In our follow-up, we asked many of these respondents if they did not see a contradiction in their attitudes. Could one really have abundant freedom in an environment of high expectations? A layperson from Lenexa Baptist Church in Lenexa, Kansas, gave a common response: "I guess the best way to express what takes place here is to say that we have great freedom within boundaries. The boundaries are making sure we are within the church's vision and that we do everything with excellence."

Noting the high energy of this layperson, the researcher asked him if he felt any constraints with high expectations. He responded, "Not really. I like knowing what is expected of me. I like to be a part of something where you can make a difference. I've been in churches where you really wonder if you count. Freedom isn't just doing anything you want. But I do have a lot of freedom within the expectations that have been given to us."

The thirteen breakout churches all demonstrated this Quadrant 2 reality. Since none of the comparison churches were in this quadrant, we concluded that the Freedom/Expectation Paradox was a characteristic unique mostly to breakout churches and great churches.[8] The other quadrants were the obvious visual descriptions for the comparison churches.

THE COMPARISON CHURCHES: NO QUADRANT 2

None of our thirty-nine comparison churches were identified by our research team members to be Quadrant 2 churches. They were identified, however, as churches clearly in the other three quadrants.

> **Keep in mind as you read all of our assessments of comparison churches that we intentionally excluded great churches from the comparison group. A great church met the same criteria as a breakout church with two exceptions. The move to greatness came with new pastoral leadership, and the church did not necessarily experience a sustained period of decline or plateau. Breakout churches moved to greatness under the same leadership. Most indications are that the great churches would have many, but not all, of the same characteristics of the breakout churches.**

Seven of the comparison churches were Quadrant 1 churches. In these churches, expectations of staff and members were high, but freedom to do the ministry was low. The leadership of these churches tended to be autocratic. Though we cannot empirically verify attitudes and dispositions, the research team members repeatedly reported that those involved in ministry seemed to work out of some legalistic obligation. Joy was not evident in their lives or in their ministries. These churches tend to have growth for a short season until disillusioned staff and members begin leaving.

Most of the comparison churches were Quadrant 3 churches. These twenty-five churches had few expectations of their members. The leadership was more concerned about filling vacant positions than seeing people involved in life-changing ministries. Each year the "nominating committee" or some similar group would attempt to fill all the vacancies, including committee memberships for committees that never met.

The sad irony of the Quadrant 3 churches is that low expectations were accompanied with low freedom. While little was expected of those filling positions, the members and staff were repeatedly constrained by any attempts to do something new, daring, or innovative. The pathetic cliché of "We've never done it that way before" doomed these churches to mediocrity.

Another seven of the comparison churches were Quadrant 4 churches. These churches really did not expect much of their members, nor did they have any compelling vision that guided and motivated the few who wanted to be involved in ministry. As a consequence, the few ministries that existed were often competitive with and antagonistic toward one another. This low expectation/high freedom combination is a formula for disaster.

Because there were no clear guidelines or vision, the environments of these churches tended to be chaotic. Ministry leaders fought for budget dollars and facility access. One ministry philosophy would compete directly with another. One frustrated member of a comparison church commented, "Everybody just seems to be doing their own thing. We don't seem like a church. We're just a bunch of people with our own agendas meeting in the same building."

THE CULTURE OF EXCELLENCE AS AUTOCRAT

The comparison churches in Quadrant 1 and the breakout churches in Quadrant 2 did have some similarities. Compared to the comparison churches in Quadrants 3 and 4, these churches did have strong leaders. There was, however, a clear and distinct difference in the leadership styles.

The Quadrant 1 leaders were autocratic. They demanded their way instead of earning their way. They tended to view losses of dissenting members not only as inevitable but desirable. They frankly had an insecurity that left little room for opinions other than their own.

In an interview with a twenty-seven-year member of a comparison church that clearly fit the Quadrant 1 paradigm, the member actually began crying as I asked perfunctory questions. With apparent disregard for the question I asked, "Sheila" began to lament: "I love this church. It is my home. But so many of my friends have left because the pastor [of two years] is such a dictator. He doesn't have any concern for us; he just has to have his way. I am really torn. I love this church, but it's really not my church anymore. I guess I will have to join some of my friends who moved to another church."

The churches in Quadrant 2, the breakout churches, did have strong leaders, but they were not autocratic. To the contrary, they had a humility that defied many stereotypes of strong leaders.

While I was in the middle of writing this book, I sent letters to each of the leaders of the breakout churches. I soon received a warm response from Won Sang Lee, the recently retired pastor of Korean Central Presbyterian Church in Vienna, Virginia. Lee served the church from 1977 to 2003.

Listen to a portion of his response to hear a clear indication of the spirit typical of the breakout church leaders: "It is my great pleasure and honor to hear that you have selected the Korean Central Presbyterian Church as one of the thirteen breakout churches. I am afraid that receiving praise in this world may reduce the real reward from the Lord in heaven. But I trust that this may also encourage and teach all of us to serve Him better as the Lord expects us to do."

As I have noted on repeated occasions, the breakout leaders exhibited a humility that humbled all of us on the research team. That humility, however, was not a sign of leadership weakness. The breakout church leaders were intensely focused on achieving excellence, and it is that environment of excellence that provided the framework and level of expectation that has shaped the thirteen churches in our study.

Researcher Stuart Swicegood put it this way: "There does seem to be an autocratic force in the church. It is not a person but an environment that demands excellence." Strong leadership produces a culture of excellence. That environment attracts those to the church who desire to make a difference. And that same culture keeps the members and staff focused on those things that really matter.

THE CULTURE OF EXCELLENCE AND THE RIGHT PEOPLE

There were points in our research at which "the chicken or the egg" query seemed to be our predicament. Were the right people attracted to the church because of the culture of excellence? Or did the culture of excellence take shape *because* the right people were on board?

Our research indicates that the likely path during the transition to greatness was first getting the right people on board. In other words, the Who/What Simultrack (see chapter 5) was one of the first steps in the move to greatness, in the same way that "First Who" was a necessary first step for the good-to-great companies studied by Jim Collins and his team.

The environment of excellence began when the leadership got the right people, laity and staff, in the right place. The men and women who began filling places of ministry were motivated to do the work to which God had called them for his glory. The right people led in the transformation of the church from an environment of mediocrity to an environment of excellence. This environment of excellence in turn attracted more of the right people.

In chapter 9 we will look at the fascinating phenomenon of the "Big Mo." Without getting too far ahead, we can say that the Big Mo refers to a momentum that accelerates the growth of the church. While several factors contribute to this increasing growth rate, the culture of excellence is certainly one of the primary causes. The right people create the environment, which attracts more of the right people, which creates an even more excellent culture, and so on.

THE CULTURE OF EXCELLENCE AND THE "NOT-TO-DO" LIST

In *Good to Great,* Jim Collins introduced the idea of a "stop doing" list. He wrote that the builders of the good-to-great companies "made as much use of 'stop doing' lists as 'to do' lists. They displayed a remarkable discipline to unplug all sorts of extraneous junk."[9] In evaluating the breakout churches on this criterion we found that the best church leaders implicitly relied on "stop doing" lists, which we are calling "not-to-do" lists. As Jim Collins wrote on page 139 of *Good to Great,* "Most of us lead busy but undisciplined lives." When I began to discover this attitude prevalent among the breakout churches, I was convicted of my own undisciplined life.

As I am attempting to meet the deadline for the submission of this book, I have the great need to prepare a sermon for next Sunday. I also have two consultation reports that are due. I need to finish some grading for the semester. And I have personal obligations that should have priority over all these demands. I need my own "not-to-do" list.

One of the reasons Xenos Christian Fellowship is a great church is the leaders' recognition that they cannot do everything well. That not only implies fierce devotion to the VIP factor; it also implies a willingness to cease any activities that are outside the vision of the church. A culture of excellence will never become a reality until a church takes the often painful step of "not doing."

Consultant Carolyn Weese has visited Xenos three times in the past ten years. She provides a set of outside eyes to the church. Her input is valuable in the "to-do" and "not doing" lists of the church.

The leaders of Xenos have made difficult decisions to discontinue ministries. When the counseling ministries did not fit the congregation's vision, the path of least resistance would have been to continue the ministries because so many people were connected to them. But the tough decision was made, and the obvious conflict ensued. The church weathered the storm and became more focused on its "to-do" list.

In the early 1990s, Xenos discontinued its ministry networking program largely based on a similar ministry at Willow Creek Community Church in South Barrington, Illinois. Nothing was inherently wrong with the ministry. The problem was that the ministry networking emphasis detracted from the primary vision of home groups.

We saw countless ministries and programs in the comparison churches that seemed to serve no real purpose. We noted other worthwhile ministries that could not be done with excellence because the churches were attempting to do too much. One of the key reasons breakout churches have a culture of excellence is because they do a few things well and are "not doing" the rest.

The thirteen breakout churches are involved in diverse ministries and programs. We did not see a clear pattern of types of ministries that may be replicated in other churches. What we did see was a culture that insisted on excellence. While it is important to discern what we are supposed to do, it is equally important to do those things well. One of the more difficult decisions for the comparison churches was not that of choosing what to do. Rather, the difficulty was choosing what *not* to do and then making the very difficult move of eliminating that which could not be done with excellence.

Though I certainly cannot know what you are thinking as you read this, I can imagine that you may be mumbling a bit at what you have read so far. "He keeps writing about these churches that made these difficult decisions and faced times of conflict. Now he says that breakout churches have to make tough choices and eliminate much of what they do. I'm not sure I'm up to this task of leading or being in a church that moves to great."

I admit that I had those same thoughts as the data, interviews, and researchers' insights were assimilated. Then I started hearing the leaders of these breakout churches talking about the supernatural strength that was given to them to move forward. I heard them speak of developments that would be described by many as miraculous. I listened to many of them tell of how God took their weaknesses and demonstrated his strengths.

Then I realized I was not so much researching breakout churches as I was hearing the stories of a great God. As we enter into the final three chapters of this book, do not forget the awesome power of the God you serve. In his strength, you can see your church break out to greatness.

IN ESSENCE, IN SUMMARY
A CULTURE OF EXCELLENCE

- The thirteen breakout churches had a passion for excellence in all they attempted. Their motivation in this quest for excellence was always biblically and theologically driven. They sought to do their best for the Savior they serve and the God to whom they give all glory.

- The VIP factor, or the Vision Intersection Profile, and the culture of excellence were integrally connected. It is at this point of vision that the passion for excellence is most obvious in the breakout churches.

- One of the common denominators of excellence is the Freedom/ Expectation Paradox. Those involved in ministry, staff and laity alike, had a great deal of freedom to carry out the ministries in which they are involved. This freedom, however, existed in the clearly known boundaries of expectations in the church. Those who minister had much freedom as long as they remained focused on the vision of the church and carried out their ministries with excellence.

- None of the thirty-nine comparison churches could be described as high expectation/high freedom churches. Twenty-five of the churches were low expectation/low freedom. Little is expected, but if someone does accept a task in these churches, he or she is bound by many rules and traditions. Seven of the churches were high expectation/low freedom churches. These churches were led by an autocratic pastor. Another seven churches were low expectation/high freedom. "Chaos" would be the best description of these churches.

- The breakout churches did not have autocratic leaders. Instead, they had autocratic cultures. In other words, it is the culture of excellence that demands much of those who minister in the churches.

- The breakout churches got the right people on board prior to the establishment of a culture of excellence.

- Almost as important as what the breakout churches did is what they did not do. The "not-to-do" list is a common feature of the churches. Often the decision to discontinue something in the church proves to be more difficult than starting something new.

CHAPTER 8

INNOVATION ACCELERATORS

He who joyfully marches in rank and file has already earned my contempt. He has been given a large brain by mistake, since for him the spinal cord would suffice.

—Albert Einstein

im Collins titled chapter 7 of *Good to Great* "Technology Accelerators." We examined the breakout churches on this dimension and came to remarkably similar conclusions as Collins and his team. Based on our findings, however, we modified the concept to reflect the fact that breakout churches are accelerated not just by technology but by innovation—thus, our focus here is on what we call "Innovation Accelerators."

In September 1995 two churches made intentional and controversial decisions that would for years determine their direction and decline. Both churches had an average worship attendance of about 750 that year. Eight years later, in 2003, the attendance of the two churches was remarkably similar—475 and 460. In just eight short years both churches had experienced declines of more than 35 percent.

Figure 8A. Innovation Acceleration

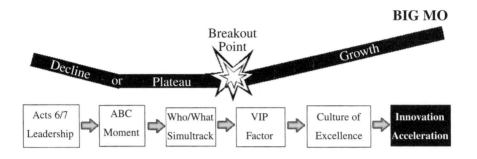

But the similarities do not end there. Both churches were in suburban areas of large cities. The 1995 to 2003 growth rate of one of the communities in which the church was located was 14 percent. The other community's growth rate was 11 percent. Simply stated, both churches were in growing communities with large population bases, and both churches experienced significant declines. But, beyond the numerical similarities, the differences become obvious. The story is truly a sad tale of two churches.

A TALE OF TWO CHURCHES

Both of the churches were among our thirty-nine comparison churches. The first church, which we will call Westmont Memorial Church, was started in 1955. The sponsoring church of Westmont purchased four acres for the new church in the mid-1950s. The church struggled for its first twelve years of existence but began a steady growth pattern as the community began to grow. By 1985 attendance was 550. Five years later in 1990 the church reached its peak attendance of 750.

The church has had only two pastors in its history. The current pastor, "Franklin Hart," led the church to most of its growth. It was he who realized that the church could not grow beyond its current level on four acres. Hart had led the church to try many different ideas to get more people on the limited available land, but four acres just could not hold more than 750. The attendance of the church from 1990 to 1994 hardly changed at all.

Pastor Hart began exploring the idea of relocating the church as early as 1985. Initial and informal conversations met with stiff resistance from many of the longer-term members. The pastor yielded to the resistance and did not attempt to explore a relocation option for a few more years.

Frustrated that Westmont could not move off its plateau, the pastor received approval to secure the services of a consultant. Hart was not surprised when the consultant said that it was physically impossible for the church to add more people. Efforts to acquire surrounding land were lackluster. Many of the members just liked things the way they were.

Pastor Hart took the recommendations of the consultant to the floor of a church business meeting. He naively thought that the voice of an outsider might sway the resistant members. Instead, a verbal fight took place between the resistant majority and the minority that desired the church to grow. One of the most sensitive issues was the stained-glass windows donated by a few key families early in the history of the church. When the pastor suggested that they could use the windows in another building in a new location, he received an angry rebuttal.

Needless to say, the church did not relocate. The pastor told us frankly that he has lost his passion for ministry. He would have retired earlier if the stock market had not decimated his 403(b) retirement. "I am just biding my time," he admitted. "They sealed their fate in that business meeting, and I can't do a thing about it."

Westmont Memorial Church has a history of resisting any significant change. It is little wonder that the congregants adamantly refused such a major change as relocation. They followed the path of least resistance where tens of thousands of churches can be found.

The second church in our tale is Fleming City Community Church, the fictional name of a real congregation that fortunately did not hinder its growth with limited acreage. The church has plenty of room for growth on its twenty-eight usable acres. Nevertheless, it has followed the same downward path as the Westmont Memorial Church.

"George Yeats" became pastor of Fleming City in 1993. He was enamored with many of the latest developments in church life, and key members of the church would learn too late that the pastor was encouraged to leave his former church after he unilaterally removed all the hymnals from the sanctuary.

Apparently the aggressive pastor did not learn his lessons. Within two weeks of arriving at Fleming City, he told the music and worship leader to make dramatic changes in the music and worship style of the church. The worship leader reluctantly made the changes, and an uproar ensued.

The pastor then attended a conference where the speaker advocated an organizational leadership structure that Yeats quickly embraced. He adopted this new structure for his church without any input from members and leaders at Fleming City. He even neglected to read the church bylaws, which clearly prohibited him from changing the structures of the church.

The stories of Pastor Yeats's infatuation with the latest fads and trends in church life seemed endless. One longtime member told us, "People refer to us as 'the church of what's happening next.' We never know what his latest idea will be. We are in a state of constant chaos."

Another member was equally blunt: "He makes decisions based on blind emotion. He never follows through on the ramifications of his ideas in the church. He can't think for himself. He always has to adopt someone else's ideas and programs."

The turmoil endured by Fleming City Community Church has been evident in the decline of the congregation. By any measure, the church has experienced a significant downturn. "People are just tired of 'the fad of the week,'" a five-year member told us. "They are going to other churches that are more stable, where pastors have more common sense. It's not that we are unwilling to change. It's just that the pastor and his little group introduce change without any explanation. I guess I will be leaving soon too."

Westmont Memorial Church and Fleming City Community Church seem to have little in common. They may be in similarly populated communities, but their personalities are significantly different. One church is stuck in tradition. The other church is enamored with new and seemingly innovative approaches. But both churches are having serious problems and are declining.

Not surprisingly, the thirteen breakout churches took neither approach. Unlike the traditional Westmont Memorial Church, the breakout churches are not adverse to change or innovation. Indeed, several of the churches made dramatic changes. But the churches are not like Fleming City Community Church either. They are sometimes surprisingly slow in adopting new and innovative approaches. They are careful, even plodding, in making major changes.

THE ROAD LESS TRAVELED

The most common bond of Fleming City Community Church and Westmont Memorial Church is the vast company they keep. Most churches in America fit one of two categories: Traditionalist/Resistor or Innovator/Embracer.

A good way to visualize each of the categories is through the use of a flowchart. The Traditionalist/Resistor model follows a common path as shown in figure 8B.

Figure 8B. The Traditionalist/Resistor Model

The Traditionalist/Resistor church is troubled by any sign of change. When an innovation is suggested or proposed, the church builds a wall of strong resistance, typically without any meaningful evaluation of the innovation. The church's ultimate desire is stability. Twenty-four of our thirty-nine comparison churches resembled this model.

The Innovator/Embracer church is enamored with innovation. The leaders return starry-eyed from a conference proposing new ways of doing church. While the ideas and innovations may actually be positive, the church does not critically evaluate the changes for the context of the church they lead. This common occurrence is illustrated in figure 8C.

Figure 8C. The Innovator/Embracer Model

Note the sequence of the embracing of innovation in this model. The churches often see the innovation as the "magic bullet" to meet all their needs. They surmise that if they just adopt this latest innovation, the desired growth will follow. Fifteen of the thirty-nine comparison churches followed this model.

The breakout churches, however, followed a road less traveled. They neither rejected innovation nor embraced it blindly. We called their deliberation "innovation acceleration" and illustrate it in figure 8D.

Figure 8D. Breakout Churches: Innovation Acceleration

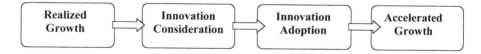

The key insight in chapter 7 of *Good to Great* is that, as Jim Collins writes, "When used right, technology becomes an accelerator of momentum, not a creator of it. The good-to-great companies never began their transitions with pioneering technology, for the simple reason that you cannot make good use of technology until you know which technologies are relevant."[1] Drawing upon that insight, the breakout churches did not blindly embrace innovation as a panacea to growth needs. Instead, the innovation typically *followed* growth. The slow, sometimes plodding process of considering innovation often began with some level of skepticism. Was the innovation truly something unique? Would it make a difference in the context of the church? Would it complement the vision or would it compete with the vision?

The breakout churches were not adverse to innovation. They may have been slow in accepting an innovation, but once they accepted a new approach, they were quick to use it for the good of the church. They viewed innovation as an acceleration of growth, not a creator of growth.[2] Let's look at how some of our breakout churches responded to innovation.

Innovation in the church is nothing new. Remember bus ministries? And the two most common responses to innovation, traditionalist/resistor and innovator/embracer, have been the most common responses. Rare is the church that takes the road less traveled demonstrated by the breakout churches.

INNOVATION AND THE VIP FACTOR

The comparison churches that blindly chased innovation seemed to be making a futile attempt to create a vision. The new innovation would be the declared vision. I cannot recall how many churches I have researched or consulted that have a borrowed vision from another church. Their hope is ever present that this new vision will be the solution to whatever ails the church.

Just as the good-to-great companies sought to adopt only those pioneering technologies that linked "directly to the three intersecting circles of the Hedgehog Concept,"[3] the breakout churches sought innovation, not to create a vision, but to enhance an existing vision. These churches' fanatical adherence to the VIP factor meant that they would embrace an innovation only if it could help them be more faithful to the vision.

You read earlier, for example, the story of the clear and determined vision of Xenos Christian Fellowship in Columbus, Ohio. The church was started in a nontraditional setting. When the informal gathering later became a church, the natural organizational structure was to maintain an informality that could be found in a home-group setting. The leaders became fanatical about home groups being the center of all ministry activity. Attempts at innovation not related to their VIP factor of home groups failed.

An extensive counseling ministry grew at Xenos when counseling ministries were first being introduced on a broad scale across America. The innovation may have been right for some churches, but it did not complement the VIP factor of Xenos.

The church also attempted ministry networking, a program designed to get large numbers of laity involved in ministry. The concept was started by Willow Creek Community Church and has been received very well by many churches, but it did not complement the vision of Xenos. Thus ministry networking was discontinued not long after its beginning.

> We want to be clear that innovation cannot be evaluated "good" or "bad" out of context. In one church, a particular innovation may be a spectacular addition for the good of the church. In another church, the adoption of that same innovation may be a formula for disaster. We noted very few innovations in our research that would always be bad or always be good. Discernment is the key.

The lessons learned by Xenos were twofold. First, do not import an innovation to the church that is not clearly aligned with the vision. Second, it is much easier to decline to implement an innovation than to implement it and then discard it. Xenos paid for introducing innovations that did not align with the vision. Today the leadership is more careful and discerning about "the latest, the newest, and the best."

The VIP factor for Lenexa Baptist Church in Lenexa, Kansas, as noted earlier, is "aggressive evangelism." This vision is modeled consistently by the pastor, Steve Dighton. It was the pastor's unwavering commitment to this vision that led to a church split near the beginning of his ministry in the early 1990s.

But the pastor remained focused on the vision beyond the split. Several times in our interview he used the phrase "aggressive evangelism" as an obvious indicator of the church's priority. Members in the church speak of the pastor's desire to engage anyone in any situation with the gospel. Years later the church has caught that same passion, and many members model the aggressive evangelistic vision today.

When the members of Lenexa Baptist talk about exciting developments of the past five years, they speak of the new building and the excitement of seeing people make sacrificial financial commitments to fund the building project.

So why did Lenexa Baptist adopt the innovation of a new building? The church was responding to the evangelistic growth that had taken place, and they wanted to be sure their evangelistic efforts were not hindered by lack of space. The embracing of innovation followed the growth of the church, unlike many churches where a new facility is constructed with the hope that it will engender growth itself.

At Korean Central Presbyterian Church in Vienna, Virginia, Pastor Won Sang Lee led his congregation to adopt the slogan "Training the Saints to Transform the World." The occasion was the twentieth anniversary of the church on November 7, 1993. For Korean Central Presbyterian Church the clever phrase was more than just an anniversary slogan. It reflected the heartbeat of the church. Pastor Lee had led the church to equip Christians to meet the spiritual and physical needs around the corner and around the world. On July 1, 1987, the church sent a team of short-term missionaries to Guatemala. By November 1990 KCPC established the Central Missionary Fellowship for the ongoing sending of both short-term and long-term missionaries.

The VIP factor included ministering to those around the corner as well. In 1994 the church was recognized by the governor of Virginia for its ministry to the elderly with the opening of the Central Senior Center. In 2000 the church purchased the Community Service Center of Washington, D.C., to have a central place to minister to the alcoholics, drug addicts, and poor in the downtown area. Hardly any of the churches we researched ever considered the somewhat radical innovation of purchasing an entire facility to do additional ministry.

The list of ministries could continue, but the point is clear. The church is fiercely devoted to its vision. Any innovation, such as the purchase of an entire facility, takes place only because it complements the vision: "Training the Saints to Transform the World."

THE TAIL AND THE DOG

I recently worked with a church that had a Christian school that, by most observers, would be deemed successful and dynamic. The leadership made the painful decision to move the school to be a freestanding institution, independent of the church.

The opposition to the leadership's decision was intense and vociferous. But the senior pastor and other leaders held firm. When we asked the pastor why the tough decision was made, he was quick to respond: "The school became the tail wagging the dog. It seemed like everything we did revolved around the school and its needs. We didn't seem like a church, just a worship center that housed a Christian school."

We followed this line of reasoning further. Would the pastor advise any church against having a Christian school? "Probably not," he responded. "I would instead recommend that the leaders begin with a clear understanding of the relationship between the school and the church. The church made the mistake of starting a Christian school without thinking of the implications."

> **The breakout churches did not suggest that any particular innovation was wrong for *all* churches. They were clear, however, that some innovations were wrong for *their* churches. The two reasons most often cited for an innovation misfit was its failure to complement the vision and the fear that the innovation would be the tail wagging the dog.**

Where's the Dog?

Many of the comparison churches seemed, on the surface, to be guilty of letting the tail wag the dog. Our team recalled several stories of churches where the "latest" innovation seemed to be the driving force for a few months, only for the excitement to fade until the next innovation came along.

Our team was enjoying sharing several stories of the comparison churches' attempts to introduce innovations. We repeatedly spoke of these churches letting the tail wag the dog. Then one of our more astute researchers spoke: "What a minute—where's the dog?"

We looked at him with blank stares that indicated we had no idea what he was saying. He clarified: "We keep talking about the tail wagging the dog. We're assuming that these churches have 'dogs.' The dog is the main vision, the main emphasis of the church. Most of these churches don't have a clue what their vision is. They have the wagging tail but no dog."

He was right. We were able to see a main vision in a few of the comparison churches. And when those churches strayed from the vision to chase the latest innovation, we could then say that the tail was wagging the dog. But in most of the comparison churches, there was no purpose or main vision. The tail could not wag the dog because there was no dog.

The breakout churches struggled with the tail and the dog as well. But we always saw the "dog" in these churches. The dog, of course, was the VIP factor.[4]

The Tail, the Dog, and the Breakout Churches

Calvary Memorial Church in Oak Park, Illinois, was one of several of the breakout churches that understood how easily the tail can wag the dog. In 1997 the church began to follow the lead of many other churches that were trying big events to reach their communities. The events were highly successful in attracting significant numbers of people, but, leadership realized, the events were not adding disciples to the church.

Many churches have attempted big events to attract the community and reach the unchurched. Some have experienced successes and seen a direct positive correlation to evangelistic growth. Other churches do not see a direct evangelistic impact from these events but continue them anyway. They see the events as a good means to create an awareness of the church and the gospel.[5]

Calvary Memorial Church not only viewed the big events as evangelistically unproductive; they also sensed the events were detracting the focus from the vision of the church. Researcher Michael McDaniel notes: "An increasing awareness of community irrelevance began to grow among members of the congregation. Leadership especially began to feel that the church was not doing enough to reach the neighborhood with the gospel."

For Calvary, the big event was the tail wagging the dog. Not only could the leadership find no direct evangelistic benefit, the resources needed to carry out the big event were actually diminishing the church's evangelistic impetus in the community. Many members saw the event as *the* evangelistic outreach of the church, so nothing more was required of them.

Bethel Temple Community Church in Evansville, Indiana, had an experience similar to that of Calvary Memorial Church. Researcher David Bell notes: "Prior to their chrysalis factor, the Bethel Temple staff discovered they were highly skilled at putting on big events. They would invest much of their time and resources into organizing and promoting events that would draw in large numbers of people. However, they were unable to come up with a workable plan to keep the crowds they drew. Consequently, they lived from one event to the next."

One of the pastors of Bethel Temple agreed. "You always felt like you were chasing a rainbow around here. We could do events, but we had no purpose or infrastructure," he said.[6]

> Breakout churches obviously are not mistake-free. This example of the churches chasing innovation without a clear objective is but one example of the fallibility of the congregations. Our purpose in presenting this research is not to highlight perfect churches, but to show how congregations moved from mistakes to corrections in becoming great.

Grace Evangelical Free Church in Allen, Texas, is another example of a breakout church that had seen the tail wag the dog until they began to focus on their VIP factor, home small groups. Pastor Joel Walters said that the worship services were seen as the single place where all ministries were to take place. "We had a change in philosophy that ignited our change and focus: we moved caring and fellowship from the worship service to small groups."

Grace Church should provide encouragement to church laity and leaders who think their church must be a megachurch to be a great church. Figure 8E shows that the church has an average attendance of nearly 300, not small or megachurch. Note the pattern of growth. After reaching 200 in attendance in 1993, the church had no growth for five years. Then a slow but steady breakout growth pattern began to emerge in 1997 and continues today. Grace Evangelical Free Church is focusing on the dog wagging the tail instead of the reverse.

Figure 8E. Average Worship Attendance at Grace Evangelical Free Church

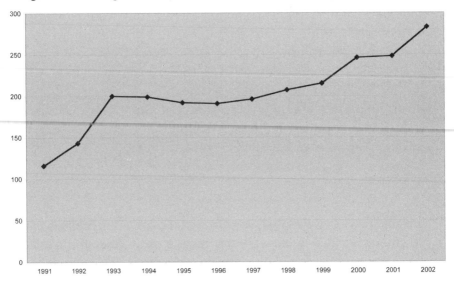

INNOVATION AND THE PURPOSE-DRIVEN FACTOR

Any serious student of the church since the mid-1990s cannot ignore the impact of Rick Warren's Purpose Driven concept.[7] Warren has his devotees and his critics. But the Purpose Driven concept is simplistic genius. It is not as much a methodology as it is a basic philosophy: The church must be driven by its purposes. Churches cannot be program-driven, building-driven, or budget-driven. They must be driven by the five purposes of the church: worship, evangelism, discipleship, ministry, and fellowship.[8]

Many church leaders have mistakenly viewed the Purpose Driven concept as an innovative methodology without regard to the philosophy behind it. They therefore believe that if they offer the courses offered by

Warren's church, Saddleback Valley Community Church, they have emulated the Purpose Driven church. Or if they create a visual of a baseball diamond and four bases, representing four levels of commitment and discipleship, they have captured the essence of the Purpose Driven philosophy. Discipleship courses and baseball diamonds may be innovative aids in grasping the Purpose Driven concept, but many churches, including several of the comparison churches in our study, adopt the methodology without grasping the philosophy.

Six of the thirteen breakout churches noted the importance of the Purpose Driven philosophy in their transition to greatness.[9] Unlike many of the comparison churches, they were focused on how the Purpose Driven philosophy could accelerate the growth and health of the church. Purpose was an innovation accelerator, not a methodological fad.

The leadership of Bethel Temple Community Church realized that they were event driven after grasping the Purpose Driven idea. They changed the church's infrastructure to reflect the church's purposes.

The breakout transition of Central Christian Church of Beloit, Wisconsin, was enhanced by the leadership's grasp of the a purposeful church. Researcher Michael O'Neal notes: "For many years, Central Christian Church lost its focus on the main reason the body of Christ exists: to make fruit-bearing disciples for Jesus Christ. In the early 1980s, during the years of renewal, Pastor David Clark preached and taught purposeful ministry. By the mid-1980s, the church began to pursue biblical purposes in its ministries."

Jon Harris, the senior pastor at Fairfield New Life Church near Sacramento, California, acknowledges his indebtedness to the Purpose Driven idea in leading his church to greatness. After attending a conference at Saddleback, the pastor could no longer be content to chase the latest fad or innovation. Harris notes, "We basically began to ask what our purposes are and does the decision at hand fit with those purposes?" The church was once struggling with breaking the 200 barrier. Today the average worship attendance exceeds 700.

The influence of the Purpose Driven concept on many of the breakout churches is significant. But unlike the comparison churches, the breakout churches adopted the philosophy of the model instead of seeing its methodology as the answer to all churches' needs and problems.

BUILDINGS AND LOCATIONS AS INNOVATION

The comparison churches either loved building programs or hated them. Some of the comparison churches refused to build or relocate because they were so adverse to almost any changes. Other comparison churches were involved in numerous building programs because they saw the new facilities as the answer to all of their needs. But the story is different for the breakout churches.

> **Constructing buildings and relocating churches are not new concepts. Some may question whether this topic belongs in a chapter on innovation. Although the concepts are not new, they are innovative and challenging to the church attempting to build or relocate.**

First Gethsemane Baptist Church of Louisville, Kentucky, grew from 135 to 2,100 in membership and from 200 in worship attendance to 1,300 in worship attendance from 1984 to 2003. During that time, construction and new buildings were not the primary focus. In 1994, the church, desperately needing ministry and education space, constructed an office, education, and family activity addition, which now doubles as a temporary weekend worship center. Several properties—including a factory warehouse next door—have been acquired for community outreach, parking, and an eventual new worship complex. In 2001 the church finally adopted and approved a new master plan for development with a commitment to remain in the center of the city, where there are so many ministry needs. It is Pastor T. Vaughn Walker's goal to have the facility expansion completed with as little indebtedness as possible. "I don't want the next pastor to have to devote energy and time to acquire property, build facilities, or pay off debt, as we have had to do," he told us resolvedly.

Southwest Baptist Church in Amarillo, Texas, began meeting in a metal warehouse building in 1974. The church began to consider buying property and constructing new facilities after the transition to greatness. Pastor J. Alan Ford led the church to a unanimous vote to take the steps of faith.

These breakout churches did not see the innovation of new building construction to be the driving force of the churches. Instead, they viewed new construction as a necessary step to move forward, not as a goal to be achieved. Sometimes the breakout churches moved ploddingly slow in constructing new facilities.

Grace Church, a Christian and Missionary Alliance Church in Middleburg Heights, Ohio, was one of five breakout churches that lamented its slow and cautious process in building. Researcher Chris Bonts described his interviews with the staff of Grace Church: "One mistake or regret that was expressed by all of the staff interviewed concerned the relocation and building programs. They did not build big enough, and even though they relocated to a new facility in 1996, they are currently in the middle of an eight-million-dollar building program because they are rapidly running out of space."

One of the most dramatic innovations adopted by five of the breakout churches was a complete relocation. Again, the leaders of the churches did not jump into a relocation decision without a lot of deliberation. But once they made the decision, the leaders moved with determination and resolve.

Grove City Church of the Nazarene in Ohio is a tale of three pastors. The current pastor, Bob Huffaker, has led the congregation since 1989. During this time, worship attendance has increased from 617 to over 2,800. But the church would not be a breakout church under Huffaker's leadership alone. The church would not have met our survey criteria for a period of decline and plateau.

Another pastor in this story is Herb Rogers. Pastor Rogers served the church from 1982 to 1988, when he left to become a district superintendent in the Nazarene denomination. When Rogers arrived at Grove City, the church was in its third year of slight decline. Thus the new pastor had several significant challenges before him. But the greatest challenge was the location of the church itself. Rogers was clear: "Relocation was a necessity; there was no parking." Not all the members were supportive of the decision, and some left the church. "Some left in connection with the financial campaign to raise money for the relocation," Rogers noted. "They were commitment-phobic."

The relocation added the needed parking spaces and increased attendance capability from 300 to 1,000. The church made 27,000 telephone calls announcing the upcoming relocation. More than 3,000 of the calls yielded legitimate prospects, people who expressed a sincere desire to attend a church service.

But the story of Grove City and its breaking out must include a third pastor. Curtis Lewis served as pastor in a short tenure from 1980 to 1983. During that period Lewis led the church to purchase property for relocation. Herb Rogers led the church to relocate. And Bob Huffaker led the church to new levels of growth to become a megachurch.

Note the growth chart in figure 8F. After a few years of struggle, the church began to break out of its plateau. Look at the nearly 100-person increase in attendance in 1989, after the church moved to its new location. Though somewhat unusual that three pastors are a part of this breakout story, there is little doubt that the relocation was an innovation accelerator for the church.[10]

Figure 8F. Average Worship Attendance at Grove City Church of the Nazarene

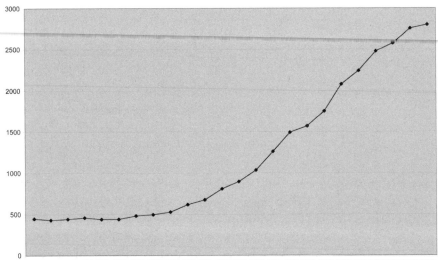

INNOVATION TRAP OR INNOVATION TRIUMPH?

A wise pastor told me early in my ministry, "Whatever you do to get them to come is what you have to do to get them to stay." The folksy wisdom of the pastor made good sense to me. If we have to try every latest fad and innovation to reach people, we will have to do one better to get them to stay and to reach the next wave of people.

This misguided strategy is called the "innovation trap." Many of the comparison churches in our study were eagerly embracing the innovation trap. Those who led these churches were guilty of lazy leadership. They would eagerly embrace someone else's idea, but they had few ideas of their own. They could have pursued their own passions, encouraged the church members to pursue their ministry dreams, and found the greatest needs of the community. Instead, they waited on the latest, the newest, and the most exciting. They chased fads instead of pursuing God's plan for their ministries and their churches. And they found themselves soon caught in the innovation trap.

But leaders and laity in other comparison churches were not lazy; they were fearful. They were fearful of change, fearful of the unknown, and too comfortable with the status quo.

One of the many reasons I was so impressed with the breakout church leaders was the way they demonstrated both wisdom and courage. They showed wisdom in the proper use of innovation. They did not see the latest fad as the answer to everything, yet they were not afraid to embrace innovation if it accelerated the growth and enhanced the health of the church. They demonstrated courage once the decision was made to move forward with innovation. They avoided the innovation trap and were rewarded with the innovation triumph.

The breakout churches moved from decline and struggle to growth. Their leaders demonstrated the legacy mind-set that we called Acts 6/7 leadership. The churches experienced that time of awakening we dubbed the ABC moment: the awareness that something is not right with the church, the belief that the difficulty can be overcome when the brutal facts are faced, and the willingness to endure conflict and to see victory beyond the conflict. The churches then proceeded along the breakout progression depicted at the beginning of this chapter. These tremendous strides were then enhanced with innovation accelerators.

By the time the churches had come this far, an unmistakable momentum was taking place. One breakout leader commented: "It seems like we are just watching all the great things God is doing." The "Big Mo" had begun. To that exciting development we now turn.

IN ESSENCE, IN SUMMARY
INNOVATION ACCELERATORS

- Most churches in America fit in one of two categories related to innovation: Traditional/Resistor or Innovator/Embracer. The former model represents churches that avoid nearly all changes, and the latter describes churches that continually chase the latest fad.

- The breakout churches, however, followed a surprisingly slow and plodding path of adopting innovations only after close scrutiny and much deliberation. They neither feared innovation nor embraced it blindly.

- The breakout churches made certain that any innovation complemented and enhanced the VIP factor.

- The metaphor we used to describe innovations is "the tail and the dog." In many churches the tail (innovations) wags the dog (the church's main vision and mission). Breakout churches kept the dog wagging the tail.

- The Purpose Driven model was a great benefit to almost half of the breakout churches. The concept helped the leadership understand more clearly how to stay true to the VIP factor.

- New construction and relocation were key innovations used by the breakout churches. The churches proceeded slowly but deliberately in their decisions to move ahead with these changes.

- An important decision for a church is to determine whether an innovation will become a trap or a triumph. Many of the comparison churches followed the path of the innovation trap as they moved from fad to fad. The breakout churches demonstrated wisdom by using the innovation as an accelerator of growth and enhancer of health.

CHAPTER 9

BIG MO OR BLIND EROSION?

The world is moving so fast that there are days when the person who says it can't be done is interrupted by the person who is doing it.

—Anonymous

One of the most important ideas to come from Jim Collins's *Good to Great* is the idea he calls "The Flywheel and the Doom Loop." (See chapter 8 of *Good to Great*.) Although we have retitled the chapter "Big Mo or Blind Erosion" it is essentially the same concept explained in *Good to Great*.

The interviews for the breakout churches project proved to be among the highlights of this project. Deborah Morton, one of the lead researchers, commented: "We needed some highlights because this project was so frustrating."

The frustration of which Deborah spoke was the process of discovering the breakout churches. The highlight that she noted was the opportunity to speak with and interview leaders and laity in the church once we knew the church had made the breakout cut.

Researcher Chris Bonts experienced the highlight of meeting breakout church leaders as well. He made the trip to the Cleveland area to

Figure 9A. The Big Mo

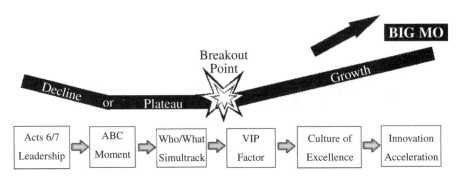

interview several people at Grace Church, Christian and Missionary Alliance. One of his favorite interviews was with a layman who had been at the church for thirteen years. "Arthur" had no church background; he came to Grace Church at the invitation of a relative and became a follower of Christ shortly after his first visits.

Like most of the laity in our breakout churches, Arthur described the senior pastor Jonathan Schaeffer with the words *approachable, humble, passionate,* and *real* and added, "Over the years he has become more transparent and his humility has increased."

But when we inquired of the key events or developments that had taken place to move Grace Church to greatness, Arthur was momentarily silent. He then spoke deliberately: "No one thing stands out, but everything stands out. The whole transition was a 'God thing.'"

A similar story was repeated in different ways by persons in all of the breakout churches. They had difficulty identifying one event or development. Instead, they spoke of a relatively slow-building momentum that now is moving at an incredible pace. Ten of the thirteen churches specifically used the word *momentum* to describe their understanding of the progress in the church. The other three indicated that they felt they were on the beginning edge of such a momentum.

UNIVERSITY OF KENTUCKY BASKETBALL AND BREAKOUT CHURCHES

In *Good to Great,* Jim Collins uses the example of the UCLA Bruins basketball dynasty of the 1960s and 1970s to illustrate a point about how many years of effort were required (15 years!) before reaching breakthrough levels of performance.[1] As a nearly twenty-year resident of

Louisville, it's impossible not to follow Kentucky basketball. I thought it would be interesting to examine one of my favorite college teams, the University of Kentucky, to see if its success followed a pattern similar to that of UCLA.

My other favorite team is Murray State University. The latter school is a mid-size university that seems to be developing a good program. The former school is rich in tradition and success.

University of Kentucky basketball began in 1903, and the team recorded the school's first victory over Lexington YMCA that year. It would not be until 1909 that Kentucky had its first winning season. Indeed, the school's basketball program struggled until a man named Adolph Rupp took the head coaching job in 1930. Though Rupp did have some early success with Southeastern Conference championships beginning in 1933, the school did not have its first national championship team until 1948.

I recently asked several Kentucky basketball devotees to guess how many years it took Rupp to win his first national championship. The longest time guessed was six years. But the reality is that Rupp did not lead Kentucky to its first National Collegiate Athletic Association championship until his eighteenth year at the helm.

Successes began to take place rapidly at Kentucky after 1948. Rupp led the team to a second and third national championship over the next three years. NCAA probation in 1952–53 set the school back a bit, but the national title returned to Kentucky in 1958. Successor coaches Joe B. Hall, Rick Pitino, and Tubby Smith have all won national championships; Smith did so in his first year in 1998.[2] While the University of Kentucky does not win a national championship every year, it does expect to be a contender. Rare is the year that pollsters do not place the Wildcats in the top ten preseason poll. The tradition is established; the momentum is obvious.

Some may fault me for using an athletic comparison for breakout churches, but I am in no way suggesting that the work of the church is analogous to competitive college sports. The sources of victory in the latter are good coaching, teamwork, and talented athletes. The source of victory in the church is a sovereign God. My point in using the sports comparison is to provide some clarity to what is taking place in these breakout churches. There is a struggle, followed by a buildup, followed by a breakout point, followed by a momentum. Whereas previous victories required laborious efforts, the "Big Mo" period seems to provide victory after victory more naturally.

Most of the breakout churches were in the Big Mo era of their recent history. One layperson at Grove City Church of the Nazarene said it well: "We just stand amazed at what God is doing. We don't know what will happen next, but we know it will be good."

> The breakout churches did not have to demonstrate evidence of a Big Mo as a criterion to make the screening cuts. We noticed this issue in the churches *after* we found the thirteen churches. At this point, we can clearly identify the Big Mo in ten of the thirteen churches. We believe that the other churches will fit the pattern and soon experience the Big Mo as well.

THE BIG MO AT GRACE CHURCH

Grace Church, CMA, in the Cleveland area has a classic pattern of struggle/build-up/breakthrough/momentum that is evident in the churches with the Big Mo.[3] This is the same buildup/breakthrough process that Jim Collins, in *Good to Great*, likened to a flywheel when he wrote that every good-to-great transformation followed the same basic pattern—accumulating momentum, turn by turn of the flywheel—until buildup transformed into breakthrough.[4] (Jim Collins makes a point of crediting David S. Landes and his book, *The Wealth and Poverty of Nations*, for the terminology of "buildup" and "breakthrough.")

Look at the worship attendance numbers for Grace Church in figure 9B. From 1980 to 1987 worship attendance declined slightly (*struggle*). From 1987 to 1990, a slight growth pattern reversed the earlier trend of decline (*buildup*). Then in 1991 the church experienced one of its largest one-year increases in its history (*breakthrough*). From that point on, every year but one has been a steady and strong growth period (*momentum*).[5]

Our team conducted numerous interviews with staff and laity at Grace Church. One of the consistently asked questions in the interviews was, "Can you name the top two factors that led to the transition to growth at Grace Church?" Some of the respondents were not even able to speculate at an answer. Others struggled but gave us responses. Interestingly, none of those who could give us an answer came up with the same explanation. Look at some of the responses:

- "We became a guest-friendly church."
- "The big issues were Pastor Don's commitment to prayer, the Billy Graham Crusade, and leadership development."
- "Probably one of the greatest developments was a greater grasp on hell and the fate of the lost in our community. The church believed in the doctrine before, but their grasp of the doctrine grew."
- "The decision to relocate was a big factor."
- "The addition of gifted staff was probably one of the turning points in the history of this church."
- "The top two factors are discontentment with standing still and accountability afforded through small groups."

Most of the people we interviewed in the breakout churches could not identify one or two reasons for their breakthrough. And those who attempted to provide reasons had such a variety of responses that we could isolate no single issue that was prominent in the transition.

Figure 9B. Average Worship Attendance at Grace Church, CMA

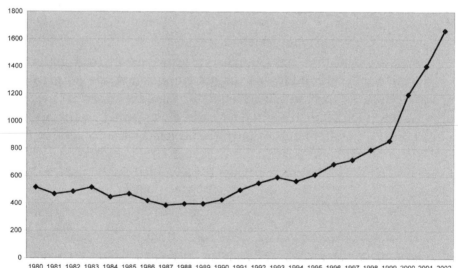

"NOT JUST ONE THING"

Church growth advocates are sometimes criticized for taking a human-centered approach to reasons behind a church's transformation. Our study never presumed that the transition to greatness was anything but God-centered. It had a clear Christian "bias" that affirmed the sovereignty of God. We did not seek, nor do we believe in, some neat formulaic approach to growing a church. We did, however, seek to discover the instruments that God used to move a church to greatness. It was our prayer that, by discovering God's instruments in this transition, we could help other churches and leaders that are struggling.

So what are these instruments that God used? Our conclusion is that simple answers cannot be deduced from our study. As Jim Collins noted in *Good to Great*, "There was no miracle moment . . . Although it may have looked like a single-stroke breakthrough to those peering in from the outside, it was anything but that to people experiencing the transformation from within. Rather, it was a quiet, deliberate process of figuring out what needed to be done to create the best future results and then simply taking those steps, one after the other, turn by turn of the flywheel. After pushing on that flywheel in a consistent direction over an extended period of time, they'd inevitably hit a point of breakthrough."[6] In our study of breakout churches we observed a similarly long and arduous process. Such is the reason that we have adopted Collins's template of illustrating the path to greatness in the diagram at the beginning of each chapter. The many issues we have noted thus far depict clearly that a multitude of factors are involved in the transition. Jim Collins noted in *Good to Great* that one of the executives interviewed for his project admonished him at one point, saying, in effect, "Look, you can't dissect this thing into a series of nice little boxes and factors, or identify the moment of 'Aha!' or the 'one big thing.' It was a whole bunch of interlocking pieces that built one upon another."[7] Astonishingly, a layperson of a breakout church told us nearly the same thing: "It's not just one thing. It's a whole bunch of things."

Interestingly, we received a greater consistency of responses from the breakout leaders when they told us the reasons they were *hindered* in the transition. One or a few issues can be readily identified as a barrier to growth, but identifying the positive reasons for growth is much more problematic. The reason for this difficulty in identifying the positive reasons was clear to us and is the topic of this section called "Not Just One Thing."

I have been with many struggling church leaders who have observed the Big Mo in a great church or a breakout church[8] and have heard many of them wonder what issues are taking place in these churches. The implication behind many of their questions is a desire to find a few, perhaps easy, methods to move their churches in the same direction. But the breakout churches showed us that the path was neither simple nor easy. And perhaps that is one key reason so few church leaders decide to pay the price to lead their churches to greatness.

THE LONG-TERM APPROACH TO THE BIG MO

In chapter 3 I noted the long tenure of the pastors of the breakout churches. At the time of the writing of this book, the average tenure was 21.6 years. That tenure is six times greater than the tenure of the typical American pastor. While longevity in itself is no guarantee of moving a church to greatness, I can state without hesitation that the process of moving a church to greatness is long-term.

Since completing this research project, I have already been able to use the information to help and encourage other church leaders. Tom Bary is the senior pastor of Neptune Beach Baptist Church in the Jacksonville, Florida, area. Tom has faithfully served at the church for a decade, and he believes a significant breakout is imminent. I concur that, with the path the church is taking, it may soon qualify as a breakout church.

Because I have this information, I am able to encourage Tom and to let him know the Big Mo may be present at Neptune Beach soon. During the past ten years, Tom has struggled with the death of his father, his own health problems, and some serious internal church matters. It would have been an easier path for him to declare that the struggles are not worth it and to move to another church that may seem more promising. But Tom believes that God has a great plan for Neptune Beach. He heard my data on the time the breakout process often takes, and he was encouraged. He is resolved to wait on God in anticipation of a Big Mo in the near future.

The move to greatness and to the Big Mo is not easy. But all of the leaders of the breakout churches will tell you that the pain and the wait have been worth it.

PREACHING, BIBLICAL AUTHORITY, PRAYER, AND THE BIG MO

I would be negligent if I failed to report a common theme among many of the breakout church leaders. In the process of leading the churches in the breakout, these leaders reported a heightened awareness of the importance of their preaching ministries. Some of them expressed a belief that the Big Mo would not have taken place if they had not given greater attention to the ministry of preaching.

This information did not surprise us. In a previous study, our research found a direct correlation between time spent in sermon preparation and evangelistic effectiveness.[9] In another study, we found that one of the key reasons the unchurched were attracted to particular churches was the quality of the preaching ministry.[10]

Consistently we heard the members of the breakout churches tell us that one of the key reasons their church is experiencing a positive momentum is the consistent quality preaching of the senior pastor. Some examples that support this thesis were evident in our interviews:

- Layperson at Southwest Baptist Church: "The faithful preaching of Reverend Ford has been a key factor in the growth of our church."
- Staff member at Calvary Memorial Church: "Pastor Ray has been zealously committed to biblical preaching and obedience no matter what the cost."
- Pastor Jonathan Schaeffer, Grace Church, Christian and Missionary Alliance (when asked if there was a change in his approach to his preaching ministry prior to and during the time of transition to greatness): "No, I am still an expository preacher who primarily preaches through books of the Bible."
- Layperson at Central Christian Church: "Pastor Clark shows his humility in the pulpit. He is so human. One of the big factors in our church is his 'down-to-earth' sermons that relate to everyday life."
- Informational packet at First Gethsemane Baptist Church, noting one of the six values you will discover at the church: "Bible-based preaching and teaching."

I have attempted throughout this book to be very careful *not* to imply that the churches that moved to greatness did so with some magical, methodological, quick-fix formula. To the contrary, the opposite was true. Because we have been careful to note unique characteristics of breakout churches, you may sometimes get the impression that these unique issues explain the totality of the move to greatness and the momentum that followed. While I hope you found these characteristics to be helpful and informative, I do not for one moment want to suggest that the basics of Christian ministry were abandoned.

> Our study of breakout churches did not measure such quantifiable factors as hours spent in sermon preparation.[11] All of the research team members, however, indicated that preaching was primary in the ministry of the breakout pastors. We would surmise that the pastors gave significant hours to sermon preparation much like leaders in other effective churches we have studied.

The breakout churches never would have sustained the momentum they have without consistent faithfulness to foundational issues. The leaders and the laity in these churches believe in the total truthfulness of Scripture,[12] and they hold to the priority of preaching and the primacy of prayer.

Researcher George Lee notes of First Gethsemane Baptist Church: "The prayer ministry had proven to be integral to the momentum of the church. Many members support the prayer ministry at scheduled times between church and home."

As George Lee further reports, the leadership of this church has been the key to its priority of prayer: "Dr. Walker continually emphasizes the necessity of prayer and fasting to combat spiritual warfare. He and his family have led the church through many corporate and private times of prayer and fasting. Dr. Walker states: 'I know the enemy is seeking to destroy us because of what God is doing in the life of the ministry of First Gethsemane. That is why I continuously fast and pray with my wife weekly that we would always be used for His glory.' "

The evidence of our research is convincing. These churches never abandoned the basics in their transition to greatness. There were obviously many methodological issues that were of great importance in their breakout. But any methodological factors were secondary to biblical fidelity, preaching, and prayer. The Big Mo cannot be sustained by methods. The breakout churches are truly Acts 6:4 churches: "[We] will give our attention to prayer and the ministry of the Word."

After more than fifteen years of researching the American church, I am convinced that all churches are in one of three categories. Some are experiencing a Big Mo, where it seems that one success easily builds upon another. Others are headed toward a Big Mo. Growth and success in ministry are not as easy to come by, but steady if not plodding progress is evident. But the third category unfortunately tells the story of eight out of ten American churches. It is the category of decline and erosion—the counterpart to Jim Collins's comparison companies that "failed to build sustained momentum and fell instead into what [he] came to call the doom loop."[13] Though this book is about breakout churches, I want you to hear the stories of the thirty-nine comparison churches. Perhaps if you recognize the signs of blind erosion in your church, you can help your church reverse its path to one of growth headed toward greatness.

BLIND EROSION: THE COMPARISON CHURCHES

I wrote a large portion of this book while on the beaches of Florida. Three beaches on the Gulf of Mexico served as my getaway places for this major writing project. My favorite coastal city, as I mentioned earlier, is Naples, Florida. I love the beauty of the city and the year-round warmth. The other two beaches are in the Florida panhandle: Carillon Beach and Cape San Blas. These two beaches have the whitest sand of any place I have ever been. Even as I write these words, I am looking at the sugar white sands and emerald green waters of Carillon Beach, near Panama City Beach, Florida.

As a devotee of beaches, I am well aware of both their beauty and the relative ease with which they can be destroyed. The constant pounding of thousands of waves each day cannot leave a beach unchanged. In some cases, the waves can actually bring in more sand and cause accretion, the building up of a beach. In other cases, the waves can take the sand away and cause erosion. Except in the case of hurricanes or other major thrusts of nature, the process of erosion is not noticeable day by day. I see no less of the beach this morning than I did yesterday. Nevertheless, the beach is experiencing slow change that is imperceptible to the naked eye.

Sometimes I think the church fares better with a "hurricane" than with "blind beach erosion." At least the hurricane gets most of the issues on the table and forces the church to deal with them for good or bad. Blind erosion, on the other hand, takes place in pseudo-comfort. Most members perceive that no change is taking place, and most of them like it that way.[14] Therein lies the danger. By the time most churches become aware of the years of slow erosion, the damage is severe and sometimes irreversible.

The breakout churches had a Big Mo that moved them forward. The comparison churches are experiencing blind erosion that is moving them toward a slow but certain death. How have the majority of American churches found themselves in this predicament? What are some reasons for this nearly imperceptible decline? We found ready answers to these questions in our thirty-nine comparison churches.

Blind Erosion and No Accountability

My first pastorate after seminary was in St. Petersburg, Florida. In my interviews with several of the lay leaders prior to my coming to the church, I noticed a recurring theme. When I would ask them about the health of the church, one word was repeated several times: *stable*.

I could not reconcile their perception of the church with the information they had sent me. The most recent year's attendance was 118; seven years earlier the average attendance had been 191. In a relatively short period, attendance had declined 62 percent, but the common consensus among the church members was that the church was "stable."

The more I looked at the reports, the more concerned I grew. The number of conversions in the church was almost nonexistent. Ministries had been discontinued. Conversations with knowledgeable people in the community indicated that the reputation of the church had suffered. But the condition of the church, according to its leaders, was "stable." From an outsider's perspective, the lack of awareness was inexplicable. But the more I have become involved in working with churches across America, the more I see this very situation manifest itself.

Xenos Christian Fellowship provides an annual report to its congregation. The twenty-page document covers the following information: student ministry, adult ministry, evangelism, large meetings, servant teams, home groups, annual planning retreats, budget, adult outreach, equipping ministries, missions, operations and administrations, pastoral ministries, average attendance, and other financial information.

There is little accountability in most churches across America. Few churches provide good information to their membership on key ministries, attendance, and growth. As a consequence, the leaders and members of the churches seem to have little awareness of the slow erosion the church is experiencing. Earlier we looked at the blind erosion of one of the comparison churches. Now let's look at another prototypical comparison church.

"Riverdale Church of the Savior" has declined in worship attendance from 355 to 239 over the past ten years. This decline of 33 percent was mentioned by none of the members we interviewed. For those members who have been at the church all of the past ten years, the decline in average attendance by eleven people each year is imperceptible. The problem is exacerbated by the complete lack of accountability of the church. None of the church's ministries report on their status to the congregation. No statistical reports are provided. No evangelistic evaluation is given. The budget is reviewed annually by the less than 5 percent of the congregation who decide to come to a budget meeting.

I keep this church anonymous because I have no desire to hurt the reputation of a well-meaning people. No one with whom I met had a malicious motive to harm the congregation. To the contrary, most of the members seemed to love their church. But there is no accountability present. When the church finally gets a wake-up call to the serious condition it's in, it may be too late for it to be restored to health.

Blind Erosion and Theology

Most of the comparison churches had articulated a conservative, evangelical theology in writing. The documents these churches provided us looked very much like the breakout churches' statements of faith. Based on the written information we gleaned, we could not discern a noticeable difference in the theologies of the two groups of churches.

> **Somewhat surprising to us was the almost equal availability of written documents of faith from both the breakout churches and the comparison churches. Almost all of the thirty-nine comparison churches and the thirteen breakout churches had some type of written information about their basic doctrinal beliefs. Several of the churches from both groups provided very detailed printed information.**

If we were to leave our analysis at the point of the written documents, we would have to conclude that there is really no difference in the theologies of the comparison churches and the breakout churches. Our interviews, however, revealed a different dynamic. Three distinct issues related to the comparison church leaders and members arose as we began to probe into matters of belief.

1. Almost all of the persons we interviewed in the breakout churches knew the basics of their doctrinal beliefs. *Very few of the laypeople in the comparison churches knew anything about their churches' doctrinal position.*

2. Unlike the laypeople in the breakout churches, those in the comparison churches would often equivocate on matters related to the doctrine of exclusivity. The laypeople in the breakout churches most often expressed certainty that explicit faith in Christ is the only way of salvation. Those in the comparison churches frequently questioned whether or not a "good" person of another religious faith might go to heaven as well. In other words, *the comparison churches' members often held theological positions in contradiction to the printed doctrinal positions of their churches.*

3. Even when the interviewees of the comparison churches expressed positions congruent with the stated doctrinal position of their churches, we often found inconsistencies in their willingness to practice their beliefs. The clearest example of this reality was in the area of evangelism. *They might believe that Christ is the only way of salvation, but they are unwilling or unable to share the gospel with non-Christians.* In contrast, the majority of those we interviewed in the breakout churches were passionate about reaching people for Christ *personally.* They did not expect all evangelism to be done by the staff or a select few in the church.

Blind erosion took place in many of the comparison churches because the members gave only mental assent to the churches' core values and doctrinal beliefs. The harsh reality is that most of the members of the comparison churches simply did not or would not grasp what the biblical role of the church and its members should be.

Blind Erosion and Ignorance

Closely related to the issues of an uncertain theology and a lack of accountability is ignorance. Our conversations with the members of the comparison churches indicated clearly that their first priority is looking after their own needs. We often heard these members speak of "the great fellowship" or how they "look after the needs of the members," but we rarely heard them express excitement about evangelistic outreach or ministry beyond the church.

Our researchers concluded that many of these members do not know what the New Testament church should look like today. Many of the comparison churches are thus inwardly focused. And a church that never looks beyond itself is a church headed toward a slow but certain erosion.

Another area of apparent ignorance among the members of the comparison churches is in basic statistical information about their churches. When we asked the members to give us the average worship attendance of the church, the most common response was "I have no idea." Among those who did venture to give us a number, their responses were, on average, 30 percent higher than the numbers reported by the churches.

While I readily concur with those who would say that numbers cannot be the ultimate measure of a church's health, I would also express concern if members were clueless about the attendance of the church. If they cannot discern that people are exiting the church on a regular basis, how can they have any type of meaningful attempts at discipleship and assimilation? Numbers are not everything, but neither are numbers unimportant.

BLIND EROSION AND RESISTANT LEADERS

Some of the lay leaders we interviewed were not ignorant; they simply did not want change. They could articulate the evangelistic purpose of the church, but they were uncomfortable if new people came into the church. They were in small groups or Sunday school classes where they were comfortable and knew everyone. Any attempts to start new groups or classes were met with anger by those who liked the groups the way they were. And a number of these resistant laypeople told us without hesitation that they liked the current size of the church. Evangelistic or other outreach attempts would meet stiff resistance because they would disturb the delicate balance of the perceived right size of the congregation.

How did these members reconcile their cognitive belief in evangelistic outreach and their own personal resistance to get involved? Typically they gave money to mission causes as their act of Great Commission obedience. They were happy to fund others in other parts of the world to reach out in Christ's name. They just did not want to mess with the comfortable status quo they had in their own churches. I am hesitant to be critical of pastors and other staff leaders of churches. As I have indicated several times, their job is the toughest in the world. They often have hundreds of "bosses" with contradictory expectations who do not hesitate to voice concerns and criticisms to them if they do not do things their way. Yet the differences between the breakout church leaders and the comparison church leaders were so significant that I cannot neglect to discuss this reality. These leaders can sometimes be the most obvious cause of blind erosion.

When the research team compared notes on the interviews with comparison church leaders, we noticed at least six issues present in resistant leadership. Sometimes only one issue would be obvious; on other occasions multiple factors were at work. We also heard many of the breakout church leaders recall times of their own failed leadership in the past. And they cited one or more of the factors listed in figure 9C that contributed to their church's blind erosion before they led the church to greatness.

Figure 9C. Blind Erosion and Resistant Leadership

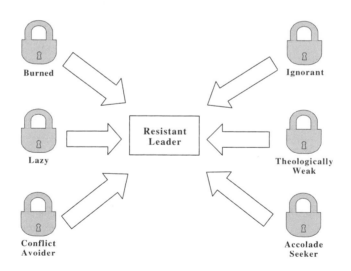

The *burned* leader has made valiant efforts to lead the church to positive change, but the resulting resistance and criticism have caused significant pain. This leader is demoralized and hurt. He is unwilling to try great things for God for fear of more conflict with people.

One of the many rewarding aspects of this project was conversing with several of the breakout church leaders after I notified them of their church's selection. Their responses of gratitude and humility were further indicators of why these leaders stand out from the crowd.

Stephen Schwambach, senior pastor of Bethel Temple Community Church, had difficulty finding the words to say and struggled to express his thanksgiving to God for what he felt was undeserved recognition. The selection was particularly gratifying because he had seriously considered leaving the church at one point.

Researcher David Bell reported on several major obstacles Schwambach faced when he had become senior pastor. Schwambach had sought the counsel of a mentor who suggested that birthing a new church would be a better path than trying to revive a struggling church. Also, as noted earlier, Stephen Schwambach had succeeded his father as senior pastor. In the early years of the son's leadership, many members compared him unfavorably with his father and criticized him often. The cumulative criticism left him deeply wounded.

Rare is the pastor who is willing to return to the battles of conflict after experiencing a severe wound. Many of the comparison churches' pastors have been burned in the past. One has to have empathy for their desire to avoid the pain they experienced in previous conflicts.

The *ignorant* leader does not have the understanding of what it takes to lead a church to greatness. He may be lacking in interpersonal skills and basic leadership abilities. As a seminary dean, I sometimes see some of our students well equipped in the classical disciplines but clueless about how to lead a church or how to relate to deacons, elders, or power brokers. The problem is not limited to neophytes, however; many long-term pastors have not learned leadership skills either.

The *lazy* leader has discovered the low accountability of ministers in many churches. Though this leader may have many "bosses" (members), day-by-day accountability is low or nonexistent. Many church leaders, because they have few people monitoring their daily efforts, can become workaholics or lazy bums. The structure of many churches leads to both extremes.

The *theologically weak* leader has some of the same doubts about cardinal doctrines we noted earlier in some laypeople. Although his church's statement of faith may be clear about the exclusivistic nature of the gospel, this leader is just not certain that "good" people of other faiths cannot go to heaven.[15] From an organizational perspective, this leader has abandoned the core values of the organization. From a theological perspective, he has abandoned the gospel.

The *conflict avoider* will steer clear of controversy and tough decisions at any cost. It is unlikely that this leader will be a burned leader, because he would not put himself in the position of engaging in a major battle. Ironically, such leaders typically are not avoiding conflict; they are just postponing it. One cannot please everyone. It is not unusual for conflict avoiders to leave the church when the first significant conflict emerges.

The *accolade seeker* thrives off the recognition and praises of the church members. This leader focuses almost all of his time on pastoral care and encouragement of those in the church. While a pastoral heart is commendable, the accolade seeker has no time to reach out to those outside the church, and he has difficulty making any decision that will lessen the praises of him and his ministry.

The comparison church pastors were resistant leaders. They exhibited at least one, and sometimes as many as three, of the six characteristics we noted. Their leadership failure is one of the primary reasons their churches were declining. And, for the most part, this decline was not obvious to those in the church. The affliction is called blind erosion, and left untreated it becomes deadly.

THE MYTH OF THE PLATEAUED CHURCH

There is no such thing as a plateaued church. A church is either growing or declining. In my research of thousands of churches, I have never seen a church maintain identical statistics for more than two consecutive years. The term "plateaued church" is commonly used to describe churches that are marginally declining or marginally growing. In fact, I have used the term many times, including a few uses in this book. And some churches may experience several years of nearly flat growth, when their attendance hovers in a tight range. But in reality a church is either declining or growing.

All of the breakout churches have broken out of the doldrums of decline, and most are experiencing the Big Mo today. There is a momentum where most decisions seem to work and few initiatives fail. A staff member of one of the thirteen churches stated the issue well: "This is the fun part of ministry."

Sadly, most churches in America are experiencing blind erosion. It is tragic that God's church is not reaching people. It is equally tragic that most of the members and leaders of these churches are blind to the reality of the erosion.

I have taken many pages of this chapter to contrast the significant differences between a breakout church experiencing the Big Mo and a comparison church suffering from blind erosion. It is my prayer that the wide chasm that exists between these two realities will provide a God-given motivation for leaders to take their churches from mediocre to good, and from there to great.

As this book nears its end, I want to encapsulate the major characteristics of the breakout church. The concluding chapter is more than a summary; I pray that it can be a blueprint for leaders to move their churches to greatness. To that final endeavor we now turn.

IN ESSENCE, IN SUMMARY
BIG MO OR BLIND EROSION?

- The "Big Mo" refers to what seems to be an inexplicable momentum in the breakout churches. It is a time when one success builds upon another and most decisions and initiatives are the right choices. The Big Mo was not a screening criterion for the breakout churches, but ten of the thirteen churches clearly had established this momentum.

- The typical process of the Big Mo came in four stages: struggle, buildup, breakthrough, and momentum.

- When we attempted to isolate the issues that led to the Big Mo, we could find no single factor or even a few factors. The issues were many and diverse.

- Long-term leadership was a key correlate in churches that achieved the Big Mo. As our study indicated earlier, the move to greatness is not achieved easily or quickly.

- Though this study has focused on many methodological issues in the transition to greatness, it is important to note that foundational issues remained the focus of the leadership. Biblical authority and the primacy of preaching and prayer moved the churches to greatness and are integral in the churches maintaining the Big Mo.

- Blind erosion refers to the slow decline in the comparison churches. I use the adjective *blind* because most of the members and leaders of these churches are unaware of the erosion.

- The key factors we noted in blind erosion were weak theology, ignorance, resistant lay leadership, and resistant staff leadership. Resistant staff leadership tended to exhibit one or more of the following characteristics: burned, ignorant, lazy, theologically uncertain, conflict avoiding, and accolade seeking.

CHAPTER 10

TO BECOME A BREAKOUT CHURCH

*Live as though Christ died yesterday, rose from the grave today,
and is coming back tomorrow.*

—Theodore Epp

I f imitation is the sincerest form of flattery, then Jim Collins should be flattery's greatest recipient. I have made no attempt to disguise my dependence on his work *Good to Great*. His method of research and his results were the cornerstones on which we relied to write this book on breakout churches.

Shortly before writing this chapter, I reread a portion of *Good to Great*, an exercise I conducted dozens of times. For the first time, I was drawn to Collins's closing paragraph. In light of the work we had conducted as a team, and with the writing of this book nearing completion, his words made more sense than ever.

> When all the pieces come together, not only does your work move toward greatness, but so does your life. For, in the end, it is impossible to have a great life unless it is a meaningful life. And it is very difficult to have a meaningful life without meaningful work. Perhaps, then, you might gain

that rare tranquility that comes from knowing that you've had a hand in creating something of intrinsic excellence that makes a contribution. Indeed, you might even gain the deepest of all satisfactions: knowing that your short time here on earth has been well spent, and that it mattered.[1]

These last words of Collins's secular business leadership book are powerful: *"Indeed, you might even gain the deepest of all satisfactions: knowing that your short time here on earth has been well spent, and that it mattered."* If making a difference in work is so meaningful, how much more meaningful is making a difference in God's work?

Two weeks before I finished this book, I spoke at the University of Kentucky at a ministry called The Rock. The purpose of this ministry is to reach fraternity and sorority members with the gospel. Every Wednesday during the regular semesters, The Rock has a worship service geared to reach these non-Christian college students. My son Art was the host and spokesperson for The Rock during his senior year of college. And on that chilly evening in early December, his dad was to be the speaker.

One of the greatest honors of my life was to be introduced by my son. Tears flowed freely down my cheeks as he spoke of me being his spiritual role model. Then he told those college students in the closing of his introduction: "I love how my dad loves the Lord. I love how he treats my mom. I love my dad. Let me introduce to you my hero and my father, Thom Rainer."

I could not speak immediately as I went to the platform. Hundreds of speaking engagements have come and gone, but I have never been more honored and moved than the way Art's words touched me.

You see, my consistent prayer for the past quarter of a century has been simple. "Lord, save my three sons through your Son, Jesus Christ." That prayer has been answered in full. "Lord, if it is your will for my sons to marry, please give them godly, Christian wives." No wives yet, but we may be getting close! And my third consistent prayer: "Father, in your power, allow me to show your love and power by the ministry I have first to my wife and my sons. Let me be a Christlike influence on Nellie Jo, Sam, Art, and Jess." And on that cold early winter evening, I began to see that perhaps that third prayer was being answered. I was humbled and grateful to God. Maybe, despite my many weaknesses and dumb mistakes as a husband and a father, God has used me to make a difference to my family.

TO BE GREAT, TO MAKE A DIFFERENCE

I have been researching churches for fifteen years. I have authored or co-authored thirteen books. But none of the work I have done in this area has impacted me like this project on breakout churches. Jim Collins wrote of making a difference through meaningful work.[2] But I have seen and spoken to men and women making a difference in God's church. The impact of their work is eternal and inestimable. I believe that deep in the heart of nearly everyone is a desire to be different, to make a difference. And I believe that the heart desire of most Christians is to make a difference for God for his glory.

There is little doubt that many American churches are sick. The documentation I cited earlier certainly paints that dismal picture. But there is no doubt that we serve a God of all possibilities. We must confront the reality of the struggles our churches face. And we must acknowledge a sovereign and omnipotent God who is the source of any solutions to the plight of the church.

> One aspect of our research that could not be captured in data or diagrams was the unmitigated excitement conveyed by our research team members when they returned from their research of a breakout church. Laura Cruse's comments below were typical. In one of our team meetings, we mused at how members and guests of these churches must feel when they attend a worship service or get involved in a ministry. There was little wonder from our perspective that the churches were attracting many people and that momentum was building.

I have seen the extraordinary differences in the breakout churches. My team members have been amazed. Researcher Laura Cruse remarked after she returned from visiting Xenos Christian Fellowship in Columbus, Ohio: "Xenos is an incredible church. I believe they are second to none in their training of leadership, and in the standard to which they hold their servant team without having been there several years." Laura enthusiastically added: "The sense of community at the church is incredible. The church has grown almost entirely from conversion growth. Xenos does not really attract transfer growth because of its countercultural feel."

Those involved in the breakout churches sensed that they were making a difference because they were working in a church that made a difference. A clear and discernible difference was evident between most of the members of the breakout churches and those in the comparison churches. The former had excitement and joy characteristic of those who have purpose and meaning in life.

Most of us who know Rick Warren and his ministry felt that his book *The Purpose-Driven® Life*[3] would be well received. But neither my peers nor I expected the book to move instantly to best-seller lists and sell millions of copies. Rick addressed a deep longing in the lives of millions. We all desire to have purpose and meaning in life. Such is the reason I am so excited about this research. It is not just about the church corporately. It is about individuals in these churches. The breakout churches have hundreds of stories of lives moving to greatness, about people who are now making a difference. And many members told us that it is the first time they felt that their lives had meaning.

WHAT IS GREATNESS?

Chapter 9 of *Good to Great* contains a section headed "Why Greatness?" In that section Jim Collins relates the following story: "During a break at a seminar that I gave to a group of my ex-students from Stanford, one came up to me brow furrowed. 'Maybe I'm just not ambitious enough,' he said. 'But I don't really want to build a huge company. Is there something wrong with that?'"[4] This story came to mind when a pastor from Michigan emailed me the following message: "Dr. Rainer, I hear you are writing a book about churches based on Jim Collins's book. I can't wait to read it. But I really don't have a desire to lead a megachurch. I hope your book will help pastors like me."

I am well aware that numerical measures have played a major role in our screening process and subsequent evaluations of the breakout churches. Just as Jim Collins was quick to assure his former student that "Greatness doesn't depend on size,"[5] it is my sincere hope that the use of such quantitative values will not lead readers to conclude that great churches are always big churches.

As you review the thirteen churches that made the breakout cut, you will see both megachurches and smaller churches.[6] We were determined not to do a study on big churches, but on great churches. And while one may question the criteria we used to determine greatness, the size of the church was not a characteristic that fit into our screening process.

Great churches were, in our study, churches that had broken out of the mediocrity of losing as many people as they were reaching. They were churches that had become outwardly focused, more intentional about evangelism than before. And they were churches where the same leader moved with the congregation during the transition. In many cases, the leaders experienced the same breakout transformation as the churches they served. In that sense we studied both breakout churches and breakout leaders.

> We are not certain of the number of breakout churches in America. As I note in the epilogue, numerous factors worked against us to get the data we needed. Based on our findings in the thirteen churches in our sampling, I conjecture that *at least* 100 churches in the United States would meet our criteria.

One pastor of a comparison church engaged me in a lengthy conversation. "James" was one of the few leaders in the thirty-nine congregations who really seemed interested in the breakout research of churches. He asked bluntly why we were looking at his church. I told him candidly that his church was a comparison church, a congregation that was not great, and one that would be compared in anonymity to the churches that met the criteria.

I was not certain James would allow the process to continue. But instead he started asking me a series of questions about the churches that made the breakout cut. After I did my best to explain the process, he stared straight at me for an agonizing few seconds.

"I once had a dream," he said softly.

"Excuse me?" I responded with uncertainty.

"I once dreamed of leading a church to become great," James said. He was speaking with difficulty. I could tell he was trying to fight his emotions. "I entered the ministry with idealistic expectations. Somewhere along the line, I got distracted. Maybe it was the critics. Maybe it was my own mixed-up priorities. Something happened though. Somewhere I lost my dream. Twenty-seven years of ministry," he said. "Now I wonder if I have made a difference or if my churches have made a difference. Is it too late for me to start over? Can I lead a church to become great? I don't want to go through this life without making a difference for God."

That powerful and poignant conversation reminded me again of the meaning of greatness. It is not the size of a church or the budget it carries. It is a congregation of God's people making a difference for his glory.

In these final few pages, I do not wish to repeat themes you have read in previous chapters. I do, however, desire to focus on the issues that really mattered the most in breakout churches. Some of what you read will be a reminder. Other parts will be new. But all will be important, because these are the issues that the breakout church leaders told us really mattered. Let's look at a blueprint for becoming a breakout church.

THE MAJOR COMMON THEMES IN *GOOD TO GREAT* AND *BREAKOUT CHURCHES*

In *Good to Great*, Jim Collins compared the Good to Great project with findings explained in his earlier book, *Built to Last*, and noted how the projects tied together: "To make a shift from a company with sustained great results to an enduring great company of iconic stature, apply the central concept from *Built to Last*: Discover your core values and purpose beyond just making money (core ideology) and combine this with the dynamic of preserve the core/stimulate progress."[7]

The breakout churches never strayed from the central doctrines of the Christian faith. These doctrines are the churches' "core values." While the comparison churches indicated adherence to these values in their written documents, their practice of the values was dubious.

As we noted earlier, Collins describes the good-to-great corporate leaders as Level 5 leaders: "In contrast to the very *I*-centric style of the comparison leaders, we were struck by how the good-to-great leaders *didn't* talk about themselves."[8] Collins then describes the "compelling modesty" of the leaders: "The good-to-great leaders never wanted to become larger-than-life heroes. They never aspired to be put on a pedestal or to become unreachable icons. They were seemingly ordinary people quietly producing extraordinary results."[9]

Our team described the leaders of the breakout churches as Acts 6/7 leaders. Their confident humility seemed remarkably similar to Collins's concept of "compelling modesty." Yet, in the final analysis, the best description of the breakout church leaders is "Christlike spirit." The apostle Paul described this attitude well: "Your attitude should be the same as that of Christ Jesus: Who, being in very nature God, did not consider equality with God something to be grasped, but made himself nothing, taking the very nature of a servant, being made in human likeness" (Phil. 2:5–7).

Good to Great is not an explicitly Christian book, and Jim Collins makes no claims in the book to being a Christian. Yet the description of the leaders of good-to-great companies seems so close to our description of breakout church leaders and the good-to-great companies themselves seem close to the churches we highlighted. The reasons for this close similarity are clear: in our research process we specifically looked for evidence of our findings outlined in *Good to Great*. Perhaps the best way to understand the similarities is in this visual depiction:

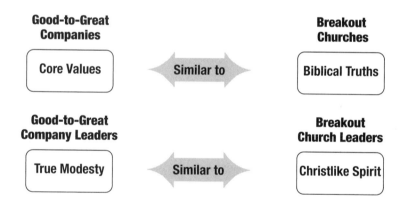

Is it possible that good-to-great companies and breakout churches have so many institutional commonalities that the leaders and central values are alike? Or is it possible that the good-to-great corporations actually assumed biblical characteristics that led them to become great companies? We on the research team believe that the presence of altruistic core values and leaders with servantlike attitudes made the corporations great. Simply stated, the more the corporations became biblical in their approaches to business practices, the higher the likelihood that they would become great businesses.

WHERE THE COST IS GREATEST

Our research demonstrates repeatedly that one of the key reasons the leaders of the comparison churches failed to move their churches to greatness was their unwillingness or inability to pay the costs necessary to do so. What I have not addressed to this point is where the cost is greatest.

Let's return to my earlier example of James, the pastor of the comparison church who was willing to discuss his church with me. I pressed him to remember where he lost his dream for his church. "I guess the first negative experience I remember was a business meeting where two families shot down every idea I suggested," he said. "I left that evening down and discouraged. That small church was so frustrating."

But James still had a dream and vision to lead a church to greatness. He left the small church thinking that a larger congregation would bring greater opportunities and less opposition. "I guess I was naive," he told me. "The bigger church just had different problems, but it still had problems."

The major conflict in the larger church was an attempt by James to lead the congregation to build a larger sanctuary. The church already had three full Sunday morning services, and growth was stymied by the lack of space.

"I was dumbfounded by the opposition," he reflected. "Looking back, I should have known that I moved too quickly. Several key families had strong emotional attachments to the building. No reasoning was going to work with them."

The more the pastor spoke, the clearer the struggle became. Every problem of which he spoke was related to problems with other Christians. Was this pattern common in the other churches we studied? We then returned to our research to identify the challenges and problems articulated by persons in both the comparison and the breakout churches.

Though I had been working on this project for several months, the results of our research surprised me. We identified 172 problems and struggles in both the comparison and breakout churches. Of the total, 171 of the problems were issues with other Christians. Only one church mentioned non-Christians as the source of the struggle, and that source was noted only once.

Jesus spoke of the importance of the unity of believers prior to his death on the cross. In the prayer to his Father in John 17, Jesus said:

> "My prayer is not for them alone. I pray also for those who will believe in me through their message, that all of them may be one, Father, just as you

are in me and I am in you. May they also be in us so that the world may believe that you have sent me. I have given them the glory you gave me, that they may be one as we are one: I in them and you in me. May they be brought to complete unity to let the world know that you sent me and have loved them even as you have loved me." (vv. 20–23)

The cost of becoming a breakout church, ironically, is most often the result of problems and conflicts with other believers. Many of the comparison church leaders grew weary of the struggle with fellow Christians. The breakout church leaders had no fewer conflicts, but they decided to persevere despite the pain and struggles.

> Why would a comparison church pastor give up after several struggles and crises when a breakout church pastor persevered? We could find no evidence of greater challenges and problems with the comparison churches. We found no evidence of lengthier challenges and problems with comparison churches. And we saw no indication that the breakout pastors had a higher threshold for pain. It just seems that the breakout church pastors made the decision to persevere, and that they sought God's strength to see them through their trials and difficulties.

RIGHT PEOPLE AND THE BREAKOUT TRANSITION

In light of our understanding that the cost of greatness is most often conflict with other believers, the need to have the right people on board is even more urgent. I earlier explained that breakout church leaders acted quickly and compassionately when making the necessary changes to move a person who might be holding the church back.

I am now going to make what may seem to be contradictory statements. Breakout church leaders make quick and compassionate people decisions, and they move deliberately and often slowly. How can a leader move both quickly and slowly?

I return to the example of one of the senior pastors of the breakout churches. At his request, I am keeping the names anonymous and modifying the details, but the essence of the story is true.

The senior pastor had several people problems prior to the church's transition to greatness. The two most prominent problems were a staff member who simply could not or would not fulfill the basic job responsibilities. He spent his time counseling members, but his job required no counseling. The other problem was an elder who always saw the worst in a situation. "He insisted that the United States never put a man on the moon," the pastor said laughing. "He said it was all staged, that it could never happen. I think he really believed that! He never could see the possibility of great things happening."

Just two people in a fairly large church were proving to be a major hindrance to the church's progress. "I made the decision to deal with those two problems immediately. It really wasn't my personality to confront people," he reflected, "but I made the tough moves despite my own discomfort."

The senior pastor and an elder met with the staff member. He was given three months' probation, in which time his performance as it related specifically to his job description would be evaluated. He was also told to stop counseling, a ministry led by another staff member. He did not stop counseling and made only a feeble effort to fulfill the responsibilities of his ministry. He was dismissed with a generous severance package.

The senior pastor and two elders met with the combative elder. They brought to his attention the negative and divisive influence he was having on the church. The elder became angry and defensive. He attempted to lead a move to force the pastor out. The move failed, and the elder and his family left the church.

"Those were some of the toughest days of ministry," the pastor told us. "We lost some good families who didn't know the full story about these two men. It was probably two years before we were able to put that behind us fully. It was really tough, but it had to be done."

Were all the people problems then resolved? The pastor laughed again, "No, we were a long way from getting our house in order. We still had a lot of people who weren't on board with us, but we had to take those situations more slowly. We dealt with the big problems quickly and then had patience with the others."

The breakout church leaders dealt quickly and compassionately with the major people problems in their congregations, but they were patient to wait on solutions for dealing with the more minor issues. Again our research of the thirteen churches showed that very few of the breakout transitions happened quickly. Long tenure and patience were thus two key components in moving to greatness.[10]

THE PEOPLE ISSUE AND THE FREEDOM/EXPECTATION PARADOX

I cannot overstate the importance of people issues in the breakout transition. But I also anticipate that many readers will wonder how they can lead their churches to make the right people decisions. The advice to move quickly but compassionately applies to only a few people in the church. How does one lead a congregation to get the right people in all ministry areas? How can a church find the right lay leaders and staff leaders when hundreds of individuals may be involved?

Interestingly, most of the breakout church leaders responded that they did not find the right people. To the contrary, the right people found the church. The Freedom/Expectation Paradox discussed in chapter 7 shapes this reality. The key to getting the right people is to create an environment that expects much of people and also gives them the freedom to do the work of the ministry to which they have been called.

The theme was clear in our interviews with the laity of the breakout churches. They desire to be a part of something that makes a difference so that they can make a difference. And in the breakout churches, these laypeople found a place where ministry really makes a difference.

But a church leader cannot simply declare that the congregation will now be a high-expectation church. Like most of the issues in the breakout churches, the transition takes time. Raising the bar of expectations is often incremental and painfully slow. The process can mean methodically increasing the expectation of a ministry position each time a vacancy occurs or a new position is added. It may mean the addition of a new members or inquirers class, so that new and prospective members can hear what is expected of them before they join the church. And it may also include new and higher standards for leaders, who in turn attract high-expectation leaders to their ministries.

> In previous research, we discovered that raising the bar of expectations was the number one requisite in member retention.[11] And perceived or real conflict with current church members was the number one stated reason most church leaders chose *not* to raise the bar. We certainly heard that concern expressed by the comparison church leaders.

The blueprint for becoming a breakout church requires becoming a high-expectation church. Only then will the right people get on board, stay on board, and remain excited about being on board.

PASSION AND CHOICES

I was recently asked the following question by a friend and colleague: "If you could do anything in the world you wanted to do, and if money was not an issue, what would you do?" My response was quick and simple: "Exactly what I am doing now." It is an immeasurable joy to wake up each morning excited about what the day holds for me.

My vocational hats may seem diverse at first glance: seminary dean, church consultant, preacher, teacher, speaker, researcher, and writer. But the different aspects of ministry in which I am involved have a common theme. I am passionate about helping Christians better understand the church and culture so that we believers can be more effective at engaging and evangelizing the culture in which we live. Other opportunities have come my way that some people may perceive as promotions, the natural step of upward mobility. But I could not get excited about any of those possibilities. I could not find myself being passionate about anything else vocationally.

I heard the word *passion* four times in our interviews with leaders of the comparison churches. And in each of those four instances, the word was used to describe an attitude of the past, an era of nostalgia and longing. For the breakout leaders, passion describes their everyday ministry. Their enthusiasm is contagious, and their visions are magnetic.

I recently had a good discussion about life after college with my oldest son, Sam. He is an incredibly gifted young man, all parental prejudice aside. He has been out of college for a few years and has done very well in his vocation. But more than the accolades and promotions that have come his way, I have been most impressed with his passion.

In a moment of father-son reflection, Sam expressed to me what passion means: "Dad, God gives us just a few years in this life. I don't want to waste them doing something that doesn't make a difference." Passion means making the choice to do that for which we can make the greatest difference. It means saying no to opportunities that may be good but not the best. It means that the best path is not always the easiest path.

Sam was right. The breakout church leaders were right. In their personal lives and in their leadership of their churches, they chose the best path. They realized that neither they nor their churches could please everyone or meet every demand. They followed the dreams God gave them. And they did so regardless of the cost. Such is the nature of passion. And such was the clear difference between the breakout leaders and the leaders of the comparison churches.

INNOVATION: OPEN BUT CAUTIOUS

The breakout churches, as a whole, were not the most innovative churches I have studied. But neither did they resist innovation just because "we've never done it that way before." The best description we developed for this attitude toward innovation was "open but cautious." The key, it seems, was that the leaders of these churches followed first the vision and passion God gave them for the church.

Some of the comparison church leaders used innovations to replace passion. They had no vision for their churches, so they used someone else's idea to fill the void. But the breakout church leaders would embrace an innovation only after careful examination. They were more concerned about the vision God had given them for their churches and about equipping the right people who were attracted to that vision. If an innovation improved that reality, they would happily adopt it.

AND THE GREATEST OF THESE ...

Our research team gathered together for what would later prove to be our last team meeting. "Have we missed anything?" I asked. "Have we failed to note anything about the churches and their leaders?" I don't recall which person spoke first. "Love," someone said. Several others nodded in agreement. I needed no explanation, for I had been with this project for several months. The team was exactly right.

> **Twenty-twenty hindsight always takes place in my research projects. If my team were to begin anew on this endeavor, I would spend a lot more time trying to understand more fully this very apparent love relationship between the leaders and the members.**

The more time we spent with breakout church leaders, the more we realized that expressive love was a vital part of their ministries. The leaders spoke without prompting about the deep love they had for their congregations. In different venues these same leaders told the members of their churches in different ways of their love for them. The love expressed was neither superficial nor syrupy. It was clear to our team and to the members of the thirteen churches that they were loved by their leaders.

An obvious response to our observation may be: "Well, I could love church members/pastors/staff members if they were like those in these breakout churches." But six of the thirteen senior pastors told us specifically of deciding to love the people during some of the most difficult days of their tenures at their churches. We on the research team believe that the leaders' decisions to love even the unlovable people in their congregations was a key factor in their churches' breakouts.

A BLUEPRINT FOR BREAKOUT CHURCHES?

I am hesitant to offer what may appear to be a step-by-step approach for churches to break out. Indeed, I hope that throughout this book you have heard the unmistakable emphasis that greatness in a church is a deeply theological issue. Great churches are great only because of the power of a great God.

In my closing pages, however, I do deeply desire to provide some practical issues for the struggling church leader or member who longs to see his or her church move to greatness. I encourage you to follow the process illustrated at the front of chapters 2 through 9. The suggestions that accompany each of the steps on the breakout transition are actual insights we gleaned from leaders in the breakout churches.

Thank you for investing your time in this book and our research project. My prayer has been that this work will somehow encourage, convict, or exhort you not only to lead a breakout church, but to become a breakout leader. Please join me in the next few pages in my own personal postscript where I share my journey toward breakout leadership.

> **Keep in mind as you view figure 10A that it is intended to be illustrative and not comprehensive. We could have cited many more examples from the leaders we interviewed.**

Figure 10A. Some Steps toward Breaking Out

Acts 6/7 Leadership	• Develop core biblical values. • Pray for a Christlike spirit in all areas. • Decide in God's power to love the people of the church no matter what. • Seek to lead your church to an outward focus, beyond the walls of the congregation. • In God's will make a commitment to stay with the church long-term.
The ABC Moment	• Seek outside counsel to help you see the church from an outsider's perspective. • Be a lifelong learner through numerous media. • Pray for your critics and maintain an attitude of love toward them. • Be prepared for the reality that most crises will be the result of conflict with Christians. • Pray that God will allow you to see beyond the crisis and see his work in the difficult moments.
Who/What Simultrack	• Deal quickly but compassionately with major people problems. • Develop a high-expectation culture in the church that will attract more of the right people. • Work on major structural needs in the church while simultaneously working on people issues.
The VIP Factor	• Discern your passions for ministry as a leader. • Discover the gifts and passions of the members of your congregation. • Discover the needs in the community. • See where the above three factors intersect, and focus many resources at this vision intersection.
Culture of Excellence	• Attempt to do all things with excellence in God's power. • If the church cannot do something with excellence, consider discarding or discontinuing the effort. • See innovation as a means, not as an end. • Carefully evaluate each innovative opportunity; be open but cautious with innovations.
Big Mo	• Learn that each success God gives is often a beginning point for another opportunity for success.

A PERSONAL POSTSCRIPT

I n 1984 I sat by my father's bedside as he ended his two-month struggle with cancer and entered into the presence of Christ. I was devastated. At age twenty-eight, I was a second-year seminary student. Dad had given me his blessing to leave the field of banking, which had been his lifelong career, to follow God's call to vocational ministry.

Dad just seemed too young to die at age sixty-two. I had lost my father, my best friend, and my hero. Sam Rainer was the mayor of Union Springs, Alabama, a small, struggling town south of Montgomery. He also was president of one of the two banks in town.

During the 1960s and 1970s my father took a difficult and unpopular stand to treat the African-American population with equality and dignity. Though the blacks in Union Springs were a majority, they were relegated to second-class citizenry at best. From my perspective, Dad was color-blind in a volatile and racially explosive time.

I did not realize the historical import of the time in which I was raised, but my father seemed to have an awareness of the moment. He introduced me to a segregationist governor named George Wallace, and he took me to the back of an African-American church to hear a powerful preacher and orator named Martin Luther King.

I have rarely known someone of my father's convictions and strength. His father was an alcoholic and his mother died when he was ten. He and his siblings virtually raised themselves. But I never heard Dad complain.

Dad was a World War II hero. He was wounded while serving his country as a top turret gunner in a B-24 Liberator. I never knew of the medals he received until I gathered his personal items after his death. He never bragged. He never considered himself a hero.

Dad had opportunities to leave the small and struggling town, but his heart was in Union Springs. He loved the people in his hometown, black and white, rich and poor. He was a man who was passionate about his place in life. He always seemed grateful.

But in April 1984 he was gone. My mother and my brother asked me to preach Dad's funeral. I had never spoken at a funeral before; now my first would be my father's.

I vividly remember telling my young firstborn son that "Daddyman" had died, and that I would preach the funeral message. Sam, named for his grandfather, spoke softly with a smile: "God will help you, Daddy."

God did help me. No church in town could hold the people who came to the funeral. For what seemed to be miles at the graveside service I saw faces of love: black, white, young, old, rich, and poor. Somehow I made it through the funeral and, to the glory of God, I would later hear of lives that were impacted by my message.

Why have I taken this personal excursion? You see, on that warm day in April of 1984, I made a decision and a commitment to God. I was reminded of the incredible brevity of life through my father's death. But I was also reminded of the difference we can make through the way he lived.

I loved my dad dearly. His Savior became my Savior. His values became my values. And his example shaped my life to this very day. Sam Rainer taught me that every day is to be lived to the fullest in God's power. No moment is to be wasted. We are to wake up with passion for God's work and go to sleep with that same passion. Life is a marvelous gift. And on that difficult day in 1984, I determined that in God's power that gift would not be wasted.

You have purchased or borrowed this book for a reason. I don't know the reason, but God does. Perhaps you have been struggling in your church and your ministry. Perhaps you are a senior pastor, a staff member, or a layperson. Maybe you were looking to these pages for hope when hope seems to have faded.

Some of you may have been attracted to the idea of greatness. You don't want to go through the rest of your days just being and doing good; you have a heartfelt desire to be great.

I don't know what brought you to this book, but I do know the God of all hope and all greatness. I remember how he took a weak and weeping twenty-eight-year-old man and gave him hope in the midst of heartache and pain.

This book has been about churches that have moved to greatness. It has been about Christians and church leaders who have moved to greatness. But above all, it has been about a great and awesome God. He is your strength. He is your source of power and hope to move you and your church from being good to becoming great.

It is a sin to be good if God has called you to be great.

In Christ's strength, may the rest of your days in life and ministry be great for his glory alone.

FREQUENTLY ASKED QUESTIONS

Q: Are the thirteen breakout churches a complete list of all the churches in America that met your criteria?

No. We had data on only 52,333 churches of nearly 400,000 churches in America. Among the 52,333 churches, 1,936 churches met the two criteria for evangelistic churches. From that point, we needed information submitted by the churches to determine further eligibility. But only 881 churches of the 1,936 responded to our requests for information. We therefore missed over a thousand churches to be considered and screened. We believe that the number of churches in America that would meet our breakout criteria would be at least 100, and that number may be conservative.

Q: Why did you have so much difficulty getting information on churches? Jim Collins, in *Good to Great*, had considerable information on the companies his team screened.

Collins's research was on Fortune 500 companies. Information on these corporations is exhaustive and available to the public. These companies must report by law detailed information on their operations. No such requirements exist for churches. Some of the denominations we asked for help flatly refused our requests. On several occasions, the data we received was insufficient. Still other churches stopped cooperating with us at a point. The process was arduous and often frustrating. There is just no good single source to get information on the vast majority of churches in America.

Q: Were any denominational churches omitted from your study?

Yes. We requested information from all the major denominations in the United States, but some of them declined to participate in this project.

Q: Why did you limit your study to churches in the United States?

First, we already knew the difficulty involved in getting good data from American churches. That problem is exacerbated when dealing with churches of different countries. Second, the comparison of data becomes more problematic when crossing international borders. Still, we believe that this research and its findings will have application in international contexts. Many of the principles we articulated do not have regional or national limitations.

Q: How did you find independent and nondenominational churches since no single data source exists for these churches?

We wrote dozens of letters to key Christian and church leaders across America for leads on the nondenominational churches. One of our primary problems was that most of the leads pointed to megachurches. While we wanted the megachurches in our study base, we also wanted to include smaller churches. As a consequence, we had to write additional letters and emails specifically seeking the smaller churches. We finally received sufficient names of churches to cause us to believe we had a valid and large sample.

Q: How did you select the comparison churches?

The 39 comparison churches were selected from our database of several thousand congregations. We found churches that were similar to the breakout churches ten years earlier. The churches were of similar size, in similar demographic locations, and had similar doctrinal beliefs. Three comparison churches were selected for each breakout church, for a total of 39 comparison churches. This process was relatively easy, because the only comparisons we needed were in size, demographics, and doctrine. We could have found many more comparison churches in our database.

Q: Why did you utilize the specific screening criteria for this project?

In earlier research projects, we have used evangelistic criteria as our initial screening priority. Such data are typically available, while other measurements, such as discipleship or worship, cannot be quantified easily. The evangelistic criteria also are good indicators of the missional effectiveness and obedience of the church. The criteria that required evidence of a decline/plateau followed by breakout growth is an integral part of the thesis of this project. We were looking for churches that had moved from being good to becoming great. That definition requires some type of quantitative reality. We also sought churches that did not change senior pastors during the transition. By design we sought to find churches that moved to greatness without dismissing the pastor or without the pastor leaving voluntarily before the transition took place. In other words, we were not looking for churches whose single answer to lack of growth was to get a new leader.

Q: Why did only thirteen churches make the cut?

Nearly 96 percent of the churches were cut for failing to make the evangelistic criteria. One-third of those churches did not respond to our requests for information. About one-half of the remaining churches did not demonstrate the requisite pattern of decline/plateau, breakout, and growth. Only 13 churches that made the previous cuts did so under the same pastoral leadership. For more details, see appendix B.

Q: Did you have any biases in your study?

Our study certainly has biases. It is difficult to remove the background and prejudices of the persons doing the research, especially in a process like ours that has so much subjective questioning. Having said that, I do believe that the research team did an incredible job of limiting their biases. Our team meetings were times when we were able to test one another's findings and interpretations. The probability of an individual researcher importing significant biases to this study was slim, since he or she was regularly checked by the other researchers.

Q: How do breakout churches compare with churches that are already great?

A great church would meet all of our evangelistic criteria and have no significant periods of decline or plateau. We also would not include pastoral tenure as one of the criteria. Nevertheless, even with these differences, the breakout churches are remarkably similar. Perhaps the single biggest difference would be the C in the ABC moment. Not all of the great churches of which we are aware have experienced a major crisis like the breakout churches. Crises are expected in the breakout churches because the congregation has to experience significant change in the transformation.

Q: What is the level of certainty a breakout church will remain great in the future?

The simplest answer is that there is no certainty. We have worked with thousands of churches and seen the tragic stories of great churches losing their focus on several occasions. Some of the more common reasons for a great-to-mediocre transition are the moral failure of leaders, failure to deal with divisive people in the church, and a slow slide to a more inward focus rather than the outward focus of the past. Having said that, we do believe that most breakout churches will remain great. The struggles that moved a church to greatness are not easily forgotten. Most leaders will do everything they can, in God's power, not to return to the days of mediocrity.

Q: Do you have any concern about how church leaders will receive and apply your research on breakout churches?

It has been my prayer that this book will be used for God's glory to provide encouragement and hope to church leaders across America and the world. We have gone through months of research to show that God can take a difficult and struggling situation and move a church to greatness. If I have a single concern, it is that the issues in this book will be perceived to be a quick-fix formula for turning a church around. What has taken place in the 13 breakout churches is God-centered, not human-centered. One cannot spend any time in these churches without sensing an extraordinary presence of God and dependence on him.

Q: What was the biggest surprise in your study?

I was surprised at several points. I expected the pastors of the breakout churches to have long tenures, but I didn't expect the average tenure to be more than two decades. I was also surprised that the churches were cautious about embracing innovations. But the greatest surprise was to hear of the cost of breaking out. My bias did not want this factor to be included in the study. I feared that describing the high price churches and leaders paid when they moved to greatness would deter and discourage others from taking this path.

Q: *Good to Great* is a secular book. Do you feel uncomfortable using its principles for a research project and a book on Christian churches?

When I shared with a group of my doctoral students the initial research and results of this project, one of the students appeared concerned and asked to meet with me. His primary issue was my taking secular principles and applying them to the church. I heard his admonitions and sought God's will to continue the project. The more we did on the research, and the more I became involved with the churches through my team, the more I became convinced that I would see this project to its conclusion. I do anticipate that the book may have some critics who express this concern. My response is simple. Most of the principles I read in *Good to Great* have biblical foundations even though they are not expressed as Christian principles. I realized that my foremost attraction to Collins's book was not its research methodology. My attraction was the research results that clearly had Christian and biblical foundations. From the humble attitude of the Level 5 Leader to the strict adherence to core values, I saw and read principles that had immediate application biblically to the churches across America and the world.

Q: I am not a senior pastor. What can I do with the findings of your research team in this book?

Take the principles of this book and apply them to the ministries where you have involvement or leadership roles. They are, for the most part, quickly transferable to youth ministry, to education ministry, to parachurch ministry, and to leadership in small groups and Sunday school classes, to name a few. You might need to make some modifications in our principles to make them fit your ministry, but most of the issues will have ready application. If you have a relationship with your senior pastor that is open and trusting, you might try giving him a copy of this book and get his response as well.

Q: How can we find the right people for our church or ministry when there is a shortage of qualified ministers and laypeople?

It would seem that there really is not a shortage of qualified people. Most people are not attracted to the mediocrity prevalent in many churches and ministries. The key, it seems, is to move your church or ministry toward excellence and high expectations. Quality people are attracted to quality ministries. People desire to be a part of something greater than themselves. They want to be involved in something where much will be expected of them. They want to be a part of something that makes a difference, and they want to make a difference in their lives as well.

Q: What do you see to be the biggest and most difficult challenge for churches to break out?

Very few churches are willing to deal with the *A* of the ABC moment. They simply do not have an *awareness* of the mediocrity in which they have become mired. The reasons for this lack of awareness are many. Some church leaders are unwilling to admit that their churches are doing poorly. They rationalize the church's poor state, or they point to supposed success factors to argue that they are not unhealthy. Other church leaders do not want to deal with the change that must come if a church has an awareness of its addiction to mediocrity. Still other leaders do not wish to create conflict that is inevitable if the church is to move to greatness.

Q: How does this project compare with your previous research efforts?

I have examined the evangelistic effectiveness of churches. My research teams of the past have looked at the issues of high expectations and assimilation. We have conducted two major research projects on the unchurched (*Surprising Insights from the Unchurched* [Zondervan, 2001] and *The Unchurched Next Door* [Zondervan, 2003]). And we have studied the cultures of four generations to see how well the church is doing reaching each generation. This project has taken these "pieces of the research puzzle" and put them together in a comprehensible whole. *Breakout Churches* affirms and complements my previous research. But even more, this project has helped me to have even greater clarity about my previous work. In some ways *Breakout Churches* is really a prequel to my other books. It represents the whole, whereas the other books represent the parts.

Q: Where and how should I begin?

I have attempted to present the key issues in chapter 10 as well as provide a summary chart for some definitive steps in moving to greatness. But if I sound redundant, forgive me; the transformation is not a quick-fix methodology. It took an entire book to describe the process because it is neither simple nor painless. If I had to advocate a point of beginning, I would begin with a look at myself. Or to be more precise, I would ask God to search me to see what I need to do to move to greatness. All of the breakout churches had Acts 6/7 leaders. Few of these leaders can be found in churches today. Whether you are a senior pastor, a youth minister, or a Sunday school teacher, God can use you to become this legacy leader. I urge you to "hang in there." The move to greatness is most often slow and arduous in our time, but it is perfect in God's time. He is watching over you. He is your strength. He is your source of hope even when all hope seems gone. I will never know the names and faces of most of you who read this book. I want you to know, however, that I prayed for you before you ever read a word. I have asked God to bless and give hope to those who read these words, not for my glory but for his alone. Thank you again for reading this book, and thank you for your heartfelt desire to do something great for God. You *are* in my prayers with the specific hope that your greatest days serving the Lord are just around the corner.

SELECTION PROCESS AND RESEARCH STEPS

STEP ONE: DETERMINE THE CRITERIA FOR SELECTION

1. We determined that we would first use evangelistic criteria to select the churches. While evangelism is not the totality of a healthy church's ministry, we do not believe that a church could be called healthy if it is not obediently responding to Christ's Great Commission. Evangelistic data is usually easy to find in churches where data is available. The most common nomenclature for evangelistic results was baptisms, conversions, or professions of faith.

2. The first evangelistic screen we used was a minimum of twenty-six conversions in at least one of the past five years of record. We felt that it was reasonable for any size church to reach at least one person every two weeks.

3. The second evangelistic screen was a ratio of worship attendees or membership (whichever is higher) to conversions. This ratio answers the question: How many members/attendees does it take to reach one person for Christ? Lower ratios are better ratios. In the screening process, the church had to have a maximum ratio of 20:1 for at least one of the past five years.

4. Because we are studying the transition of churches to greatness, the screening criteria included evidence of decline in worship attendance in past years followed by a sustained period of growth of at least five years. The church also had to demonstrate that the most recent year was a growth year in worship attendance.

5. The decline, breakout, and growth all had to take place under the same pastor. We believed that this criterion was absolutely necessary. The common prescription for a declining church is to get a new pastor. Unfortunately, only two out of ten pastors are leading churches to growth. There are not enough "turnaround" pastors to lead even one-third of America's 400,000 churches. We thus sought churches whose pastors had changed rather than churches that changed pastors.

STEP 2: LOCATE A DATABASE OF CHURCHES

This portion of the process was frustrating. While we did get data on 52,333 churches, we could have had significantly more with greater cooperation from several denominations. The source of our data at this point was cooperating denominations and responses to 117 inquiries we sent to key church and denominational leaders around the nation. From this database we were able to apply our evangelistic screening.

STEP 3: APPLY THE TWO EVANGELISTIC SCREENS

Both evangelistic screens were applied and reduced the number of churches from 52,333 to 1,936.

STEP 4: SEEK OTHER SCREENING DATA FROM REMAINING CHURCHES

We requested from the 1,936 churches at least ten years of statistical data. Only 881 churches responded.

STEP 5: APPLY BREAKOUT SCREEN

From the 881 churches, we selected those congregations that had shown historical attendance declines, followed by breakout growth, followed by at least five years of worship attendance growth. Lack of sufficient data eliminated some of the churches. The remaining churches did not meet the breakout criteria. This screen left us with 211 churches.

STEP 6: APPLY CONSISTENT LEADERSHIP SCREEN

We then looked at the 211 churches to determine if a change in senior pastors precipitated the breakout growth. Such was the case with 194 of the churches. We were down to 17 churches.

STEP 7: BEGIN INTENSIVE RESEARCH ON SCREENED CHURCHES

We began the process of gathering historical documents from the 17 churches, interviewing laypeople and staff members and, in many cases, conducting on-site visits. In this process we discovered that 4 of the churches really did not meet the previous screening criteria. We had been given incomplete or inaccurate information. This unexpected screen left us with the 13 breakout churches.

STEP 8: RESEARCH THE BREAKOUT CHURCHES

At this point we began even more intensive research on the church, including but not limited to the following:

1. Gathering internal and historical documents on the churches.
2. Gathering published material on the churches where available.
3. Conducting interviews with staff and laity.
4. In most cases, traveling on-site to the selected churches.
5. Testing Collins's key principles on the Fortune 500 companies from *Good to Great* with the 13 churches.
6. Comparing our results with a similar process on 39 comparison churches. I have provided an overview of the comparison churches in appendix C.

The screening can be illustrated as follows:

Beginning Database: 52,333 churches

⇓

Evangelistic Screen: 1,936 churches

⇓

Received Historical Data: 881 churches

⇓

Reported a Decline/Breakout/Growth Pattern: 211 churches

⇓

Reported Breakout under Same Pastor: 17 churches

⇓

Verified Data to Qualify: 13 churches

SELECTION PROCESS OF COMPARISON CHURCHES

The selection of comparison churches proved to be surprisingly easy. The purpose of the comparison analysis is to create a historical control group. By finding very similar churches to compare to the breakout churches, we were able to conduct comparative analysis in our research, distinguishing variables that might explain the transformation to greatness. Our objective was to find churches that had the same opportunities to make the transition but failed to do so. Our key question then in looking at the two sets of churches was: "What is the difference between a comparison church and a breakout church?" Because we already had data available from churches that did not meet the criteria for the screening process, we had many churches that we could have used as comparison churches. Admittedly we did not conduct as extensive an interview process as we did for the breakout churches, but we did get basic information that allowed for the comparison. In all cases, the senior pastor was interviewed. We indicated to these senior pastors that we were gathering research material for a project, and that the information they provided would be used in anonymity. We ultimately decided to use three comparison churches for each breakout church, using the following criteria:

Size Fit

The comparison church had to have an average worship attendance within 10 percent of the breakout church at a point prior to the breakout growth of the breakout church.

Geographic Fit

The comparison church had to be located in the same state as the breakout churches or in a contiguous state.

Demographic Fit

The demographics of the two churches had to be similar. The population of the defined communities of the churches had to be within 20 percent of each other prior to the breakout and after the breakout of the breakout church.

Doctrinal Fit

The comparison church and the breakout church had to have similar doctrines. When the breakout church belonged to a denomination, we typically took comparison churches of the same denomination, since doctrinal agreement should be common within the same denominational entity. When the church was independent or nondenominational, we looked at the written doctrinal statements of the churches to make certain they were congruent.

SYNOPSIS OF CHURCHES SELECTED

Though you have become familiar with the breakout churches throughout this book, all of the churches are listed together in this appendix, with a summary narrative of each congregation. The churches are listed in alphabetical order.

BETHEL TEMPLE COMMUNITY CHURCH / EVANSVILLE, INDIANA

Bethel Temple Community Church (formerly Bethel Tabernacle) was organized in 1933 by Albert F. Varnell, an evangelist and radio Bible teacher in Evansville, Indiana. In 1936 Varnell brought together a group of five "Bethel" churches into the Bethel Ministerial Association. Bethel would remain a part of this association until 1983, at which time, because of doctrinal and directional differences, it became an independent congregation. Although Bethel is still independent today, the church works closely with other evangelical churches in the area.

In 1946 Varnell invited R. R. Schwambach to join him at Bethel Temple as associate pastor. Schwambach had been active in the United Methodist Church, but he was increasingly troubled by what he perceived to be a liberal drift in the denomination. Schwambach was encouraged by Varnell's adherence to the biblical inerrancy and his commitment to the essential truths of the Christian faith, and he accepted the invitation.

Bethel Temple named Schwambach as pastor in 1951 following Varnell's retirement. The church enjoyed tremendous growth under the new pastor's leadership. For example, Sunday school attendance grew from 135 in 1951 to over 1,000 by 1979. The church relocated in 1967.

For the next three years the church plateaued in attendance. This lack of growth and the energies expended in a building program took a physical and emotional toll on Pastor Schwambach. Feeling that at age fifty-five he was too young to retire, he asked the congregation in 1981 to allow him to "trade places" with his son, Steve, who had been one of his associate pastors since 1970.

Steve Schwambach had a very difficult time stepping into his father's shoes. The continued presence of his father on the pastoral staff made it hard for many in the congregation to accept that a real change of leadership had taken place. The younger Schwambach's controversial strategies to reach the unchurched were met with increasing resistance.

During the early years of Schwambach's leadership, attendance quickly fell from about 1,000 to below 800. The attendance would remain in that range until 1989, when the number reached 900 and then above 1,000 in 1990. But attendance fell back to the 900s again until the year 2000, when a real transition began.

Pastor Schwambach had already begun his own life transition. He describes his early years as pastor as a time "when I was supremely confident in the rightness of my mission—so much so that I came across as arrogant. I was so sure I was leading us where I sensed God wanted us to go that I simply could not understand why everyone didn't agree. I would sit down in the homes of angry members and plead with tears for them to stay the course—to no avail."

Finally, the years of giving his all just to maintain the status quo shattered his confidence in his own abilities. "I came face-to-face with the inescapable fact that in my own strength I simply wasn't good enough to lead this church where I sensed God wanted it to go," the pastor told us. "Repeatedly, God had to use a ball bat to break my sinful pride and stubborn will." A member of his leadership team reports that today he is "very humble and self-deprecating."

Following an extended time of prayer and fasting in the early 1990s, Schwambach finally came to grips with the assignment God had given him. He came to believe it was his task to lead Bethel Temple all the way through the treacherous waters of transition, no matter how long it took. On June 2, 1993, Schwambach challenged his congregation to become "a church of passionately committed believers." Instinctively, he knew this was the only way Bethel Temple Community Church would ever be able "to inspire unchurched people to become everything Jesus created them to be."

In 2000 the leadership of Bethel Temple realized they "were struggling to go nowhere." Nothing had really changed, but now they were keenly aware that they were just going through the motions of doing church. It was truly an ABC moment, but the pastor and leadership were uncertain where to turn.

In 2001 Brad Johnson, then a teaching pastor at Saddleback Valley Community Church, recommended that the staff read *Good to Great* by Jim Collins. (Johnson had been a student in Bethel Temple's youth ministry during Schwambach's tenure as associate pastor there.) The church had already been influenced by the Purpose Driven model of Rick Warren and Saddleback, but it was *Good to Great* that proved to be the turning point. One pastor called Collins's work "the most transforming book." Another said, "We were trying to find solutions to a problem we couldn't define." Now *Good to Great* principles are a natural part of the vocabulary of most of the leadership team of Bethel Temple. Employing those principles is a conscious effort on their part.

The church broke the 1,000 barrier in 2003 and sees no reason for the trend to slow. So far in 2004 the growth rate has doubled from the previous year. Bethel Temple is a classic breakout church with one exception. We would like to see a longer period of growth and recovery beyond the breakout point. From what we have observed thus far, we have a high level of confidence that this growth will continue.

CALVARY MEMORIAL CHURCH / OAK PARK, ILLINOIS

Calvary Memorial Church began in 1915 in Oak Park, Illinois. The founders' purpose was to start a nondenominational congregation founded on solid biblical principles. The church grew steadily from its founding as the Oak Park community became a growing suburb of metropolitan Chicago.

The Oak Park area is probably one of the most liberal communities in the United States. The town boasts one of the largest gay and lesbian communities and may have the largest percentage of gay population outside San Francisco. Of the fifty-five churches in Oak Park, only two or three would be considered evangelical or conservative.

When researcher Mike McDaniel presented to me the data on Calvary Memorial Church, I was hesitant to accept the congregation as a breakout church. Though the church demonstrated classic breakout patterns, it had only one recent year of attendance decline. I was not certain that we could call that brief period of time a true struggle. It appeared to be more of a blip in a sustained growth pattern rather than a time of decline or plateau.

Mike demonstrated to me rather convincingly that Calvary did have a plateau of a different sort. From 1994 to 1999 the church experienced declining rates of growth with each consecutive year. During that time the church was attempting to find the right infrastructure, particularly in staffing. From 1999 on, the growth of the church has been remarkable. Worship attendance grew from slightly above 900 in 1999 to almost 1,500 in 2003.

Also the church struggled in the early years of Ray Pritchard's ministry, specifically from 1989 to 1992. The pastor had to deal with several divisive issues in the church, particularly whether the church would have women elders (the church chose to keep the eldership limited to males), and worship styles (the church added a contemporary worship service on Saturday evening).

Once the church got past its controversies in 1992, it experienced good but not spectacular growth. But the true breakout growth began to take place after 1999. The church for many years had been a refuge for conservative Christians in a liberal area, but by 1999 the leadership began to see the fruit of an intentional outreach into the Oak Park community. The chrysalis factor for Calvary Memorial Church was its intentional desire to be community focused. The congregation would not be content merely to be an island for conservative Christians in a sea of liberalism.

Today Calvary is a biblical church that seeks to let its light shine in a very difficult environment. Pastor Ray Pritchard gives thanks to God that the church is no longer "lily white" in its composition, but reflects the diversity of race and ethnicity of Oak Park. More than one-third of the congregants are nonwhite. The church is also reaching into the liberal community with ministries of caring and love. One woman in the church directs a large counseling ministry that, among meeting many other needs, has reached out positively into the homosexual community.

One drawback for Calvary Memorial has been a long history of inadequate facilities. In 1979 it purchased the former building of First Presbyterian Church, doubling the size of its old facilities. This additional space, however, would prove inadequate to handle the continued growth of the church. Despite significant facility limitations, however, this clear example of a breakout church may see its best days yet ahead.

CENTRAL CHRISTIAN CHURCH / BELOIT, WISCONSIN

Central Christian Church's history dates back to 1911, but its breakout did not take place until 1989. The church reached about 200 in attendance by 1960, but it saw no significant growth from that level for the next twenty-eight years.

David Clark was called as senior pastor of the church in 1981. His first seven years as pastor were a struggle as the church did not move off its 200 plateau. By 1989 a breakout took place that can be partially explained by the relocation of the church. But that factor alone cannot explain the dramatic growth of the church. After hovering around the 200 attendance level for most of its history, the numbers more than doubled to 500 in 1991. By 2003 average worship attendance was over 1,600.

And the growth cannot be attributed to transfers of Christians from other churches alone. In fact, the conversion growth rate is much higher than the transfer growth rate. In 2002, for example, the church had 172 baptisms and 32 transfers.

The story of David Clark's ministry at Central Christian is fascinating. When the pastor first came to Central, he was still in his twenties. Reflecting back, Clark recognized that he tried to make too many changes too quickly. We interviewed a longtime member of the church who explained that the senior minister had tried to bring his personal agenda into the church at too rapid a pace, and some of the church leaders had resisted the change. Six months into his ministry at Central Christian, Clark was fired by the church board.

An elderly woman in the church led the congregation to petition for Clark's reinstatement. The petition was successful, and the minister stayed. The next four years were a time of healing and reconciliation.

Despite the period of healing, however, the church still experienced no net growth. David Clark became increasingly frustrated and seriously considered leaving. Then the church leader had a true ABC experience that convinced him that better days were ahead. From 1911 to 1988 Central Christian Church averaged about 200 in worship. But from 1989 to 2003 attendance increased dramatically from 200 to 1,600. What factors explain the significant increase?

During the mid-1980s David Clark determined that the church could not continue business as usual. He and the church leaders began to dream about what the church could be and what it could do. The year 1986 was pivotal. The church leaders, both staff and laity, began to dream of Central becoming more than just a neighborhood church. Many major decisions were made that would impact the church positively for the decades to come.

Among the major decisions were the relocation of the church, an unswerving discipline to remain focused on the purposes of the church, the creation of a culture that encourages every member to be involved in ministry, and the addition of several key staff persons. The church also became intensely aware of the community in which it served. Today many in the community recognize Central Christian Church as a servant and friend.

Central Christian Church, an independent Christian congregation, is a classic breakout church. Its pattern of decline, plateau, and breakout growth under the same pastoral leadership fits our criteria well.

FAIRFIELD NEW LIFE CHURCH / FAIRFIELD, CALIFORNIA

Fairfield New Life Church is a Nazarene congregation started in 1956. When Jon Harris became pastor in 1992, average Sunday worship attendance was only 94. After one year of ministry at Fairfield, the pastor saw attendance decline to 90. Five years into his ministry, the church had virtually no growth.

As I noted earlier in this book, the influence of Rick Warren, Saddleback Valley Community Church, and the Purpose Driven Church model is inestimable. Often, when church leaders begin to ask basic questions of the church's reasons for existence, mental bells ring. Pastor Harris's listening to an audiotape by Warren on the Purpose Drive Church in 1996 proved to be his ABC moment. The board members were invited to listen to tapes from the Purpose Driven Conference, and the vision was birthed. A group from the church attended the Purpose Driven Conference later that year.

The ABC moment for Fairfield New Life Church was like that experienced in several of the other breakout churches. The leaders began evaluating virtually all aspects of their ministries and structures to see if they were doing everything possible to be the church God called them to be. They reached a conclusion that the church had to start over in many ways. Two of the more prominent symbols of this new beginning were relocation and a new name. Fairfield First Church of the Nazarene thus became Fairfield New Life Church. New Life Church also focused on transitioning from an Anglo congregation to a multicultural church in order to reach the increasingly diverse community. Today New Life is a very ethnically mixed congregation, and the professional staff reflects this diversity.

From the outset, however, the church leaders were not content to rest on their new insights. They knew that a church could quickly lapse into business as usual. For six months before the relocation, the entire congregation read the Great Commission every Sunday during worship services. During this time Pastor Harris also preached exclusively on the purposes of God's church. Also, they shared an insight from George Barna's book *The Turn Around Church*: Although fewer than 10 percent of churches succeed in a restart venture, there is a common characteristic in the churches that do. That is, *they are almost ready to die to see people come to Jesus.* Through this challenge and prayer, a passion for evangelism ignited the congregation.

Like many of the breakout churches, Fairfield New Life Church experienced an exodus of some key members. Though the number of losses was not great, many of those who left were influential in the church.

Worship attendance in 1996 was 115, but the number increased 58 percent to 182 in 1997. One year later the church broke the 200 barrier for the first time in its history. By 2003 the average attendance was 712.

One of the greater challenges facing the church today is the need for their own property and buildings. They currently meet in a high school on Sundays, and they have 5,000 square feet of office space for their staff. Indeed, the pastor reflects that "not getting land soon enough" was one of the mistakes they made during this time of new vision and new growth.

Fairfield New Life Church fit well our criteria of a breakout church. Interestingly, Pastor Jon Harris did not come to the church in 1992 with any visions of growth or significant ministry in the community. To the contrary, he was attracted to the church because of its small size. He was seeking a church that would not interfere with his plans to pursue a Ph.D. Pastor Harris did not plan to lead in the growth of a great church. God had other plans.

FIRST GETHSEMANE BAPTIST CHURCH / LOUISVILLE, KENTUCKY

When Dr. T. Vaughn Walker became the senior pastor of First Gethsemane Baptist Church in 1984, he knew he was preparing to lead a congregation that had been through a number of struggles. Numerous members had already left the church to start another church in Louisville. The average worship attendance in 1984 was 135.

During the first seven years of his ministry, Walker saw modest growth and harmony among the fellowship, but had little confidence that they could ever do great things for the Lord. Frustrated that the church might never break out of comfort and routine, the pastor considered leaving the predominantly African-American church. One large and prominent church began to talk seriously with Walker about his leaving First Gethsemane to become their pastor. He met with the deacons, and they heartily recommended Walker to the church. The church soon held a business meeting at which the members voted overwhelmingly to call him as pastor. For some reason, Walker could not give the church a definitive response at that moment.

He drove home from that meeting struggling for an answer. He stopped at a rest area and spent most of the evening in prayer. He continued to struggle on through the next day and evening. Finally, Walker realized that he had no peace about changing churches. He sent a letter to the large church, indicating his decision to remain at First Gethsemane. The chairman of the deacons received the letter but refused to read it to the congregation. Despite the chairman's persistence, Walker remained convinced—he was to stay at First Gethsemane Baptist Church.

"Immediately after I finally surrendered to God's will and decided to stay at First Gethsemane," Walker commented, "things began to happen. The church began to grow, and there was a new enthusiasm in the air." The ABC moment for this church was a pastor making a commitment to stay. By 2003 attendance had moved from less than 200 to over 1,300.

When Vaughn Walker made his commitment to stay at First Gethsemane, he saw many changes that had to be made. Expanded leadership and new staff were high on his agenda. In the beginning there was no paid staff other than the pastor and a part-time secretary. Extending the control of the church's finances and budgeting process beyond the deacons and trustees to include broader ministry needs and priorities was one of the more important changes. This change was gradual, and it took nearly nine years to fully implement this approach. Today this process continues to work with great harmony and accountability.

First Gethsemane Baptist Church is dually affiliated with both the Southern Baptist Convention and the National Baptist Convention, USA, Inc. It is fast becoming recognized as a premier church in both denominational entities. But Walker is not satisfied with the progress that has been made thus far. He is constantly leading the congregation to see beyond the present and look to God's possibilities for the future. He initiated a semi-annual, churchwide ministry update and evaluation to give the entire congregation the opportunity to evaluate and give feedback in numerous areas, including staff, facilities, ministries, and programs.

I am grateful that George Lee of the research team "discovered" First Gethsemane. It is a church located only miles from the seminary where I serve as dean, yet I was unaware of the recent exciting history of this congregation. The church fits our criteria as a breakout church in all areas. It powerfully depicts the story of perseverance and patience coupled with visionary leadership as a catalyst for growth in a great church.

GRACE CHURCH, CHRISTIAN AND MISSIONARY ALLIANCE / MIDDLEBURG HEIGHTS, OHIO

Grace Church, affiliated with the Christian and Missionary Alliance denomination, was one of the larger evangelical churches in the greater Cleveland area. The church was particularly well known and influential in the Cleveland suburb of Middleburg Heights. In 1979 the growth of the church began to slow, and Grace Church entered a period of plateau.

Donald Schaeffer was pastor at that point. He was the founding pastor and would ultimately serve the church a total of forty-one years. In 1985 Schaeffer and some key lay leaders attended a Church Growth Institute seminar led by Bill Orr. The seminar leader told them that churches do not remain plateaued; they either begin to grow again or they begin to die. That seminar proved to be a wake-up call for the senior pastor. He returned to the church with a new desire and vision to reach greater Cleveland with the gospel.

The attendance of Grace Church was 500, and Schaeffer thought that was all he could handle. He was diligent in sermon preparation each week, and the pastoral demands of the church consumed the remainder of his ministry time. Nine children at home kept him rather busy as well.

But the conference shook the young pastor from his leadership complacency: "By the time I went to that conference," Schaeffer told the researcher, "I had gotten comfortable in ministry. Prior to that point in my ministry, there was a certain amount of self-satisfaction with the job I had done. God used that conference to create dissatisfaction. I had a drastic change in attitude toward the church's responsibility to proclaim the gospel and reach a lost world for Christ."

After the seminar, Grace Church slowly began to implement some changes that would lead to breakout growth in the 1990s. The church learned more about developing skills to take it to a new level. They sought to increase lay involvement in ministry and leadership. They increased their budget contributions to international missions. And they made major infrastructure decisions, including relocation and the adoption of a dying congregation just fifteen minutes away from the church.

Grace Church's attendance climbed to 2,000 by 2003, and the church today reaches nearly 100 people for Christ annually. But the breakout growth of the church did not take place overnight. As indicated at numerous points throughout this book, pastoral commitment, tenacity, and tenure are critical issues in breakout churches. Indeed, we believe that we found those elements as a part of the chrysalis factor in all of our churches. This thesis was clearly evident in Grace Church. While the leadership awakened to the need to change, the breakout did not occur for another eight years. Pastor Schaeffer had already been at the church for twenty-five years in 1985. Still another eight years would pass before significant positive change took place.

Schaeffer had numerous opportunities to leave for another church during the difficult times of plateau and transition, but he was certain of his call to Grace Church. "I had several opportunities to leave, but I knew God had called me here," he told us. "I wanted to stay and see the work through."

Grace Church is clearly a breakout church. Indeed, it was one of our first to make the cut with the multiple criteria we established. Donald Schaeffer retired as senior pastor in 1998 and was succeeded by his son Jonathan. The church's rate of growth has continued to increase under the son's leadership, going from almost 800 in 1998 to over 2,000 in 2003.

GRACE EVANGELICAL FREE CHURCH / ALLEN, TEXAS

Grace Evangelical Free Church sits in the shadow of some of the largest and best-known churches in America. Allen is a northern suburb of the Dallas–Fort Worth metroplex. With an attendance of approximately 300, the size of the church is dwarfed by such megachurches as Prestonwood Baptist Church, located just ten miles from Grace.

But the story of Grace Evangelical Free Church definitely fit our criteria for breakout churches. Indeed, the size of this church was encouraging to the research team because it is more like the vast majority of the 400,000 churches in the United States.

Senior Pastor Joel Walters arrived at Grace in 1992, when attendance was less than 150. By 2003 worship attendance reached 283, but the breakout did not occur until 1998. After the first year of Walters's ministry at Grace, attendance jumped to 200, an increase of more than 33 percent. But for the next four years, attendance actually declined to 196. From 1998 to 2003 worship attendance has increased unabated.

The history of Grace Evangelical Free Church is not unlike many churches in America today. The church began in the Plano/Allen suburbs of Dallas. Five couples were commissioned to start home Bible studies in the area in March of 1977. By November of the same year, the church held its first worship service in Allen High School.

The original name of the church was Allen Community Evangelical Free Church, which would be changed to its present name in 1982. Like many struggling churches, Grace would have little stability in the tenure of its pastors. In the first ten years of Grace's history, ten men served as senior pastor. With a tenure of over a dozen years, Senior Pastor Joel Walters has finally provided the church with some stability and a base for future growth.

The chrysalis factor in the breakout churches includes some type of crisis with the church, the pastor, or both. The apparent severity of the crisis varied in each of the thirteen churches. For Grace Evangelical Free Church, the crisis seemed to be one of relatively small magnitude.

The ABC moment took place when the leaders of the church realized that Grace had hit the 200-attendance ceiling. The reason for the ceiling was obvious to many of the members. The majority of those attending Grace expected Pastor Walters to meet their ministry needs. After all, such had been the pattern when the church was smaller. Walters realized, however, that the church would remain in its business-as-usual pattern unless some changes took place.

The pastor knew that the laity of the church would have to assume responsibility for much of the ministry. He saw two immediate actions that could move Grace in this direction. First, new staff had to be added soon. The church was accustomed to the solo pastor model, and many members liked that apparent close relationship between the people and one pastor. But the biggest change was moving the primary responsibility of ministry from the pastor to small groups. The church already had a small-group ministry in place, but the people in the groups did little or no ministry.

They enjoyed the fellowship and the Bible studies, but they did little intentional ministry.

The transition to equipping the small-group members for ministry went fairly well. Pastor Walters noted that the change was not traumatic because "we took an existing structure and gave it new meaning. We also got a great deal of input from our small-group leaders and our elders."

Still some members did not like the change. Pastor Walters noted that "a few people left the church not because of change in structure, but because of change in the church."

The pastor does regret that the church did not build bigger facilities, because today space needs are hindering the church from more significant growth. The church has a stated goal to reach 500 in attendance and then to start new churches. This vision is communicated regularly to the elders and to the entire congregation.

GROVE CITY CHURCH OF THE NAZARENE / GROVE CITY, OHIO

Grove City Church of the Nazarene is a tale of three pastors. The present pastor, Bob Huffaker, led the church to new levels of growth. His predecessor, Herbert Rogers, led the church to its breakout point. But many of the church members point to Pastor Curtis Lewis, who preceded Rogers, as a key person in purchasing property for the new location. Under Rogers's leadership, the church purchased property to which they would ultimately relocate.

In 2004 Grove City Church of the Nazarene reached an all-time high average worship attendance of 3,126, which would rank the church as the largest in its denomination in the United States and Canada. There were times, however, when many members in the church could not ever see the possibility of the church becoming such a potent ministry force in the Columbus, Ohio, area.

From 1980 to 1985 worship attendance actually declined slightly from 445 to 440. For six full years the church experienced no growth. From our interviews with laity in the church, we heard that the church had a classic ABC moment. The leadership realized that the church's facilities were not sufficient for future growth and that the church needed to relocate. They began to look at the church from the perspective "of those who were not there yet," one of the associate pastors recalled. That same pastor said that "passionate leaders drive the ministries at Grove City, and most of those are driven to reach the lost."

Pastor Huffaker recalled that a major change in his own life was his attendance at a James Robison conference. The church would soon after shift to a more celebratory style of worship, much to the consternation of some of the members.

Grove City Church of the Nazarene has had its detractors within the membership. Change has been a constant in the past several years. The church relocated. Worship styles shifted. Staff was added. Ministries that did not fit the vision and purpose of the church were discarded. Some members expressed concern, while others were more outspoken in their grumblings. And some left the church. But Grove City continued its passion and vision to be a missionary outpost in the Columbus area.

In our interviews, we asked for key indicators of the church's success, and the responses had a unified theme. Some of the members and staff spoke of the various ministries of the church, with a strong emphasis on children's and youth ministries. Other indicators include starting a child care center, starting a school, and hiring two full-time children's pastors. There are large events that draw new people into the church: an Easter drama (20,000 people), a Hallelujah Party (an alternative to Halloween, between 3,000 and 4,000 people), a biker ministry, and RIOT (a youth outreach that attracts unchurched youth and has 500 people weekly). There are also multiple services, small-group ministry, Compassionate Ministry to the homeless, and FamJam (a family vacation Bible school that draws more than 1,500 children). Newer ministries include Saturday Night Church (which averaged more than 550 the first year) and the Journey (a postmodern service for young adults that averaged 150 the first year).

The unifying theme has been an outward focus. When the leadership of Grove City made the decision some twenty years ago to look beyond their own needs, great things began to take place. Keeping the outward focus remains the great challenge today. The church has had its share of critics over the years, both within the church and from the outside. Its success comes from an unswerving desire to ask what God would desire, rather than to seek to placate the critics.

Grove City Church of the Nazarene meets our criteria to be a breakout church. The congregation has been blessed to have more than one senior pastor who has been a good leader. But we see in Pastor Huffaker more of the Acts 6/7 leadership characteristics that should continue to move this church to greater heights.

KOREAN CENTRAL PRESBYTERIAN CHURCH / VIENNA, VIRGINIA

Won Sang Lee pastored Korean Central Presbyterian Church from 1977 to 2003. The church experienced a split in 1977 just prior to Lee's arrival. Average attendance was about 30 people. By 1979 attendance had increased more than fourfold to 130.

By the time attendance had reached the 130 mark in 1979, some of the elders in the church began to question the pastor's leadership style, theology, and preferred worship style. The issues were mostly trivial, such as the pastor allowing members to clap while singing hymns. The power struggle continued unabated for two years. Pastor Lee found himself discouraged and seriously considering leaving Korean Central Presbyterian for another church. Many of the deacons supported him, however, and convinced him to stay. They also made a commitment to pray for him with greater fervency each day.

The problems were not over for the young pastor. The dissenting elders and one-third of the members left the church in 1981. Many of the statistical gains were lost and attendance dropped to 100. As researcher Joong Shik Kim noted, "The attendance of Korean Central Presbyterian Church began to grow significantly after the critics left and the crisis was resolved."

By 1982 attendance was up to 207. The growth continued unabated and attendance reached 539 by 1985. In 2003 the average worship attendance was approaching 4,000. Won Sang Lee retired in September 2003 and was succeeded by Chang Soo Ro.

The growth of KCPC brought about the need for more space. The church has consistently purchased more property over the years, and additional worship services have provided more space as well. In 1986 the church started an English-speaking worship service. By 2003 KCPC had seven worship services on Sunday, beginning at 7:45 a.m. and concluding at 3:30 p.m. In 2001 the church purchased seventy-four acres for new facilities and a school.

The church established the Central Missionary Fellowship in 1990 and sent its first missionary that same year. Currently the church has twelve missionary families serving in eight countries. All of the families are fully supported financially by the church. Another forty-one associate missionaries are partially supported by KCPC.

Korean Central Presbyterian Church is also very mission-focused in its own locality. In 2000 the church purchased the Community Service

Center in Washington, D.C., to minister to the alcoholics, drug addicts, and poor in the downtown area. The congregation also has specific missions and ministries focused on the large population of indigent African Americans in the inner city.

Pastor Lee's original plans were to affiliate the church denominationally with the Presbyterian Church, USA. Before that tie was made, however, he began to have concerns about what he perceived to be a leftward shift in that denomination. Consequently, the affiliation never took place. In 1985 the church finally did make a formal denominational tie, this time with the more conservative Presbyterian Church in America.

Korean Central Presbyterian Church fits well our criteria for a breakout church. As is common in the churches represented in this book, a crisis precipitated the breakout growth. Also this church scenario demonstrated the common pattern of the pastor facing severe conflict and considering leaving the church. I would have liked to have had more specific data on conversion growth in the church. The anecdotal evidence, however, is convincing that many people are being reached for Christ in this church. It is a clear case study of a breakout church.

LENEXA BAPTIST CHURCH / LENEXA, KANSAS

Lenexa Baptist Church is located in the largest county in Kansas. The church is well known by many in the area as a fast-growing evangelistic congregation. Lenexa's average worship attendance now exceeds 1,200, and new building programs seem to be under way constantly. But the story of Lenexa has not always been so positive.

Lenexa began in 1988 as a mission sponsored by Emmanuel Baptist Church. Two years later the church called Steve Dighton as pastor. The church's average worship attendance was 150 when Dighton, who is defined as "aggressively evangelistic" by many members and by himself, came as pastor in 1990. The first two years of Dighton's ministry saw modest growth, as worship attendance climbed to almost 200 and budget receipts increased from $150,000 to $237,000. Then everything seemed to unravel. By 1994, four years into the pastor's ministry at Lenexa Baptist, the church had declined by half. Attendance was down to only 111 persons.

Some of the founding members had become nervous about the new growth the church experienced from 1990 to 1992. The new members were seen as a threat to the way they had become accustomed to doing church. Secret, closed-door meetings began to take place. It seemed as if the church was equally divided between those who supported the pastor and those who opposed him. At one point Pastor Dighton offered to resign rather than hurt the church.

Many members, however, encouraged the pastor to stay with the church. They reminded him of God's call to Lenexa and of his vision for the church. Many of the early members of the church began leaving. The next effect was a church split that left only half of the membership supporting the pastor and staying at Lenexa.

Many of the members told us that the difficulties and the pain in the church actually had some positive benefits. "Going through the test and tragedy of the church split had a way of making us stronger," one layman commented. "The struggle gave us a stronger faith that God was there with us."

By the time the full effect of the split could be felt, the remaining members realized the church would not survive unless each member took personal responsibility for ministry. Pastor Dighton led the way. He and his wife even cleaned the church during a time when the congregation could not afford custodial help.

If it was the pastor's evangelistic passion that led to the church split, it was that same passion that would move the church to health. Most of the members who remained with the church had come under Dighton's ministry. They knew the type of leader he was, and they desired to follow his leadership. The church would have more than just one "aggressive evangelist."

Though the pastor remained with the church through the difficult times, he freely admits that he considered moving to another church. He wonders if he might have done so had the right opportunity presented itself. He stayed, and the church has experienced the "Big Mo" ever since.

Lenexa Baptist Church believes lost people matter to God. They continuously seek ways to reach the lost and minister to the community. They call themselves "low-tech, high-touch" and are considered a "friendly and welcoming" church. They have more traditional approaches to evangelism, such as FAITH, an evangelistic program devised by the Southern Baptist Convention, with which Lenexa is affiliated. They intentionally seek to make their Sunday school classes evangelistic, and they are highly intentional about reaching those who visit the church a first time.

There was a point at which many of the members wondered whether the church would survive. But by 1999 attendance was approaching 400. By the end of 2003 attendance was approaching 1,400 with no signs of abating. This church went from almost nonexistent to good and then to great.

SOUTHWEST BAPTIST CHURCH / AMARILLO, TEXAS

Southwest Baptist Church started as an independent Baptist church in 1973 and remained independent until 2003 when it dual-aligned with the Southern Baptist Convention. The first worship service was held in the conference room of a motel; Sunday school classes met in cars of the members. Within a year the congregation was meeting in a metal warehouse building. By 1975 the church had purchased an old Church of Christ building. The auditorium could seat 1,000, so the 200 worshipers sat in a section marked by ropes.

Alan Ford was called as associate pastor and worship leader in 1974 and was called as the senior pastor in 1976, though a number of members questioned the ability of the twenty-eight-year-old minister to lead the congregation.

Southwest Baptist saw no growth in its early years after Ford became pastor. Power struggles in the church resulted in several influential and wealthy families leaving. An economic downturn in the area exacerbated the growth struggles. It was at this point that the pastor was influenced by the first of three events.

We have noted at points in this book that a conference, a book, or some other outside influence impacts the life of a church leader. As you have seen in this book, that outside resource becomes part of the ABC moment that moves the pastor to lead the church differently. In Pastor Ford's case, he notes three influences.

The first influence was a John Maxwell seminar at which Maxwell explained that many church leaders never take the time to develop lay leaders. Ford commented that his independent Baptist background caused him to believe that the pastor should do the bulk of ministry. He then asked a few of the key influencers in the church to take ownership and leadership of significant ministries in the church. It was his first attempt to turn ministry over to the laity.

The second influence was my book, *High Expectations* (Broadman & Holman, 1998). He knew that he needed to turn the rest of the ministry over to the laity and have high expectations that they would be involved in and lead the ministries. Ford commented that he "unleashed a monster.

People took ownership of the church, and the church began to grow. When people take ownership, it empowers them to make it happen."

After these two influences engendered change, the church began to grow. Attendance would finally break the 300 barrier in the late 1980s. By 1993 the average worship attendance exceeded 650. By 2003 that number had grown to about 1,300.

During this period of "Big Mo," the pastor told us that Rick Warren became the third major influence on his ministry. Warren's conferences helped Ford have a greater appreciation and understanding of the culture of the community. He consequently led the church to even more ministries of caring and outreach in the community they served.

Like many of our breakout churches, infrastructure changes helped accelerate the growth of the church. In the case of Southwest Baptist Church, relocating to a new facility was a key factor. In addition the church has added new ministry staff with the fast-paced growth of recent years.

Southwest Baptist Church is clearly a breakout church. Early struggles eventually led to key decisions that led to breakout growth. And the man who became pastor when the church was two years old has stayed with the congregation. Once again we have seen the impact of a long-term pastorate and a visionary ministry.

THE TEMPLE CHURCH / NASHVILLE, TENNESSEE

When Michael Graves became pastor of The Temple Church, a National Baptist congregation in Nashville, Tennessee, he had visions of a rapidly growing church reaching across multiple racial and ethnic lines. The vision would not come without great cost, the leader of the African-American congregation would soon learn.

Graves is the first and only pastor of The Temple Church. The congregation would meet in a number of facilities from its founding in 1977 until the completion of its first facility in 1980. The megachurch congregation now meets in a large facility on seventy-seven acres.

From its inception, The Temple Church has had a passion to reach the community in which the church is located. Samaritan Ministries is the church's primary community ministry, focusing on the inner city of North Nashville. On a daily basis the center provides hot meals, medical assistance through a well-honed screening process, and ongoing counseling. Indeed, the counseling ministry employs eleven full-time staff members who specialize in traditional, educational, and vocational counseling.

Another significant ministry of The Temple Church is Project SEE (Support, Education, and Empowerment) directed toward inner-city youth in the Cumberland View Housing Development. Since its inception in 1990, the ministry has had a significant influence in the dramatic decline of drug and gang violence.

The Bethesda Ministry of the church provides pastoral care to persons experiencing illness or grief and to the homebound and those living in extended care facilities. The prison ministry of Temple has been very successful in restoring formerly incarcerated persons to society and in reaching many of the prisoners for Christ.

These ministries are but a sampling of more than fifty ministries the church has in its community. In addition Temple has a large teaching ministry, a television ministry that reaches all of the Nashville metropolitan area, and a direct evangelistic ministry.

The average worship attendance of the church exceeded 2,000 in 2003. The growth of the church, however, has not always been dramatic, nor has the church always had a plethora of growing ministries. In fact, there have been years of decline when Bishop Graves wondered if he could even remain in pastoral ministry at The Temple Church or anywhere else.

The point of crisis for Bishop Graves and the church began to manifest in 1985. The church had grown steadily, and the pastor saw the clear possibility of reaching a multiracial and multiethnic community. But the limited seating capacity of the worship center precluded future growth. Attempts at multiple worship services were not successful. Then the pastor proposed the construction of a 2,500-seat sanctuary; that idea, like the attempts earlier to provide additional capacity, also met resistance.

Bishop Graves would soon learn that the resistance he sensed was not due to any concerns about building programs or added services. Rather, the opposition took hold when a large group of leaders began to express openly that The Temple Church might look different if further growth took place. It may no longer be just middle-class and upper-middle-class African Americans. In other words, they were worried that the church might really become the pastor's vision.

Opposition became more vocal and more resistant. More than 300 members in the church threatened to withhold their financial support unless Graves changed his plans to reach others in the community. Most of them eventually left the church, and it took Temple a few more years to recover and regain a momentum of growth. By 1989 attendance had dropped 30 percent from its high of 1,000 in 1985.

Bishop Graves reflects on this period as his most difficult in ministry. He internalized much of his pain, resulting in several weeks of hospitalization. His physician recommended he leave the ministry altogether. But leaving the church was never an option for the pastor.

Eventually the church did recover, and today it is one of the great churches in America. The church truly moved to greatness under the same pastor but at a great personal cost to him. As I have noted throughout this book, churches that break out often experience times of significant conflict and pain.

XENOS CHRISTIAN FELLOWSHIP / COLUMBUS, OHIO

In 1970 a group of Ohio State University students began printing an underground newspaper called *The Fish*. Although underground newspapers were popular among college students in the late 1960s and the early 1970s, an explicitly Christian publication was unusual. Among those students who started the paper was the current lead pastor of Xenos, Dennis McCallum.

The newspaper was printed in the basement of a boardinghouse, and that site soon became the home of regular Bible studies. The meetings, soon dubbed the Fish House Fellowship, attracted students searching for answers during turbulent times. Among those students was Gary DeLashmutt, who would later become the other lead pastor at Xenos.

For many years the church operated on a volunteer basis with no paid staff and no budget. The meeting space was made available at no charge. In 1982 the gathering changed its name to Xenos Christian Fellowship and hired the first of its paid staff. The name of the church comes from the Greek word *xenos*, which refers to a sojourner in a foreign land.

Today Xenos is a thriving evangelical church with an attendance of 4,200. The budget exceeds $5 million, and the staff includes 160 full-time and part-time employees. The number of ministries and mission opportunities seems countless. On the surface, Xenos looks like a church with a great beginning and an exciting ministry today, with few difficulties in between. The reality, however, is a different story.

Neither of the lead pastors expected Xenos to become a church, but the number of people attending the fellowship grew dramatically in the late 1970s and the early 1980s. Those who began to act as leaders over the flock had no real leadership experience. The church also had somewhat of an antileadership and countercultural ethos that would prove problematic in 1991.

In that year the lack of accountability among the churchgoers engendered some deep concerns by the leadership. Some in the fellowship were attracted to a growing hypercharismatic movement that was similar to the Toronto movement. The counseling ministries in the church had moved in unbiblical directions as well. They had become greatly influenced by the secular, pop psychology movement that was growing in the 1980s.

The leaders of the church decided to confront these aberrant movements in the church directly. At about that same time, the leaders began encouraging biblical financial stewardship. Many people in the church thought the leadership was accommodating a secular and worldly mentality.

These three issues were the major reasons for a conflict that lasted for three years and resulted in 1,400 people leaving the church and causing attendance to drop from 3,800 to 2,400. The elders asked lead pastor Dennis McCallum to write a vision paper to clarify the direction of the church. A servant team was put into place that added structure and accountability.

The establishment of the Servant Team also met opposition because the concept seemed too structured to many of the members. Today the number of leaders on the Xenos Servant Team totals 850, including all home-group leaders. These lay leaders have to meet the character qualifications found in 1 Timothy 3, and they must maintain regular prayer and Bible study times, as well as be faithful givers.

Xenos Christian Fellowship emerged from the crisis years as a much stronger church. The leadership speaks freely of the pain they experienced during this time but also of the necessity of the decisions they made. The evangelistic ministry of the church is strong. Ministries to the community, particularly to the inner city, are strong. Mission activity in the church is vibrant. Xenos Christian Fellowship is not a typical or traditional church. But the decisions the leaders made and the struggles they experienced to move to greatness are lessons for any church.

CHURCH READINESS INVENTORY

T he following inventory is designed to provide a guide to discover the level of readiness of a church to move to greatness. We use this instrument in our consultations with churches. The key is to provide your best answer with total candor and honesty. Many churches may want to have several of their leaders or members take the inventory to see if the people are thinking similarly. Take your time. Read each statement carefully.

Instructions: Give your best response to each statement as follows:

1. Strongly disagree
2. Disagree
3. Uncertain
4. Agree
5. Strongly Agree

Circle the number that best describes the church and issues related to the church.

1. The attendance of the church is on a positive trend. 1 2 3 4 5
2. The pastor of the church is a strong and biblical pulpit communicator/preacher who has a high view of Scripture. 1 2 3 4 5
3. Prayer has a high priority in the ministries of the church. 1 2 3 4 5
4. The church clearly and accurately reports numerous statistics regularly. 1 2 3 4 5
5. Most of the people in the church know the church's doctrinal positions. 1 2 3 4 5
6. Members in the church are willing to start new groups and classes to reach people. 1 2 3 4 5

7. The pastor is willing to lead the church in needed changes even if the attempted changes result in significant opposition.   1   2   3   4   5

8. The church examines the newest and latest methodologies carefully before considering adopting them.   1   2   3   4   5

9. The pastor of this church is humble, gracious, and modest.   1   2   3   4   5

10. The pastor of the church is certain of God's call to ministry.   1   2   3   4   5

11. The church is keenly aware of its weaknesses, challenges, and needs.   1   2   3   4   5

12. The church is willing to confront the difficult issues and seek remedies.   1   2   3   4   5

13. The pastor leads the church to be outwardly focused—to seek, to serve, and to minister to those who are not in the church.   1   2   3   4   5

14. Among the leadership of the church, there is a keen desire to improve and better one's self.   1   2   3   4   5

15. The church often takes major steps of faith.   1   2   3   4   5

16. The pastor of the church is passionate about ministry, the church, and serving God.   1   2   3   4   5

17. The leaders of the church often attend conferences, read books, and seek outside consultations.   1   2   3   4   5

18. The church is willing to see the negative issues it faces with a great belief that God will see them through any difficulty.   1   2   3   4   5

19. The pastor of the church often mentions and thinks about what the church will be like in another generation, even after the pastor's own lifetime.   1   2   3   4   5

20. The leadership of the church will accept slow progress as long as progress is being made.   1   2   3   4   5

21. The pastor obviously loves the church, as evidenced in the pastor's words, attitude, and actions.   1   2   3   4   5

22. The pastor does not attempt to lead as a dictator.   1   2   3   4   5

23. The pastor is committed to stay at the church for the long term.   1   2   3   4   5

24. The pastor is persistent in leading the church.   1   2   3   4   5

25. This church tends to attract gifted and highly competent people to serve as pastor and staff.   1   2   3   4   5

26. The church is willing to take on multiple major projects at one time.   1 2 3 4 5

27. The organizational structure of this church is healthy.   1 2 3 4 5

28. The physical facilities and grounds of the church are in very good condition and are cared for well.   1 2 3 4 5

29. If a new staff member is needed, the church is willing to wait a long time for the right person to hire or call.   1 2 3 4 5

30. The church is willing to deal with problem staff members quickly, even if the result is dismissal of the staff person.   1 2 3 4 5

31. The church is compassionate but firm in dealing with problem staff members.   1 2 3 4 5

32. The church leadership communicates well on issues, particularly on personnel issues.   1 2 3 4 5

33. The staff members and/or lay leaders are very compatible.   1 2 3 4 5

34. The leadership of the church does not attempt to micromanage the staff.   1 2 3 4 5

35. The staff and/or lay leaders are given great freedom to lead and carry out their ministries.   1 2 3 4 5

36. A climate of trust is evident in the church.   1 2 3 4 5

37. The church members know the purposes of the church.   1 2 3 4 5

38. The church uses its buildings wisely.   1 2 3 4 5

39. Small groups and/or Sunday school classes have a high priority at the church.   1 2 3 4 5

40. This church is a fun place to work or serve.   1 2 3 4 5

41. This church understands clearly its vision—the specific plan that God has given it.   1 2 3 4 5

42. Most of the members of the congregation know and use their spiritual gifts in ministry.   1 2 3 4 5

43. This church makes a concerted effort to minister to needs in the community.   1 2 3 4 5

44. This church chooses a few areas in which to excel.   1 2 3 4 5

45. This church attempts to do most everything with excellence.   1 2 3 4 5

46. This church expects much of its members.   1 2 3 4 5

47. This church is willing to eliminate ministries and activities if they cannot be done with excellence.   1 2 3 4 5

48. This church is willing to build quickly if the ministries and growth demand it.   1 2 3 4 5
49. Innovation is a means, not an end, at this church.   1 2 3 4 5
50. The leaders of the church use each success that God gives as a beginning point for another opportunity for success.   1 2 3 4 5

Add all the numbers you circled and put the total here. _____

See where your score falls in the following descriptions.

240 to 250. Church is displaying clear signs of moving toward greatness. We estimate that less than 1 percent of churches will score this high. A church in this category should keep doing what it is presently doing.

200 to 239. Church has significant potential to move to the breakout class. Leadership should look at those statements that did not score a 5 and see what remedies are possible to move to a higher level.

175 to 199. A church at this level needs significant work to move into the breakout category. So many deficiencies exist that multiple remedies are needed. Though the church should seek to move all statements to a score of 5, it particularly needs to give attention to those statements that were scored 3 or less.

50 to 174. Any church that has a score this low is very unhealthy. The possibility of moving to greatness, outside of miraculous intervention, is remote. The church should begin focusing on the many statements where a score of less than 4 was assigned. Though nothing is impossible with God, we rarely see churches in this category have any significant growth or meaningful ministries.

[Individuals who purchase this book are granted permission to make photocopies of this instrument for use in their local church.]

NOTES

CHAPTER 1. WHY GOOD IS NOT ENOUGH: THE CHRYSALIS FACTOR

1. Jim Collins, *Good to Great* (New York: HarperBusiness, 2001), 24.
2. Rick Warren, *The Purpose-Driven® Church* (Grand Rapids: Zondervan, 1995).
3. Collins, *Good to Great*, 27.
4. Ibid.
5. Ibid., 37.
6. Interview with Jim Collins, 4 April 2003.

CHAPTER 2. ACTS 6/7 LEADERSHIP

1. Most of the direct quotes in this book come from interviews by research team members with leaders and laypersons in the breakout churches. Other sources, such as published material, will be cited in notes, but quotations from interviews or in-house publications of the churches will not usually be identified hereafter.
2. Jim Collins, *Good to Great* (New York: HarperBusiness, 2001), 27.
3. Ibid., 21.
4. Ibid., 22.
5. This entire research project is published in Thom S. Rainer, *Effective Evangelistic Churches* (Nashville: Broadman & Holman, 1996), with subsequent research in Thom S. Rainer, *High Expectations* (Nashville: Broadman & Holman, 1997). The research team continues to update our findings, and we see no significant changes as of 2004.
6. These 427 churches are in our files regarding congregations for which we have provided consultations or where we have research data. We have not subjected the churches to sampling criteria to determine a margin of error.
7. Of the churches for which we have data, 84 percent are declining or experiencing a growth rate below the population growth rate for their communities. The latter is defined as a plateaued church. The number of 400,000 churches is an estimate based on a 2003 sampling of churches by population density and geographical location. We estimate the possible range to be between 375,000 and 450,000 churches.

8. Collins, *Good to Great*, 28.

9. These words were made popular by C. Peter Wagner in his book, *Church Planting for a Greater Harvest* (Ventura, CA: Regal, 1991), 32.

CHAPTER 3. EIGHT KEYS TO ACTS 6/7 LEADERSHIP

1. See especially Thom S. Rainer, *Effective Evangelistic Churches* (Nashville: Broadman & Holman, 1996), 130–34.

2. These 553 churches represent current information on churches for which we have research data and an additional random survey of 121 churches conducted in 2003.

3. Noted at several points in my *Effective Evangelistic Churches* and *High Expectations* (Nashville: Broadman & Holman, 1997).

4. We looked at 84 churches in the Southern Baptist Convention with records prior to 1950. The average tenure of the pastors of these churches at the point for which there was data was more than twelve years.

5. Jim Collins, *Good to Great* (New York: HarperBusiness, 2001), 34–35.

6. Ibid., 38.

CHAPTER 4. THE ABC MOMENT

1. See, e.g., George Barna, "Americans Draw Theological Beliefs from Diverse Points of View," www.Barna.org, October 8, 2002.

2. Further details on the Church Health Survey™ can be found at www.ChurchCentral.com.

3. From U.S. Census data, 1990 and 2000.

4. Based on a sampling of 1,522 churches in America in 2003. Research by the Rainer Group.

5. Based on a sampling of 1,337 churches in America in 2000, 2001, 2002, and 2003. Research by the Rainer Group.

6. Based on a survey of 877 church members, 2002 and 2003. Research by the Rainer Group.

7. Based on a sampling of 1,522 churches in America in 2003. Research by the Rainer Group.

8. Charles Haddon Spurgeon, *The Soul Winner: How to Lead Sinners to the Saviour* (Grand Rapids: Eerdmans, 1963), 17.

9. Jim Collins, *Good to Great* (New York: HarperBusiness, 2001), 86.

CHAPTER 5. THE WHO/WHAT SIMULTRACK

1. Jim Collins, *Good to Great* (New York: HarperBusiness, 2001), 41.

2. Ibid.

3. Ibid., 53.

4. See chapter 2 for an explanation of the study that produced the percentages for each level.

5. Again, our relatively small database precludes our making any dogmatic conclusions. Among the breakout churches, we were able to get tenure data from thirty-eight staff members. Among the churches with Acts 5 leaders, we received tenure data from seventy-one staff.

6. I use the term *articulator* rather than *originator*, since Rick Warren's model has its origin in Scripture, particularly Acts 2:42–47. My terminology in no way detracts from the incredible insights Dr. Warren has provided the church.

7. The Purpose Driven® model was articulated for many years by the name CAMEO (Contemporary Approaches to Ministry, Evangelism and Organization). The Purpose Driven name became well known internationally with Warren's influential books *The Purpose-Driven Church* (Grand Rapids: Zondervan, 1995), and *The Purpose-Driven® Life* (Grand Rapids: Zondervan, 2002). The latter book has sold millions of copies and continues to be a powerful influence in local churches around the world.

8. The Purpose Driven model articulates five purposes of the church: worship, evangelism, discipleship, ministry, and fellowship. I would argue that Acts 2:42 clearly defines prayer as a sixth purpose of the church.

9. Most of the churches that use the Great Commission to define their reasons for existence state that Matthew 28:18–20 is an evangelistic impetus for certain but is also far more. Both explicit and implicit with the passage is discipleship, worship, and ministry. In other words, the Purpose Driven model and the Great Commission model are very similar in the ways churches use them.

10. In my research of the formerly unchurched, published in *Surprising Insights from the Unchurched* (Grand Rapids: Zondervan, 2001), I note the critical importance of facilities in reaching non-Christians. See also my book *The Unchurched Next Door* (Grand Rapids: Zondervan, 2003) for further research on the unchurched.

11. See my research on this issue in *High Expectations* (Nashville: Broadman & Holman, 1999).

CHAPTER 6. THE VIP FACTOR

1. Though I will explain these definitions within this chapter, I want to be clear and specific about the meanings of the words I am using. *Vision* is God's specific plan for a specific church at a specific time. *Mission* is God's purposes for all churches, including worship, evangelism, discipleship, prayer, ministry, and fellowship. *Vision* is thus unique to each church, while *mission* should be common to all churches.

2. Jim Collins, *Good to Great* (New York: HarperBusiness, 2001), 95.

3. The manifestation of sign gifts typically includes speaking in tongues, interpretation of tongues, miracles (often demonstrated in healing services), and prophetic utterances. This group within the Xenos fellowship also was attracted

to the Toronto Vineyard church, which reportedly included unusual and unbiblical manifestations within their services. These manifestations have been called "the Toronto blessing."

4. The process included biblical preaching and teaching on spiritual gifts and the unleashing of the laity, assembling a number of church leaders to attend a two-day seminar on spiritual gifts, and asking several hundred members to take a spiritual gift inventory to help them in the process of spiritual gift discovery.

5. The two-thirds estimate is based on the number of members who chose to stay after the crisis period and who obviously were enthused about the original vision of the church.

6. Willow Creek Community Church is a well-known congregation in South Barrington, Illinois. At no point did I hear the leaders of Xenos make disparaging remarks about Willow Creek. They simply decided that the model offered by Willow Creek did not fit the culture and structure of Xenos Christian Fellowship.

7. The in-house document of the Xenos Servant Team pulls no punches. It states that "joining the Xenos Servant Team is extremely difficult."

8. See http://www.xenos.org/admin/steam.htm for the complete discussion of the Xenos Servant Team.

9. This quote also comes from the church's internal documents.

10. A complete description of this ministry can be found at www.urban concern.org.

11. See chapter 2, note 5, for research methodology issues.

12. The center was physically located in the state of Virginia rather than in the city limits of Washington, D.C.

CHAPTER 7. A CULTURE OF EXCELLENCE

1. In each of the thirteen breakout churches, the research team found some clear indication that excellence was a driving factor in the ministry. Sometimes this evidence was prominent in written documents. At other points, we were able to see clearly this passion in the interviews with key leaders. In none of the thirty-nine comparison churches, however, did we find such a drive or passion. Even when we returned to our research a second and third time, we saw nothing in the comparison churches' written material or in the interview process with the leaders that indicated a quest for excellence in any issue.

2. The influence of Rick Warren's Purpose Driven model was evident in these years and even today in many of the ministries of the church.

3. See chapter 4 for the earlier description of this issue.

4. Our latest data show the annual baptisms of 2002 to be 172 for Central Christian Church.

5. The Pareto Principle is cited frequently, but few persons understand its origin or impact. In 1897 Italian economist Vilfredo Pareto (1848–1923) noted a fascinating pattern in the distributions of wealth and income. His observations

did not change, even for different nations and different time periods. He found that uneven distributions of income and wealth always took place. A small number of individuals always accounted for a large majority of wealth. The pattern became so reliable that Pareto was able to predict income distributions before looking at the data. The essence of his principle was that 80 percent of wealth and income ends up in the top 20 percent of wage earners.

Pareto's concept did not make its mark in his lifetime. The 80/20 concept was popularized by Joseph Moses Juran, one of the gurus of the quality control movement in the twentieth century. Juran made a major contribution to the Japanese economy, which grew faster than any other industrial economy between 1957 and 1989.

The United States and Europe adopted this concept in the 1960s and gave rise to the commonly held phrases of the "80/20 rule" or the "80/20 principle." This principle basically asserts that 80 percent of results flow from 20 percent of causes.

The first book on this subject, *The 80/20 Principle* (New York: Currency/Doubleday) was written by Richard Koch in 1997. Hundreds of articles, however, have been written on and about this subject since the early 1960s.

6. Jim Collins, *Good to Great* (New York: HarperBusiness, 1991), 134.

7. Grove City Church of the Nazarene was one of the thirteen churches that engendered some debate among our team for its inclusion as a breakout church. The church began in 1963 and hit a barrier of 450 from 1980 to 1985. Since most of the growth has taken place under the current pastor, Bob Huffaker, some on our team argued that this church's breakout can be explained by the new pastor's leadership beginning in 1989. The breakout, however, occurred *four years* before the arrival of the new pastor. In other words, this church *did* meet all of our strict requirements of being a breakout church, including a breakout taking place without changing pastors. In fact, the growth of the church (worship attendance) from 1985 to 1989 was 40 percent. While we concur with the assessment that the leadership of Huffaker has been vital to the growth from 1989 to the present, the breakout took place under the leadership of his predecessor, Herbert Rogers.

8. The high expectation reality of healthy churches was noted in my book of that title, *High Expectations* (Nashville: Broadman & Holman, 1999). What my research failed to note was the presence of freedom to do ministry at these churches. Much of the satisfaction of the breakout churches research I have experienced is the tying of many loose ends from previous projects.

9. Collins, *Good to Great*, 139.

CHAPTER 8. INNOVATION ACCELERATORS

1. Jim Collins, *Good to Great* (New York: HarperBusiness, 2001), 152–53.

2. Jim Collins notes a very similar phenomenon with the eleven good-to-great companies in the adoption of technology. He discusses this issue in his chapter 7, "Technology Accelerators." For the breakout churches, technology was not the complete issue. Technology was a factor if the technological adaptation was a clear innovation in the church. The churches adopted numerous innovations that were not related to any technological issues.

3. Ibid., 153.

4. Keep in mind that the VIP factor is the intersection of three factors: the passion of the leadership, the passion and gifts of the community, and the needs of the community. It is the intersecting point, the vision, that we are calling the "dog." Typically when a breakout church let the tail wag the dog, it was the result of the leaders' passion not intersecting with the other two factors.

5. In my research on evangelistic methodologies (see my *Effective Evangelistic Churches* [Broadman & Holman, 1996]), I found no direct correlation between big events and evangelistic effectiveness. My subsequent research on the unchurched (see my *Surprising Insights from the Unchurched* [Grand Rapids: Zondervan, 2001] and *The Unchurched Next Door* [Grand Rapids: Zondervan, 2003]) indicates a possible positive "pre-evangelistic" relationship with big events. At this point, I have to conclude that such evidence is possible but only anecdotal.

6. A major resource in helping Bethel Temple Community Church break out of its dependence on the big-event innovation was Jim Collins's *Good to Great*.

7. Warren's *The Purpose-Driven Life* (Grand Rapids: Zondervan, 2002) has far exceeded the sales of *The Purpose-Driven Church* (Grand Rapids: Zondervan, 1995). The former book is a personal devotion and discipleship book, and the latter is a book for corporate church strategy. Still, it would appear that *The Purpose-Driven Church* has been the paradigmatic book for churches since 1995.

8. As I noted earlier, I believe that Acts 2:42 clearly indicates that prayer is a sixth purpose of the church.

9. It must be noted that some churches made the transition well before Rick Warren articulated and gave a name to the Purpose Driven philosophy. Therefore I sometimes use the term "purposeful" when appropriate to indicate a more generic concept.

10. Technically, Herb Rogers is the pastor of the breakout transition at Grove City Church of the Nazarene, according to our established criteria. The church was in slight decline during his tenure, and it eventually broke out of the decline into healthy growth. Grove City was one of the churches that we felt was on the bubble to make the breakout cut, but ultimately we had to remain true to our criteria and include it. After the church made the screening and we began to research the church, we saw that it did indeed exhibit many of the characteristics of a

breakout church. The significant difference is that, in the other breakout churches, the pastor who led the church through the breakout was also the pastor who got to enjoy the fruit of the growth for many years after the breakout. In the case of Grove City Church of the Nazarene, three pastors contributed in different ways to the breakout transition.

CHAPTER 9. BIG MO OR BLIND EROSION?

1. Jim Collins, *Good to Great* (New York: HarperBusiness, 2001), 171.

2. This information can be viewed at various points at the University of Kentucky Athletic Department website: www.UKathletics.com. See particularly the information under "Basketball" and "History and Records."

3. The CMA following the church name represents the denomination, Christian and Missionary Alliance, and is a common way for churches in this fellowship to identify themselves with their denomination in much the same way as Methodist, Baptist, Presbyterian, Lutheran, and other churches identify their denominations. Most of the literature we received from this church simply had "Grace Church," so we will omit the denominational identification from this point forward.

4. See especially page 172 in *Good to Great*. See also David S. Landes, *The Wealth and Poverty of Nations* (New York: W. W. Norton, 1998), 200.

5. We do not have data for 1992, so we are assuming that the worship attendance was halfway between the previous year and the subsequent year. The midpoint between the 1991 worship attendance of 498 and the 1993 worship attendance of 592 is 545. That is the number we used for the average worship attendance in 1992.

6. Collins, *Good to Great*, 169.

7. Ibid., 168.

8. A great church had most of the same characteristics of a breakout church with two notable exceptions. First, the great church has not necessarily experienced any plateau or decline. Second, the changing of a senior pastor may be the clear method God has used to move the church to greater health.

9. See Thom S. Rainer, *Effective Evangelistic Churches* (Nashville: Broadman & Holman), 1997. Correlation is not the same as causation. *Correlation* demonstrates some type of relationship: If one thing takes place, then another thing is likely to take place. *Causation* indicates a direct cause-and-effect relationship—for example, if I hit you on the head with a hammer, the blow will cause pain. In our studies, we demonstrate correlative relationships. We therefore cannot make a definitive causative statement that more time spent in sermon preparation will produce greater evangelistic results. We can say that the preachers who spent more time in sermon preparation were more likely to see better evangelistic results. This relationship was also noted in another research project: Thom S. Rainer, *High Expectations* (Nashville: Broadman & Holman, 1999).

10. See Thom S. Rainer, *Surprising Insights from the Unchurched* (Grand Rapids: Zondervan, 2001).

11. In *Surprising Insights from the Unchurched* our research actually did measure time allocation in a full 168-hour week for a sample of senior and solo pastors.

12. The breakout church leaders and laity used different words to describe their belief in the total truthfulness of Scripture: *inerrancy, infallibility, authority, veracity*, and others. But more than the words they used, we on the research team sensed a submissive attitude to God's Word. One researcher commented, "These leaders don't have to tell us what they believe about the Bible; you can tell it in everything they say and do."

13. Collins, *Good to Great*, 178.

14. I address this issue extensively in my book coauthored with Chuck Lawless, *Eating the Elephant* (rev. ed., Crestwood, KY: Pinnacle, 2003).

15. An excellent brief book on this topic is Ronald H. Nash, *Is Jesus the Only Savior?* (Grand Rapids: Zondervan, 1994).

CHAPTER 10. WHEN GOOD CHURCHES BECOME GREAT

1. Jim Collins, *Good to Great* (New York: HarperBusiness, 2001), 210.

2. Ibid., 208–10.

3. Rick Warren, *The Purpose-Driven Life* (Grand Rapids: Zondervan, 2002).

4. Collins, *Good to Great*, 204.

5. Ibid.

6. I have fought the seemingly futile effort to define megachurches as those churches that average at least 1,000 in worship attendance over a one-year period. I prefer that standard because less than .5 of 1 percent of churches would qualify. Unfortunately, most pundits now declare the attendance level to be at least 2,000. The number of American churches among the 400,000 congregations that have attained such a level is so small (fewer than 700) that the few in this category defy any clear categorization.

7. Collins, *Good to Great*, 190. The earlier book is Jim Collins and Jerry I. Porras, *Built to Last* (New York: HarperBusiness, 1998).

8. Collins, *Good to Great*, 27.

9. Ibid., 28.

10. I again refer to my book with Chuck Lawless, *Eating the Elephant* (rev. ed., Crestwood, KY: Pinnacle, 2003), for an expanded discussion of taking incremental steps for long-term benefit in a congregation.

11. See Thom S. Rainer, *High Expectations* (Nashville: Broadman & Holman, 1997). As I indicated at the onset of this book, the research and conclusions of *Breakout Churches* put the pieces of research from previous projects into a comprehensible whole. This issue was but one more example of this.

NAME AND SUBJECT INDEX

Surprising Insights from the Unchurched and Proven Ways to Reach Them

Thom S. Rainer

Thom S. Rainer
*Dean of the Billy Graham
School of Missions, Evangelism and Church Growth*

We've read all the hot books on evangelism, we've attended scores of seminars—and still we're not reaching the unchurched. Eighty to ninety percent of churchless Americans will never darken our culturally relevant, seeker-sensitive doors. What are we missing?

Maybe we've been asking the wrong people. It's time we heard what the small but important minority who have recently begun attending a church have to say. What made the difference for them? What critical factors helped spark their faith in Jesus and drew them into the community of believers?

Thom S. Rainer, dean of the Billy Graham School of Missions, Evangelism and Church Growth, shares the results and conclusions of a groundbreaking survey of the formerly unchurched. At last, here are proven insights into what evangelistically effective churches are doing right. Filled with charts, graphs, and other visual aids, plus an abundance of true-life accounts, this book explodes common myths about the unchurched. You will discover

- Why pastors and doctrinal preaching are critical
- The enormous influence of family and relationships
- Which things matter more than we thought, and which matter less
- What causes visitors to return
- The traits of unchurched-reaching leaders
- How to preach effectively to the unchurched
- How to become a church for the unchurched

and much, much more.

This resource includes reproducible appendices such as the Unchurched-Reaching Readiness Inventory and the Church Health Survey.

Hardcover: 0-310-23648-7

Pick up a copy today at your favorite bookstore!

ZONDERVAN™

GRAND RAPIDS, MICHIGAN 49530 USA

WWW.ZONDERVAN.COM

The Unchurched Next Door
Understanding Faith Stages as Keys to Sharing Your Faith

Thom S. Rainer

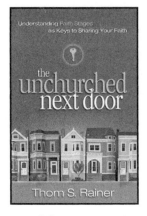

If You Invite Them, They Will Come

It's true. In a national survey conducted by author Thom Rainer and his staff, eight out of ten unchurched men and women said they would come to church—if only someone would invite them. When and how is the next big question. Rainer helps you figure out where your neighbors, friends, and coworkers are in their spiritual quest, and how you can know who among the unchurched people in your life are receptive to Christ.

"A discovery we made is that reaching lost and unchurched people is not always best accomplished with some cookie-cutter strategy," Rainer writes. "The unchurched are different in how they respond to the gospel." How different? Rainer identifies five "faith stages"—levels of responsiveness:

U1 Highly receptive to hearing and believing the Good News
U2 Receptive to the gospel and church
U3 Neutral, with no clear signs of being interested yet perhaps being open to discussion
U4 Resistant to the gospel, but with no antagonistic attitude
U5 Highly antagonistic and even hostile to the gospel

Once you recognize which stages your unchurched friends and family are in, you can much more effectively connect them with Christ. Open this book, and open your mind and heart to the powerful new possibilities of reaching *The Unchurched Next Door*.

Hardcover: 0-310-24860-4

Pick up a copy today at your favorite bookstore!

ZONDERVAN™

GRAND RAPIDS, MICHIGAN 49530 USA

WWW.ZONDERVAN.COM

Your online source for church health info...

www.churchcentral.com

- Stay up-to-date with daily church health news
- Read free articles on church health and leadership issues
- Learn about the Church Health Survey™ to help determine your church's strengths and areas of improvement
- Find suppliers of church products and services
- Browse hundreds of church job classifieds

Also Subscribe to *Church Health Today*
Dr. Thom Rainer's free, weekly e-newsletter
(sign up now by sending an email to admin@churchcentral.com)

CHURCH ✝ CENTRAL

Equipping Leaders to Grow Healthier Churches

We want to hear from you. Please send your comments about this book to us in care of zreview@zondervan.com. Thank you.

ZONDERVAN™

GRAND RAPIDS, MICHIGAN 49530 USA

WWW.ZONDERVAN.COM